The Desolate South: 1865–1866

THE
DESOLATE
SOUTH
1865-1866

*A Picture of the Battlefields
and of the Devastated Confederacy*

by

JOHN T. TROWBRIDGE

Edited by

GORDON CARROLL

DUELL, SLOAN AND PEARCE
New York

LITTLE, BROWN AND COMPANY
Boston   *Toronto*

DUELL, SLOAN AND PEARCE—LITTLE, BROWN
BOOKS ARE PUBLISHED BY
LITTLE, BROWN AND COMPANY
IN ASSOCIATION WITH
DUELL, SLOAN & PEARCE, INC.

Published simultaneously in Canada
by Little, Brown & Company (Canada) Limited

PRINTED IN THE UNITED STATES OF AMERICA

Introduction

WHEN the Civil War ended in the spring of 1865, the coterie of reporters and correspondents who had followed the Union forces were as eager to get home as were the men who had done the fighting. By midsummer, the journalistic front had more or less collapsed: Washington was now the news center, and curious Northern tourists were doing a better job of "covering" the South than were many of the newspapermen, who, after four years of war reportage, were quite happy to forget the battlefields.

John Townsend Trowbridge was a special case. When he set out from Boston for Gettysburg in the late summer of 1865, he was entering territory which he knew only from reading wartime dispatches in the metropolitan newspapers. However, he was a professional writer, and he carried a special directive in his pocket. L. Stebbins, the Hartford publisher, had had an idea: why not send an observer through the Confederacy to file a human-interest report on what he found there? There were, of course, the battlefields to tour, but there were many other subjects of interest: the plight of the defeated people, their conditions of living and working, the temper of Southern thought, and above all, the situation of the Negro, lately freed from servitude.

Trowbridge accepted the assignment with enthusiasm, for it fitted well with his background and his talents. At thirty-eight, he had come to journalism by a curious route: first as a poet, then as a newspaper contributor, then as a novelist and playwright, finally as a magazine editor. Yet, during the war just ended, he had not served with the Union correspondents. Despite bids from several newspapers, he had spent the war years in Boston, where, already acclimatized to the abolitionist atmosphere, he had helped the Northern cause by writing antislavery tracts and books. Now, with the war over, he had his chance to go South and see at first hand the places and people that had been uppermost in his mind since 1861.

Trowbridge was peculiarly well equipped to survey the defeated Confederacy. In addition to a flair for clear and crisp writing, he had a tolerant mind, an understanding of human frailties, an ability to get along with people, and a reporter's instinct for what is important, what is trivial. When he had completed his Southern travels, he was able to deliver to Stebbins a two hundred thousand-word manuscript which he could rightfully term "almost photographic and stenographic" in its content. The book was published under the title *A Picture of the Desolated States and the Work of Restoration*.

Now Trowbridge's volume was not the only one of its kind to appear in the period immediately following the war. The publishing business being what it is, other observers went South after 1865, and filed various reports in various styles and measures. But Trowbridge's effort stood out from its competitors. Because of the author's character, he could find grave fault in the attitudes and actions of many followers of the late Rebellion, but he could also find cause to praise, when praise was owing. He did not carry with him a pattern of preconceived notions and then fit the people and the events and the trends to the pattern. On the contrary, he sought to have his travels shape his thoughts, and when he had finished his assignment, he was more concerned about the future welfare of a restored Union than he was in recounting the fears and terrors of a cruel war so recently won by the cause in which he believed.

Upon publication, the book received praise, and not only from Northern readers. Far more detailed than other contemporary works, it gave an intimate picture of the Confederate elements which were working for political realignment and economic reconstruction. But because the output of Stebbins's publishing company was mostly sold by "subscription" — the house-to-house canvassing method employed so widely in those days — Trowbridge's volume did not make a deep impression on the ordinary channels of the book trade. Indeed, in later life, the author preferred to recall some of his other literary efforts, especially his volumes of poetry. This attitude was not surprising, in view of his formative years and his affinity for forms of writing other than narrative reporting.

Trowbridge's ancestors were of English stock, the family having emigrated to Massachusetts in 1634. His father was born in Framingham, but moved with his family to Oneida County, New York, while still a child. There, after his mother's death, he was bound out to a Westmoreland farmer, John Townsend, whose name he later gave to his own son. When, at twenty-one, he had served his apprenticeship with Townsend, he married a local girl and they set up housekeeping in a log cabin in what was called "the Genessee country." In Ogden township, Monroe County, John Townsend Trowbridge was born in September, 1827.

John was a typical boy in a typical rural community of his

time. He went to school in winter, worked on the farm in summer, and picked up certain items of culture in his spare time, for he was brighter than average and wanted to outshine the other youngsters. At fifteen, he had already written some verses, and when he inherited a thin shelf of French books from a cousin's estate, he taught himself the language, meanwhile bettering his English through intensive reading of the classics.

Three years later, the elder Trowbridge died, and John went to live with a married sister in Lockport, New York. He resumed his schooling there, and in January, 1845, he had his first public success — a literary prize from the Niagara *Courier* for his poem celebrating the New Year. In 1846, he visited another married sister in Illinois, taught school for twelve dollars and fifty cents a month, tried his hand at farming on shares with his brother-in-law. When he returned to Lockport, he was still a schoolteacher, but he was through with farming for good.

The spring of 1847 found him in New York City. He had decided to become a writer, and since he had an introduction to Major Mordecai Noah, editor of the *Weekly Messenger*, he persuaded this Manhattan figure to introduce him to other editors, one of whom bought a story for the remarkable sum of twenty-five dollars. Before long he was a contributor to *Holden's Dollar Magazine* — a profitable enterprise which charged its subscribers a dollar a year and paid its authors a dollar a page. It was around this time that Trowbridge began writing under the name of Paul Creyton, at first applying it to what he called his "apprentice work," then using it for earning power, since his work was growing in popularity and other editors began asking for his manuscripts.

A year in New York was enough for Trowbridge: he had won editorial recognition, but the competition with other young writers was too brisk to be profitable. He visited Boston, found it congenial, and decided to settle there, living, as he had in Manhattan, in boardinghouses, where he could keep his expenses in line with the checks earned from Boston weeklies. Not long after his arrival, two new-found friends had a proposition: why not put out a weekly of their own, they to furnish the cash, Trowbridge to furnish the brains? Soon the *Yankee Nation* appeared, but the backers gradually lost interest, the funds vanished, and Trowbridge was out of an editorship.

In between contributing to the *Yankee Blade* and the *Carpet Bag,* he turned to novel writing. The first book failed to find a publisher; but in 1853, *Father Brighthopes* appeared, a full-length novel which was described as "an embodiment of practical Christianity." A year later, Trowbridge pridefully announced his first "real novel." Under the title *Martin Merrivale,* it told of the struggles and adventures of a young writer — a theme on which the author could write with plausible authority.

With a successful book to his credit, Trowbridge decided to widen his ideas through travel; he went to Paris and stayed there ten months, perfecting his French and writing another novel. This was *Neighbor Jackwood,* inspired by the experiences of Anthony Burns, a Negro slave whose trial had been a celebrated case in Boston the year before. Although the book was denounced in Southern quarters for its antislavery theme, *Neighbor Jackwood* was Trowbridge's greatest success to date. He dramatized it for the stage: it opened in March, 1857, and relished a long run in Boston, a town whose abolitionist sentiments were in tune with the author's.

In the fall of that year, when the first issue of the *Atlantic Monthly* appeared in Boston, Trowbridge was the youngest contributor to its soon-to-be-famous pages. For some time he continued to write for the *Atlantic,* ranging his efforts from poems, stories and travel sketches to papers on current politics. Oddly enough, the most popular of his contributions — a poem called "The Vagabonds" — failed to bring him immediate praise, since it had been published anonymously.

When the Civil War came in 1861, Trowbridge did not volunteer for active service: he stayed in Boston where his pen served as a sword in the writing of antislavery books, of which *Cudjo's Cave,* published in 1863, was the most famous. In January, 1865, the proprietors of the *Atlantic,* interested in widening their field, designed a magazine for younger people; and when the first issue of *Our Young Folks* appeared, Trowbridge was among the editors. The distinguished contributors included Harriet Beecher Stowe, Louisa May Alcott, Edward Everett Hale, Lucretia Hale, Dickens, Lowell, Whittier and Longfellow.

Our Young Folks flourished, as did its staff, and by 1870, Trowbridge had not only been made managing editor but had begun to write the "Jack Hazard" serials, which added many youthful readers to an already prosperous circulation. Eventually the series comprised five books: *Jack Hazard and His Fortunes, A Chance for Himself, Doing His Best, Fast Friends,* and *The Young Surveyor* — all of which foreshadowed the Horatio Alger tradition of a later day. When *Our Young Folks* was sold to Scribner's and merged with *St. Nicholas,* Trowbridge gave up his editorship, but continued to write for a younger audience, mostly through the pages of the successful *Youth's Companion.*

In 1860, Trowbridge had married a girl from Lowell, Massachusetts. She died in 1864, leaving one child, a boy, who was to survive her by only twenty years. In 1869, Trowbridge married again, and of this union there were several more children. With his family, he went to Europe in 1888 and remained there for three years, traveling in various countries and making new literary friendships. When, at seventy-five, he turned at last to his autobiography, a recounting of these friendships, as well as of those he had formed in New England, took up a considerable portion of the book.

My Own Story, with Recollections of Noted Persons, was published by Houghton Mifflin in 1903, and Trowbridge felt that it was a suitable close to an active life. But the end was still distant, for not until another fifteen years did death come. On February 12, 1916, John Townsend Trowbridge died at eighty-eight in Arlington, Massachusetts, not far from the spot where his English ancestors had landed almost three centuries before.

*   *   *   *   *   *

In the editing and condensing of *The Desolate South,* I have removed nothing of significance from the original manuscript, as published by Stebbins. In the interests of brevity, repetitious text has been eliminated: several chapters have been removed and a few others transposed for the sake of continuity; and many footnotes have vanished, since these were written at a time when neither the author nor the historian of the 1860's was accurately informed of certain events which had recently transpired in the Confederacy. In the light of today's knowledge, such footnotes can serve no useful value. But other than the changes I have cited, the book stands just as it was written, and therein lies perhaps its major attraction, since had it been published yesterday, it could hardly be bettered as an example of competent, comprehensive and colorful journalism.

Because the original book contained a selection of steel engravings, none of which succeeded in bringing people and places to life, they have been replaced by a selection of photographs which symbolize, if they do not always represent, the areas through which Trowbridge traveled. In the captions, each photograph has been identified as to period and place, so that the reader may compare the camera image with the word picture drawn by the author.

In the selection of the photographs, I was aided vastly by the Prints and Photographs Division of the Library of Congress, where the staff is more than helpful and hospitable in answering queries. To them, I owe sincere thanks.

GORDON CARROLL

March 1, 1956
Greenwich, Connecticut

Preface

IN THE summer of 1865, and in the following winter, I made two visits to the South, spending four months in eight of the principal states which had lately been in rebellion. I saw the most noted battlefields of the war. I made acquaintance with officers and soldiers of both sides. I followed in the track of the destroying armies. I traveled by railroad, by steamboat, by stage-coach, and by private conveyance; conversing with all sorts of people from high state officials to "low-down" whites and Negroes; endeavoring at all times to receive correct impressions of the country, of its inhabitants, of the great contest of arms just closed, and of the still greater contest of principles not yet terminated.

This book is a record of actual observations and conversations, free from fictitious coloring. Whenever practicable, I have stepped aside and let the people speak for themselves. Notes taken under all sorts of circumstances — on horseback, in jolting wagons, by the firelight of a farmhouse or Negro camp, sometimes in the dark or in the rain — have enabled me to do this in many cases with absolute fidelity. Idiomatic peculiarities, so expressive of character, I have reproduced without exaggeration. To intelligent and candid men, it was my habit to state frankly my intention to publish an account of my journey, and then, with their permission, to jot down such views and facts as they saw fit to impart.

Sometimes I was requested not to report certain statements of an important nature, made in the glow of conversation. These, not without regret, I have suppressed; and I trust that in no instance have I violated a confidence reposed in me.

J. T. TROWBRIDGE

May, 1866

Contents

	Introduction	v
	Preface	xiii
I.	Gettysburg	3
II.	Chambersburg	16
III.	Antietam	21
IV.	Harpers Ferry	30
V.	Charlestown	39
VI.	Washington, D.C.	45
VII.	Bull Run	50
VIII.	Fredericksburg	57
IX.	Chancellorsville	66
X.	The Wilderness	72
XI.	Spotsylvania	75
XII.	Richmond	83
XIII.	Fair Oaks	106
XIV.	Petersburg	112
XV.	Fortress Monroe	118
XVI.	East Tennessee	124
XVII.	Chattanooga	129

XVIII. Chickamauga 137

XIX. Murfreesboro 143

XX. Nashville 149

XXI. Corinth 154

XXII. Shiloh 169

XXIII. Memphis 177

XXIV. Vicksburg 185

XXV. Natchez 200

XXVI. New Orleans 207

XXVII. Mobile 216

XXVIII. Alabama 220

XXIX. Atlanta 236

XXX. Macon 242

XXXI. Andersonville 247

XXXII. Sherman in Georgia 253

XXXIII. Savannah 270

XXXIV. Charleston 273

XXXV. The Sea Islands 284

XXXVI. Sherman in the Carolinas 294

XXXVII. The Desolate South 314

A corner of the Gettysburg battlefield, 1864

Gateway to the old cemetery, Gettysburg, 1863

Antietam Cemetery, 1865, with South Mountain in background

Graves on the battlefield of Bull Run, 1863

Ruins of the Harpers Ferry Armory, 1864

Unidentified Confederate dead on the battlefield of Gaines's Mill, 1863, where the troops of A. P. Hill, Jackson and Longstreet attacked Porter's corps

Burned-out ruins of Richmond, 1865

Confederate shell in tree at Spotsylvania, 1865. A rare instance of "close-up" photography by a cameraman of the Civil War period

Unburied dead on the Chancellorsville battlefield, 1865

Ruins of the Norfolk Navy Yard, 1865

Section of the battlefield of Atlanta, 1865

Ruins of the Richmond & Petersburg Railroad bridge, 1865

Breastworks hurriedly thrown up by Union soldiers on the slope of Little
Round Top at Gettysburg, 1865

Ruins of burned church at Columbia, 1865

Ruins of burned railroad depot at Charleston, 1865. A good example of
G. N. Barnard's skill with the wet-plate camera

Typical railroad pass in northern Georgia, 1865

Burned-out ruins at Columbia, 1865

The capitol at Nashville, 1865. Trowbridge's comment: "The Capitol is said to be the finest in the United States."

The battle-scarred
Potter house in
Atlanta, 1865

The battlefield of Missionary Ridge, 1865

Typical farmhouse
in Rossville,
Georgia, 1865

Ruins of railroad roundhouse in Atlanta, 1865

The new capitol building in Columbia, 1865. It was virtually undamaged by the fires that ravaged other sections of the town

Ruined sea wall of Fort Sumter at Charleston, 1865

Battlefield of New Hope Church in Georgia, 1865

This is the "hacked and barkless" tree which Trowbridge describes in Chapter XI, covering his visit to the battlefield of Spotsylvania in 1865

The Desolate South: 1865-1866

I
Gettysburg

IN AUGUST, 1865, I set out to visit some of the scenes of the great conflict through which the country had lately passed. On the twelfth I reached Harrisburg — a prosaic town of brick and wood, with nothing especially attractive about it except its broad-sheeted, shining river, flowing down from the Blue Ridge between pleasant shores.

It is in this region that the traveler first meets with indication of recent actual war. The Susquehanna forms the northern limit of Rebel military operations. The "high-water mark of the Rebellion" is here: along these banks its uttermost ripples died. The bluffs opposite the town are still crested with the hastily constructed breastworks on which the citizens worked night and day in June, 1863. These defenses were of no practical value. They were unfinished when the Rebels appeared in force in the vicinity: Harrisburg might easily have been taken, and a way opened into the heart of the North. But a Power greater than man's ruled the event.

The surrounding country is full of lively reminiscences of those terrible times. Panic-stricken populations flying at the approach of the enemy; flocks and herds, horses, wagonloads of heaped household stuffs and farm produce — men, women, children, riding, walking, running, driving or leading their bewildered four-footed chattels — all rushing forward with clamor and alarm under clouds of dust, crowding every road to the river and thundering across the long bridges — such were the scenes which rendered the Rebel invasion memorable.

The thrifty Dutch farmers of the lower counties did not gain much credit for either courage or patriotism. It was a panic, however, to which almost any community would have been liable. Stuart's famous raid of the previous year was well remembered. If a small cavalry force had accomplished so much, what was to be expected from Lee's whole army? Resistance to the formidable advance of one hundred thousand troops was out of the question. The slowness, however, with which the people responded to the state's almost frantic calls for volunteers was in singular contrast with the alacrity each man showed in running off his horses and goods out of Rebel reach.

From Harrisburg I went, by way of York and Hanover, to Gettysburg. Having secured a room at a hotel in the square (the citizens call it the "Di'mond"), I inquired the way to the battleground.

"You are on it now," said the landlord with proud satisfaction. In proof, he showed me a Rebel shell imbedded in the brick wall of a house close by. (N.B. The battlefield was put into the bill.)

Gettysburg is the capital of Adams County — a town of about three thousand souls. It has no especial natural advantages, owing its existence probably to the fact that several important roads meet at this point. The circumstance which made it a burg made it likewise a battlefield.

The town consists chiefly of two-story houses of wood and brick, in dull rows with thresholds elevated above the street. Rarely a front yard or blooming garden relieves the dreary monotony. In this respect Gettysburg is but a fair sample of a large class of American towns, the builders of which seem never to have been conscious that there exists such a thing as beauty.

John Burns, the "hero of Gettysburg," was almost the first person whose acquaintance I made. He was sitting under the thick shade of an elm in front of the tavern. The landlord introduced him as "the old man who took his gun and went into the first day's fight." He received me with sturdy politeness, his evident delight in the celebrity he enjoys twinkling through the veil of a naturally modest demeanor.

"John will show you the different parts of the battleground," said the landlord. "Will you, John?"

"Oh, yes," said John quite readily; and we set out.

A mile south of town is Cemetery Hill, the head and front of an important ridge running two miles farther south to Round Top — the ridge held by General Meade's army during the great battles. The Rebels attacked on the west, north and east, breaking in vain upon this tremendous wedge. A portion of Ewell's corps had passed through the town several days before and neglected to secure that very commanding position.

With the old "hero" at my side I ascended Cemetery Hill, the view from which is beautiful and striking. It was a peaceful summer day, with scarce a sound to break the stillness save the perpetual click-click of the stonecutters at work on the granite headstones of the soldiers' cemetery. There was nothing to indicate that so tranquil a spot had ever been a scene of strife.

"It don't look as it did after the battle," said Burns. "Sad work was made with the old tombstones. The ground was covered with dead horses, broken wagons, pieces of shells and battered muskets, not to speak of heaps of dead." But now the tombstones have been replaced, the neat iron fences have been mostly repaired, and scarcely a vestige of the fight remains. Only the burial places of the slain are there. *Thirty-five hundred and sixty slaughtered Union soldiers lie on the field of Gettysburg.* This number does not include those whose bodies have been claimed by friends and removed.

The new cemetery, dedicated with fitting ceremonies on November 19, 1863, adjoins the old one. In the center is the spot reserved for the monument, the cornerstone of which was laid on the fourth of July, 1865. The cemetery is semicircular, in the form of an amphitheater, and side by side, with two feet of ground allotted to each and with their heads towards the monument, rest the three thousand five hundred and sixty. The name of each, when it could be ascertained, together with the number of company and regiment, is lettered on the granite. But the barbarous practice of stripping such dead as fell into their hands, in which the Rebels indulged here as elsewhere, rendered it impossible to identify large numbers. The headstones of these are lettered "Unknown."

I looked into one of the trenches where workmen were laying foundations for headstones and saw the ends of coffins protruding. It was silent and dark down there. Side by side the soldiers slept, as side by side they fought.

Eighteen loyal states are represented by the tenants of these graves. New York has the greatest number — upwards of eight hundred; Pennsylvania comes next, having upwards of five hundred. Tall men from Maine, young braves from Wisconsin, heroes from every state between, met here to defend their country and their homes. Sons of Massachusetts fought for Massachusetts on Pennsylvania soil. If they had not fought, or if our armies had been annihilated here, the whole North would have been at the mercy of Lee's victorious legions.

As Cemetery Hill was the pivot on which turned the fortunes of battle, so Gettysburg itself was the pivot on which turned the destiny of the nation. Here the power of aggressive treason culminated; and from that memorable fourth of July when the Rebel invaders, beaten in the three days' previous fight, stole away down the valleys and behind the mountains on their ignominious retreat — from that day, signalized also by the fall of Vicksburg in the west, it waned and waned, until it was swept from the earth.

Cemetery Hill should be visited first by the tourist. Here a view of the entire field, and a clear understanding of the military operations, are best obtained. Looking north, away on your left lies Seminary Ridge, scene of the first day's fight, in which the gallant Reynolds fell and from which our troops were driven back in confusion through the town. Farther south spread the beautiful woods and vales that swarmed with Rebels on the second and third days, and from which they made such desperate charges. On the right is Culp's Hill, scene of Ewell's furious but futile attempts to flank us. You are in the focus of a half circle, from all points of which was poured in upon this now silent hill such an artillery fire as has seldom been concentrated in any great battle upon this planet. From this spot extend your observations as you please.

Guided by sturdy old Burns, I proceeded first to Culp's Hill, following a line of breastworks into the woods. A rude embankment of stakes and logs and stones, covered with earth, forms the principal work; aside from which you meet with little private breastworks consisting of rocks heaped by a tree or beside a larger rock, or across a cleft in the rocks, where some sharpshooter exercised his skill at his ease. A more fitting spot for a picnic, one would say, than for a battle.

Yet here remain more astonishing evidences of fierce fighting than anywhere else about Gettysburg. The trees in certain localities are scarred, disfigured, and literally dying or dead from wounds. Here are limbs, and yonder are whole treetops, cut off by shells. Many of these trees have been hacked for lead, and chips containing bullets have been carried away for relics.

Past the foot of the hill runs Rock Creek, a muddy, sluggish stream — " great for eels," said Burns. Big boulders and blocks of stone are scattered along its bed. Plenty of Rebel knapsacks lie rotting on the ground; and there are Rebel graves nearby in the woods. By these I was inclined to pause longer than Burns. I felt a pity for these unhappy men which he could not understand. To him they were dead Rebels, and nothing more; and he spoke with great disgust of an effort which had been made by certain "Copperheads" of the town to have all the buried Rebels gathered together in a cemetery near that dedicated to our own dead.

"Yet consider, my friend," I said, "though they were altogether in the wrong, and their cause was infernal, these, too, were brave men; and under different circumstances they might have been lying in honored graves up yonder, instead of being buried in heaps, like dead cattle, down here."

Is there not a better future for these men also? The time will come when we shall at least cease to hate them. . . .

Next morning, I went to call on Burns in a little whitewashed house west of town. A flight of wooden steps outside took me to his door. John is a stoutish, slightly bent, hale old man, with a light-blue eye, a firm-set mouth and a choleric temperament. His hair is bleached with age; and his beard, once sandy, covers his face with fine silver stubble.

A short, massy man, about five feet four, I should judge. He was never measured but once in his life — when he enlisted in the War of 1812. He was then nineteen years old, and stood five feet. "But I've growed a heap since," said John. Then, at my request, he told his story.

On the morning of the first day's fight he sent his wife away, telling her he would take care of the house. The firing was nearby, over Seminary Ridge. Soon a wounded soldier came into town and stopped at an old house on the opposite corner. Burns saw the poor fellow lay down his musket, and the inspiration to go into battle seems to have seized him. He went over and demanded the gun.

"What are you going to do with it?" asked the soldier.

"I'm going to shoot some of the damned Rebels!" replied John.

Having obtained the gun, he pushed out on the Chambersburg Pike and soon was in the thick of the skirmish. "I wore a high-crowned hat and a long-tailed blue; and I was seventy year old."

The sight of so old a man, in such costume, rushing fearlessly forward to get a shot in the very front of the battle, of course attracted attention. He fought with the Seventh Wisconsin, the colonel of which ordered him back and questioned him, and finally, seeing the old man's patriotic determination, gave him a good rifle in place of the musket he had brought.

"Are you a good shot?"

"Tolerable good," said John, an old fox hunter.

"Do you see that Rebel riding yonder?"

"I do."

"Can you fetch him?"

"I can try."

The old man took aim and fired. He does not say he killed the Rebel, but simply that his shot was cheered by the Wisconsin boys, and that afterwards the horse the Rebel rode was seen galloping with an empty saddle.

"That's all I know about it."

He fought until our forces were driven back in the afternoon. He had already received two slight wounds, and a third one through the arm, to which he paid little attention. "Only the blood running down my hand bothered me a heap." Then, as he was falling back with the rest, he received a final shot through the leg. "Down I went, and the whole Rebel army run over me."

Helpless, nearly bleeding to death, he lay upon the field all night. "About sunup I crawled to a neighbor's house and found it full of wounded Rebels." The neighbor afterwards took him to his own house, which had also been turned into a Rebel hospital. A Rebel surgeon dressed his wounds; and he says he received decent treatment at the hands of the enemy until a Copperhead woman living opposite "told on him."

"That's the old man who said he was going out to shoot some of the damned Rebels!"

Some officers questioned him, endeavoring to convict him of bushwhacking. But the old man gave them little satisfaction. This was Friday, the third day of the battle; and he was alone with his wife in the upper part of the house. The Rebels left; and soon after two shots were fired. One bullet entered the window, passed over Burns's head and penetrated the wall behind the lounge on which he was lying. The other shot fell lower, passing through a door. Burns is certain that the design was to assassinate him. That the shots were fired by the Rebels there can be no doubt; and as they were fired from their own side, towards the town, John's theory seems the true one.

Burns went with me over the ground where the first day's fight took place. He showed me the scene of his hot day's work — pointed out two trees behind which he and one of the Wisconsin boys "picked off every Rebel that showed his head," and the spot where he lay all night under the stars and dew.

This act of daring on the part of so aged a citizen naturally caused him to be looked upon as a hero. But a hero, like a prophet, has not all honor in his own country. There is a widespread, violent prejudice against Burns among that class of townspeople termed "Copperheads." The young men especially, who did *not* take their guns and go into the fight but who ran when running was possible, dislike Burns, some averring that he did not have a gun that day but that he was wounded by accident, happening to get between the lines.

Of his going into the fight and *fighting*, there is no doubt whatever. Of his bravery, amounting even to rashness, there can be no reasonable question. He is a patriot of the most zealous sort, a hot, impulsive man, who meant what he said when he started with the gun to go and shoot some of the Rebels qualified with the strong adjective.

Burns is a sagacious observer and makes shrewd remarks like this: "Whenever you see the marks of shells and bullets on a house all painted and plastered over, that's the house of a Rebel sympathizer. But when you see them all preserved and kept in sight, as something to be proud of, that's the house of a true Union man! . . ."

Next day I mounted a hard-trotting horse and rode to Round Top. On the way I stopped at the historical peach orchard known as Sherfy's, where Sickles's corps was repulsed after a ter-

rific conflict on the second day of the battle. The peaches were
green on the trees then; but they were ripe now, and the
branches were breaking with them. One of Sherfy's girls — the
youngest, she told me — had rareripes to sell. They were large
and juicy and sweet — all the redder, no doubt, for the blood of
the brave that had drenched the sod.

Between fields made memorable by hard fighting I rode eastward and, entering a pleasant wood, ascended Little Round
Top. Nearby is Devil's Den, a dark cavity in the rocks, interesting on account of the fight that took place for the possession of
these heights. A photographic view, taken the Sunday morning
after the battle, shows eight dead Rebels tumbled headlong with
their guns among the rocks below the den.

A little farther on is Round Top itself, a craggy tusk of rock-
jawed earth, covered with boulders and fields of stones. It is a
natural fortress, which our boys strengthened still further by
throwing up the loose stones into handy breastworks. I rode the
whole length of the ridge held by our troops, realizing more
and more the importance of that extraordinary position. It is
like a shoe, of which Round Top represents the heel, Cemetery
Hill the toe.

Here all our forces were concentrated on Thursday and Friday, within a space of two miles. Movements from one part to
another of this compact field could be made with celerity. Lee's
forces, on the other hand, extended over a circle of seven miles
or more around, in a country where all their movements could
be anticipated.

At a point well forward on the foot of this shoe, Meade had
his headquarters. I tied my horse at the gate and entered the little square box of a house which enjoys historical celebrity. It is
scarcely more than a hut, having but two little rooms on the

ground floor and I know not what narrow, low-roofed chambers above. Two small girls with brown German faces were paring apples under the porch; and a round-shouldered, bareheaded and barefooted woman, also with a strong German accent, was drawing water at the well. I asked her for drink, which she kindly gave, and invited me into the house.

The little box was whitewashed outside and in. The woman sat down to some mending and entered freely into conversation. She was a widow, and the mother of six children. The two girls cutting apples at the door were the youngest, the only ones left to her. A son in the army was expected home in a few days.

She ran away at the time of the fight, but was sorry afterwards she did not stay home. The house was robbed of almost everything. "Coverlids and sheets, and some of our own clo'es, all carried away. They got about two ton of hay from me. I owed a little on my land yit, and thought I'd put in two lots of wheat that year, and it was all trampled down, and I didn't git nothing from it. I had seven pieces of meat yit, and them was all took. All I had when I got back was jist a little bit of flour yit.

"The fences was all tore down and the rails burnt up. One shell come into the house and knocked a bedstead all to pieces for me. One come in under the roof and knocked out a rafter for me. The porch was all knocked down. There was seventeen dead horses on my land. They burnt five of 'em around my best peach tree and killed it, so I ha'n't no peaches this year. They broke down all my young apple trees for me. The dead horses sp'iled my spring, so I had to have my well dug."

I inquired if she got anything for the damage.

"Not much. I jist sold the bones of the dead horses. I couldn't do it till this year, for the meat hadn't rotted off yit. I got fifty cents a hundred. There was seven hundred and fifty pounds. You can reckon up what they come to. That's all I got."

The town is full of similar reminiscences; and it is a subject which everybody except the "Copperheads" likes to talk about. Shortly after the battle, sad tales were told of the cruel inhospitality shown to wounded Union troops by the people of Gettysburg. Many of these stories were doubtless true; but they were true only of the more brutal of the Rebel sympathizers. Union men threw open their hearts and their homes to the wounded.

One afternoon I met a soldier on Cemetery Hill who had been in the battle and was now revisiting the scene of that terrible experience. Getting into conversation, we walked down the hill together. As we were approaching a double house with high wooden steps, he pointed out the farther one and said:

"Saturday morning after the fight, I got a piece of bread at that house. A man stood on the steps and gave each of our fellows a piece. We were hungry as bears, and it was a godsend. I should like to see that man and thank him."

Just then the man himself appeared at the door. We went over and I introduced the soldier, who, with tears in his eyes, expressed his gratitude for that act of Christian charity.

"Yes," said the man, "we did what we could. We baked bread night and day to give to every hungry soldier who wanted it. We sent away our own children to make room for wounded soldiers, and for days our house was a hospital."

Of the magnitude of a battle fought so desperately during three days, by armies numbering not far from two hundred thousand men, no adequate conception can be formed. One or two facts may help to give a faint idea of it. Culp's meadow below Cemetery Hill — a lot of near twenty acres — was so thickly strewn with Rebel dead that Culp declared he "could have walked across it without putting foot upon the ground." Upwards of three hundred Confederates were buried in one hole. On Gwynn's farm below Round Top, some five hundred sons of the South lie heaped in one huge sepulcher.

Of the quantities of iron, arms, knapsacks, haversacks and clothing which strewed the country, no estimate can be made. The government set a guard over these, and for weeks officials were busy gathering the more valuable spoils. The harvest of bullets was left for the citizens to glean. Many of the poorer people did a thriving business picking up these missiles of death and selling them to dealers — two of whom alone sent to Baltimore fifty tons of lead collected from the battlefield.

II
Chambersburg

ON AUGUST 18, I left Gettysburg for Chambersburg by
stage over a rough turnpike, broken to pieces by Lee's artillery and army wagons two years before. We traversed a
sleepy-looking wheat and corn country, where few signs of life
and enterprise were visible. Crossing the Blue Ridge, we passed
through a more busy land and entered the pleasant suburbs of
Chambersburg at sunset.

On every side were the skeletons of houses burned by the
Rebels, and we looked across their roofless and broken walls at
the red sunset. Dead shade trees stood solemn in the dusk beside the dead, deserted streets. In places, the work of rebuilding
had been vigorously commenced; and the streets were to be
traversed only by narrow paths between piles of old brick saved
from the ruins, stacks of new brick, beds of mortar and heaps
of sand.

Our driver took us to a new hotel erected on the ruins of an
old one. The landlord, eager to talk, told me his story while
supper was preparing.

"I had jeest bought the hotel that stood where this does and
paid eight thousand dollars for it. I had laid out two thousand
dollars fitting it up. All the rooms had been new papered and
furnished, and there was three hundred dollars' worth of carpets

in the house not put down yet, when the Rebels they jeest come in and burnt it all up."

I found everybody full of talk on this great and absorbing topic. On the night of July 29, 1864, Rebel cavalry appeared before the town. Some artillery boys went out with a fieldpiece to frighten them and fired a few shots. That kept the raiders at bay till morning, for they had come not to fight but to destroy; and it was ticklish advancing in the dark. Next morning, however, before the alarmed inhabitants had thought of breakfast, they entered — the fieldpiece keeping judiciously out of sight.

They had come with General Early's orders to burn the town in retaliation for General Hunter's spoliation of the Shenandoah Valley. That they would commit so great a crime was hardly to be credited, for what Hunter had done towards destroying that granary of the Confederacy had been done as a military necessity, and there was no such excuse for burning Chambersburg. It seemed a folly as well as a crime; for, with our armies occupying the South, and continually acquiring new districts and cities, it was in their power, had they been equally barbarous, to carry on this game of retaliation until the whole South should have become as Sodom.

Chambersburg had suffered from repeated Rebel raids but it had escaped serious damage, and the people were inclined to jeer at neighboring towns which had been terrified into paying heavy ransoms to the marauders. But now its time had come. The Confederate leaders demanded of the authorities one hundred thousand dollars in gold, or five hundred thousand dollars in United States currency, promising that if the money was not forthcoming in fifteen minutes, the torch would be applied. I know not whether it was possible to raise so great a sum in so short a time. At all events, it was not raised.

Then suddenly from all parts of town went up a cry of horror
and dismay. The infernal work had begun. The town was fired
in a hundred places at once. A house was entered, a can of kero-
sene emptied on a bed, and in an instant up went a burst of
flame. Extensive plundering was done. Citizens were told that
if they would give their money, their houses would be spared.
The money was in many instances promptly given, when their
houses were as promptly fired.

Such a wail of women and children, fleeing for life from flaming houses, has seldom been heard. Down the hardened cheeks
of old men who could scarce remember that they had ever wept,
the tears ran in streams. In the terrible confusion nothing was
saved. In many houses money, which had been carefully put
away, was abandoned and burned. The heat of the flames was
fearful. Citizens who described those scenes to me considered it
miraculous that in the midst of so great terror and excitement,
not a life was lost.

The part of town east of the railroad is said to have been
saved by the spirit of a heroic lady. As her house was about to
be fired, she appealed to a Rebel cavalry captain, and showing
him the throngs of weeping women and children seeking refuge
in the cut through which the railroad passes, said to him with
solemn emphasis:

"In the day of judgment, sir, you will see that sight again.
Then, sir, you will have this to answer for!"

The captain was touched. "It is contrary to orders," said he,
"but this thing shall be stopped." And he stationed a guard
along the track to prevent further destruction of the city in that
direction.

The homeless citizens crowded to a hill and watched the completion of the diabolical work. The whirlwind of fire and smoke

that went roaring up into the calm, blue heavens was indescribably appalling. Fortunately the day was still; otherwise not a house would have been left standing. As it was, three hundred and forty houses were burned, comprising about two thirds of the town.

The raiders were evidently afraid of being caught at work. The smoke, which could be seen thirty or forty miles away, would doubtless guide our cavalry to the spot. Having hastily accomplished their task, with equal haste they decamped.

Three of their number, however, paid the penalty of the crime on the spot. Two, plundering a cellar, were shot by a redoubtable apothecary — a choleric but conscientious man who was much troubled afterwards for what he had done, for it is an awful thing to take human life even under circumstances the most justifiable. "He was downhearted all next day about it," said one. Meanwhile the dead marauders were reduced to indistinguishable ashes, in the pyre they had themselves prepared.

A major of the party, who had become intoxicated plundering liquor shops, lingered behind his companions. He was surrounded by the incensed populace and ordered to surrender. Refusing, and drawing his sword with maudlin threats, he was shot down. He was then buried to his breast outside of town, and left with just his shoulders protruding from the ground, with his horrible lolling head drooping over them. Having been exhibited in this state to the multitude, he was granted a more thorough sepulture. A few weeks before my visit to the place, a gentle-faced female from the South came to claim his body; for he, too, was a human being, and no mere monster, as many supposed, and there were those that did love him.

The distress and suffering of the burned-out inhabitants of Chambersburg can never be told. Besides the charity of other towns, the state granted one hundred thousand dollars for the relief of sufferers. This was but as a drop to them, for those who had property remaining got nothing. The appropriation was intended for those who had lost everything — and there were hundreds of such, some of whom had been stopped in the streets and robbed even of their shoes, after their houses had been fired.

"This was jeest how it worked. Some got more than they had before the fire. A boardinghouse girl that had lost say eight dollars would come and say she had lost fifty, and she'd get fifty. But men like me, that happened to have a little property outside, never got a cent."

It will always remain a matter of astonishment that the great and prosperous State of Pennsylvania did not make a more generous appropriation. The tax necessary for the purpose would scarcely have been felt by anyone, while it would have been but a just indemnification to those who had suffered in a cause which the whole loyal North was bound to uphold. But there is no loss without gain. Chambersburg will in the end be greatly benefited by the fire, inasmuch as the old two-story buildings are being replaced by three-story houses, much finer and more commodious. So let it be with our country. Fearful as our loss has been, we shall build better anew.

III

Antietam

NEXT DAY I took the cars for Hagerstown, and then set out by stage for Boonsboro. Our course lay down the valley of the Antietam, a fertile valley lined with fields of tall and stalwart corn. At Boonsboro, time was consumed in finding a guide to take me over the battlefields. At length I encountered Lewy Smith, light and jaunty Lewy Smith with his light and jaunty covered carryall — whom I would recommend to travelers. Immediately after dinner he was at the tavern door, snapping his whip.

The traveler's most pleasant experience of Boonsboro is leaving it. The town contains about nine hundred inhabitants, and the wonder is how so many human souls can rest content to live in such a moldy, lonesome place. Leave it behind you as soon as convenient, and turn your face to famed South Mountain, where the prologue to Antietam was enacted.

"I never heard it called *South Mountain* till after the battle," said Smith. "It was always the *Blue Ridge* with us." He had never heard of Turner's Gap, or Frog Gap, either. "We always called it just the gap in the mountain."

The road to the gap stretched pleasant before us. "The night before the battle," said Smith, "this road was lined with Rebels, I tell ye! Both sides were covered with them about as thick as they could lie. It didn't seem to us there were men enough in the Union Army to fight them. We thought the Rebels had got possession of Maryland, sure. They just took what they pleased and paid in Confederate money; they had come to stay, they said, and their money would be better than ours in a little while. Some who got plenty of it did well; for when the Rebels slaughtered cattle, they would sell the hides and take their own currency for pay."

The mountain rose before us, leopard-colored, spotted with sun and cloud. Lewy left his horse at a stable and we entered the woods, pursuing a mountain road which runs south along the crest. A tramp of twenty minutes brought us to the scene of General Reno's brilliant achievement and heroic death. A rude stone set up in the field near a spreading chestnut marks the spot where he fell. A few rods north of this, running east and west, is the mountain road, with a stone wall on each side, where the Rebels fought furiously until driven out by our boys coming up through the woods. The few wayside trees are riddled with bullets. A little higher up the crest is a log house, and a well in which fifty-seven dead Rebels are buried.

"The owner of the house was offered a dollar a head for burying them. The easiest way was to pitch them into the well. But he don't like to own up to having done it now."

We pushed through the woods to the eastern brow of the crest, where a superb scene opened before us — Catoctin Valley, like a poem in blue and gold, with its patches of hazy woods, sunlit misty fields, and the Catoctin Mountains rolling up beyond. The bridge across Catoctin Creek, half a mile west of Middletown, where the fighting began on September 14, 1862, could be seen far below. Standing on the brow of the commanding crest, you would say that ten thousand men might here check the advance of ten times their number, hold the gap on the left, and prevent the steep mountainsides from being scaled.

In a barren pasture above the slope climbed by Reno's men, we came upon a little row of graves under some locust trees. Several were of the Twenty-third Ohio, the impetuous regiment that had its famous hand-to-hand conflict with the Twenty-third South Carolina, in which each man fought as though the honor of the nation depended upon his individual arm. Here lay the victorious fallen. A few had been removed from their rude graves. The headboards of others had been knocked down by cows. We set them up again, and left the field to the pensive sound of cowbells.

Walking back through the gap, and surveying the crests commanding it, which were held by the Rebels but carried with irresistible impetuosity by the men of Burnside's and Hooker's corps, one is still more astonished by the successful issue of that terrible day's work. Long after the battle, explorers of the woods were accustomed to find, in hollows and behind logs, the remains of some poor fellow, generally a Rebel, who, wounded in the fight or on the retreat, had dragged himself to shelter and died there alone, in the gloomy and silent wilderness.

Next morning, our course lay along the line of the Rebel retreat and of the advance of the right wing of our army. A pleasant road brought us to Keedysville, a cluster of brick and log houses which were turned into hospitals after the battle. At the farther end of the town is a brick church.

"That was a hospital, too. Many an arm, a leg, a hand, was left there by our boys. There's a pit behind the church, five feet long, five feet deep and two feet wide, just full of legs and arms."

We rode on until we obtained a view of the hillsides where

Porter lay with his reserves while the other army corps did the fighting on the day of Antietam, then turned to the right down a little stream and past a dam, and soon came in sight of the fields where the great fight began. There they lay, over the farther bank of the Antietam, some green, some ploughed, the latter turning up yellow as ripe grain in the morning light.

"We used to could drive all over this country where we pleased. The fences were laid down, and it was all trampled and cut up with the wagons, and soldiers, and artillery." But the fences had been replaced, and now Lewy was obliged to keep to the open road.

At a turn we came to a farmhouse. "It was a sight to behold, passing yer after the battle!" said Smith, shaking his head sadly. "All in and around these yer buildings, all around the haystacks and under the fences, it was just nothing but groaning, wounded men!"

Leaving the course of the creek, we reached a still and shady grove, beside which, fenced in from a field, was a little burying ground of half an acre. In the center was a plain monument constructed of boards painted white, the pedestal bearing this inscription: "Let no man desecrate this burial-place of our dead."

And on the side of the shaft towards the fence, these words: "I am the resurrection and the life: he that believeth in me, though he were dead, yet shall he live."

This was the hospital cemetery. The graves were close together in little rows running across the narrow field. They were all overgrown with grass and weeds. Each was marked by a small headboard, painted white, and bearing the name of the soldier sleeping below.

Pursuing a road along the ridge in a southwesterly direction, Lewy at length reined up his horse in another peaceful little grove. Without a word he pointed to the rotting knapsacks on the ground, and to the scarred trees. I knew the spot; it was the boundary of the bloody "cornfield." We had approached from the side on which our boys advanced to that frightful conflict, driving the Rebels and being driven back in turn in horrible seesaw, until superior Northern pluck and endurance finally prevailed.

In a field beside the grove we saw a man ploughing with three horses abreast, and a young lad for escort. We noticed loose headboards, overturned by the plough and lying half imbedded in the furrows.

"A power of 'em in this yer field!" said the ploughman as I questioned him. "I always skip a Union grave when I know it, but sometimes I don't see 'em, and I plough 'em up. Eight or ten thousand lays on this farm, Rebels and Union together."

I picked up a skull lying loose on the ground like a cobblestone. It was that of a young man; the teeth were all splendid and sound. How hideously they grinned at me! and the eye sockets were filled with dirt.

Torn rags strewed the ground. The old ploughman picked up a fragment. "This yer was a Union soldier. You may know by the blue cloth. But then that ain't always a sign, for the Rebels got into our uniform when they had a chance, and got killed in it, too."

We found many more bones of Union soldiers rooted up and exposed as we ascended the ridge. "The Rebs had all the fence down 'cept a strip by the pike," said the ploughman. "That was jist like a sifter. Some of the rails have been cut up and carried away for the bullet holes."

He showed me marks still remaining on the fence. Some of our soldiers had cut their names upon it, and on one post some pious Roman Catholic had carved the sacred initials "I. H. S."

"I reckon that was a soldier's name, too," said my honest ploughman.

While I was exploring the fields with my ploughman, Smith brought his horse around by the roads. "The last time I drove by yer," he said, " there was a nigger ploughing in that field, and every time he came to a grave he would just reach over his plough, jerk up the headboard and stick it down behind him again as he ploughed along; and all the time he never stopped whistling his tune."

We drove on to the Dunker church, a square, plain, white-washed, one-story brick building without steeple, situated in the edge of the woods. No one, from its appearance, would take it to be a church; and I find that soldiers who fought here still speak of it as "the schoolhouse."

"The Dunkers are a sect of plain people," said one of the old Dutch settlers. "They don't believe in any wanities. They don't believe in war and fighting."

But their church had got pretty seriously into the fight. It had been patched with brick and whitewash, however, and the plain people, who "did not believe in wanities," once more held their quiet meetings there.

As it was beginning to rain, Smith carried me on to Sharpsburg and there left me. A more lonesome place even than Boonsboro, a tossed and broken sort of place, that looks as if the solid ground swell of the earth had moved on and jostled it since the foundations were laid. As you go up and down the hilly streets, the pavements, composed of fragments of limestone slabs, thrust up such abrupt fangs and angles at you that it is necessary to tread with exceeding caution.

As Sharpsburg was in the thick of the fight, the battle scars it still carries add to its dilapidated appearance. After dinner I started to walk to the bridge known henceforth and for all time as "Burnside's Bridge," but a shower coming up, I sought shelter at a stone house near the edge of town. I had scarcely mounted the steps when a woman with cordial hospitality urged me to enter the sitting room. I accepted her invitation, having found that every dweller on a battlefield has something interesting to tell.

She and her neighbors fled their homes on the Tuesday before the battle and did not return until Friday. She, like nearly every person I talked with, was sorry she did not remain in the cellar. "When we came back, all I could do was jist to set right down and cry." The house had been plundered, their provisions swept away by the all-devouring armies. "Them that stayed at home did not lose anything; but if the soldiers found a house deserted, that they robbed."

I inquired which plundered the most, our men or the Rebels.

"That I can't say, stranger. The Rebels took; but the Yankees took right smart."

She showed me in an adjoining room a looking glass hanging within an inch or two of a large patched space in the wall. "That glass was hanging on that nail, jist as it hangs now, when a shell come in yer and smashed a bedstead to pieces for me on that side of the room, and the glass wasn't so much as moved."

By this time the rain had ceased, so I continued to the bridge, a mile farther on. If the tourist is surprised at the strength of the positions on South Mountain from which the Rebels were dislodged, he will be no less amazed at Burnside's achievement here. Above the road as it approaches the bridge, and above the creek below the bridge, rises a high steep bank, like a bluff. To approach from the opposite side, exposed to a concentrated in-

fantry and artillery fire flashing all along this crest — to carry
the bridge, and drive the enemy from their vantage ground —
one would say was a feat for the heroes of the age of fable. But
the truth is, though men are slow to receive it, there never was
any age better than this — none that produced a more heroic
race of men. We have worshiped the past long enough; it is time
now to look a little into the merits of the present. Troy, and
Greece, and Rome were admirable in their day, and the men of
Israel did some doughty deeds; but the men of New England, of
the great Middle States, and of the vast Northwest, what have
they not done?

That Burnside's command could ever have crossed this bridge
in the face of superior numbers pouring deadly volleys upon
them, that is what astonishes you; and what grieves you is that
reinforcements were not sent to enable him to hold what he
gained. If Porter, who had the reserves, had been a man of right
courage and patriotism, he would have gone into the fight when
needed — for reserves were not invented merely to be kept nice
and choice — and the results of that day would have been very
different.

I spent some hours about the bridge, the Antietam Creek
singing all the while its liquid accompaniment to my thoughts.
I sat down on a rock and watched a flock of buzzards perched on
the limbs of a dead tree, looking melancholy — resembling
greedy camp followers and army speculators, who remembered
with pensive regret the spoils of the good old war days.

Returning to the village, I visited the spot chosen as a national cemetery for the slain. The ground had been purchased,
but work upon it had not yet commenced. In the Antietam
cemetery it is understood that the Rebel dead are to be included. Many object to this; but I do not. Skeletons, rooted up

by hogs and blanching in open fields, are not a sight becoming a country that calls itself Christian.

Here let the dead rest together, they of the good cause and they of the evil; I shall be content. For neither was the one cause altogether good nor was the other altogether bad: the holier being clouded by much ignorance and selfishness, and the darker one brightened here and there with glorious flashes of self-devotion. It was not, rightly speaking, these brothers that were at war. The conflict was waged between two great principles — one looking towards liberty and human advancement, the other madly drawing the world back to barbarism and the Dark Ages. America was the chessboard on which the stupendous game was played, and those we name Patriots and Rebels were but the pawns.

IV

Harpers Ferry

SHARPSBURG is not a promising place to spend the night, and I determined to leave it that evening. Entering a confectioner's shop, I asked a young lady if she knew any person who would take me to Harpers Ferry.

"Yes, Mr. Bennerhalls," she replied. "I reckon ye can get him."

I went up one of the broken pavements in search of him. To my surprise I was told that Mr. Bennerhalls did not live on that street; further, that no person of that name was known in Sharpsburg. I returned to the confectioner's shop.

"You said *Mr. Bennerhalls?*"

"Yes, sir. Mr. Bennerhalls, and Mr. Cramerhalls, and Mr. Joneshalls. I should think you might get one of them."

Bennerhalls, Cramerhalls, Joneshalls — what outlandish cognomens were these?

"I *know* Mr. Joneshalls," said the young lady as I stood with an amused expression which she mistook for sarcastic incredulity.

"Jones *hauls*," thought I. That is, Jones hauls people over the road in his wagon. And the first-mentioned individual was not *Bennerhalls*, but one Benner who *hauled*.

I thanked the young lady for her courtesy and went to find

Mr. Benner. He was sitting on a doorstep, and scratched his head over the odd patronymic. "Yes, I have hosses, and I haul sometimes, but I can't put one over that road to Harpers Ferry, stranger, nohow!"

I got no more satisfaction out of Cramer, and still less out of Jones, who informed me that not only he would not go but he didn't believe there was a man in Sharpsburg that would. I returned to the tavern and appealed to the landlord. To my surprise, he said if I could find no one else to haul me, he would.

At five P.M. we left Sharpsburg in an open buggy under a sky that threatened rain. Black clouds and thundergusts were all around us. Through occasional spatters of rain and angrily spitting squalls, we whipped on. It was a fleet horse my friend drove. He was pleased to hear me praise him.

"That's a North Carolina horse. I brought him home with me."

"You have been in the army?"

And out came the interesting fact that I was riding with Captain Speaker of the First Maryland Cavalry, a man who had seen service and had things to tell.

Everybody remembers, in connection with the shameful surrender of Harpers Ferry just before Antietam, the brilliant episode of twenty-two hundred of Federal cavalry cutting their way out and capturing a part of one of Longstreet's trains on their escape. Captain Speaker was the leader of that expedition.

"I was second lieutenant of the First Maryland Cavalry at the time. I knew Colonel Davis very well; and when I heard Harpers Ferry was to be surrendered, I remarked to him that I would not be surrendered with it alive. He asked what I would do. 'Cut my way out,' I said. When he asked what I meant, I told him I believed I could not only get out myself, but that I could pilot out with safety any number of cavalry that would take the same risk and go with me. I had lived in the country all my life, and knew every part of it.

"Colonel Davis saw that I knew what I was talking about, so he applied to Colonel Miles for permission to put it into execution. 'It's all talk,' said Miles. 'Put him to the test, and he'll back down.'

" 'Just try him,' said Davis.

"So Miles wrote on a piece of paper: 'Lieutenant Speaker, will you take charge of a cavalry force and lead it through the enemy's lines?'

"I just wrote under it, 'Yes, with pleasure,' signed my name, and sent it back to him."

At ten o'clock the same night they started. It was Sunday, the fourteenth of September, the day of the battle of South Mountain. The party consisted of twenty-two hundred of cavalry and a number of mounted civilians who took advantage of the expedition to escape the town before it was surrendered. Speaker and Colonel Davis rode side by side at the head of the column. They crossed on the pontoon bridge, which formed the military connection between Harpers Ferry and Maryland Heights, and turned up the road which runs between the canal and the heights, riding at full charge along the left bank of the Potomac. It was a wild road; the night was dark; only the campfires on the mountain were visible; and there was no sound but the swift clatter of thousands of galloping hoofs.

Four miles from the ferry, Speaker and Davis were challenged by Rebel pickets.

"Who goes there?"

"Second Virginia Cavalry," said Davis — which was true, the

Second Virginia *Union* Cavalry being of the party, while the Second Virginia *Rebel* Cavalry was also in the vicinity. "Who are you?"

"Louisiana Tigers."

"All right. We are out scouting."

"All right," said the pickets.

The leaders rode back, formed their party, gave the word, and charged. They went through the Rebel line like an express train. A few shots were fired by the astonished pickets, but they got through almost without loss. Three horses were killed and three men dismounted, but the latter escaped up the mountainside and afterwards made their way into Union lines.

They galloped on to Sharpsburg, keeping the same road all the way by which Captain Speaker was now conveying me to the ferry. The enemy held Sharpsburg. Fortunately in every street and byroad, Speaker was at home. He called on a well-known Union citizen, from whom he obtained important information. "The Rebels are in strong force on the Hagerstown Road. They have heavy batteries, too, posted on the Williamsport Pike." There was then but one thing to do. "Down with the fences and take to the fields," said the pilot of the party.

"We struck the pike between Hagerstown and Williamsport about two o'clock. We came to a halt pretty quick, though, for there was a Rebel wagon train several miles in length, passing along the pike. Our line was formed along by the pike, extending some three quarters of a mile. Then we charged. The first the guards and drivers knew, there were sabers at their heads; and all they had to do was to turn their wagons right about and go with us. We captured over seventy wagons, all the rear of the train."

It was just daylight when they arrived at Greencastle and

turned the wagons over to the Federal quartermaster there. "Then you should have seen each fellow tumble himself off his horse! Remember, we had been fighting at the ferry, and this was the third night we had had no sleep. Each man just took a turn of the bridle around his wrist and dropped down on the pavement, anywhere, and in three minutes was fast asleep."

It is eleven miles from Sharpsburg to Harpers Ferry. After striking the Potomac, we continued down its left bank, with the canal between us and the river on one side, and Maryland Heights, rising even more and more rugged and abrupt, on the other; until, as we approached the bridge at the ferry, we looked up through the stormy dusk at mountain crags rising several hundred feet above our heads. Crossing the new iron bridge, near the ruins of the old one destroyed by the Rebels, Captain Speaker landed me near the end of it on the Virginia side.

"Where is the hotel?" I asked, looking round with some dismay.

"That is it, the only hotel at Harpers Ferry now" — showing me a new, unpainted, wooden building, which looked more like barracks than a hotel. There was not a blind or shutter to be seen. The main entrance from the street was through a barroom where men were clicking glasses and sucking dark-colored stuff through straws. And this was a "first-class hotel kept on the European plan." I mention it as one of the results of war — as an illustration of the mushroom style of building which springs up in the track of desolation, to fill temporarily the place of the old that has been swept away and of the better growth to come.

After supper a "room" was shown me, which turned out to be a mere bin to stow guests in. There was no paper on the walls, no carpet on the rough board floor, not so much as a nail to hang a hat on. The bed was furnished with sheets which came down just below a man's knees, and a mattress which had the appearance of being stuffed with shingles. Finding it impossible, by dint of shouting and pounding, to bring a servant to my assistance, I went on a marauding expedition through the unoccupied rooms and carried off a chair, a dressing table, and another bed entire. Yet no devices availed to render the Shenandoah House a place favorable to sleep.

On the river side, close by the door, ran the track of the Baltimore and Ohio Railroad. How often during the night the trains passed I cannot now compute, each approaching and departing with clatter and clang and shouts of men and bell ringing and sudden glares of light, and the voice of the steam whistle projecting its shrill shriek into the ear of horrified night, and setting the giant mountains to tossing and retossing the echo like a ball.

Next morning I was up at dawn, refreshing my eyesight with the natural beauties of the place. At Harpers Ferry, the Potomac and the Shenandoah unite their waters and flow through an enormous gap in the Blue Ridge. The angle of land thus formed is a sort of promontory, around the base of which, where the rivers meet, the curious little old town is built. Higher up the promontory lies Bolivar Heights. On the north, just across the Potomac from the ferry, rises Maryland Heights; while on the east, across the Shenandoah, is Loudon Heights, an equally precipitous and lofty crag. With sublime rocky fronts these two mountains stand gazing at each other across the river which has evidently forced its way through them here.

In the morning I climbed Maryland Heights by the winding military road which owes its existence to the war. I have seen nothing since the view from Mount Washington to be compared with the panorama which unrolled itself around me as I ascended. Pictures of two states were there, indescribably tinted in the early-morning light — beautiful Maryland, still more beautiful Virginia, with the green Potomac Valley marking the boundary between.

Yet it was war and not beauty which led man to these heights. The timber which once covered them was cut away when forts were constructed, in order to afford free range for the guns; and a thick undergrowth now takes its place. There are strong works on the summit, the sight of which kindles anew one's indignation at the imbecility which surrendered them, with Harpers Ferry and a small army, at a time when such an act was sufficient to prolong the war perhaps for years.

It is a steep mile and more by road from the ferry to the top of the cliffs: a mile which richly repays the travel. Whichever way you turn, river or rock or wild woods charm the eye. But while the region presents such features of beauty and grandeur, the town is the reverse of agreeable. It is said to have been a pleasant and picturesque place formerly, but war has changed all.

Freshets tear down the streets, and the dreary hillsides present only ragged weeds. The town itself lies half in ruins. The government works were destroyed by the Rebels; of the extensive buildings which comprised the armory, rolling mills, foundry and machine shops, you see little more than burned-out, empty shells. Of the bridge across the Shenandoah only the ruined piers are left; still less remains of the old bridge over the Potomac. And all about the town are rubbish, filth and stench.

Almost alone of the government buildings, John Brown's "Engine House" has escaped destruction. It has come out of the ordeal of war terribly bruised and battered, its windows blackened and patched like the eyes of a pugilist; but there it still stands, with its brown brick walls and little wooden belfry, like a monument which no Rebel hands were permitted to demolish. It is now used as a storehouse for arms.

The first time I visited this scene of the first bloodshed in the great Civil War, a genial old gentleman, coming out of the government repair shop close by, accosted me and told the story of John Brown at Harpers Ferry.

"So they took the old man and hung him; and all the time the men that did it were plotting treason and murder by the wholesale. They did it in a hurry, because if they delayed, they wouldn't have been able to hang him at all. A strong current of public feeling was turning in his favor. Such a sacrifice of himself set many to thinking on the subject who never thought before — many who had to acknowledge in their hearts that slavery was wrong and that old John Brown was right.

"I speak what I know, for I was here at the time. I have lived in Harpers Ferry fifteen years. I was born and bred in a slave state, but I never let my love of the institution blind me to everything else. Slavery has been the curse of this country, and she is now beginning to bless the day she was delivered from it."

"Are there many people here who think as you do?"

"Enough to carry the day at the polls. Most of them are coming round to right views of Negro suffrage, too. That is the only justice for the blacks, and it is the only safety for us. The idea of allowing the loyal colored population to be represented by the whites, most of whom were traitors — of letting a Rebel just out of the Confederate Army vote, and telling a colored man just out of the Union Army that he has no vote — the idea is so perfectly absurd that the Rebels themselves must acknowledge it."

I was hardly less interested in the conversation of an intelligent colored waiter at the hotel. He had formerly been held as a slave in the vicinity of Staunton. At the close of the war he came to the ferry to find employment.

"There wasn't much chance for me up there. Besides, I came near losing my life before I got away. You see, the masters, soon as they found out they couldn't keep their slaves, began to treat them about as bad as could be. Then, because I made use of this remark, that I didn't think we colored folks ought to be blamed for what wasn't our fault, for we didn't make the war, and neither did we declare ourselves free — just because I said that, not in a saucy way but as I say it to you now, one man put a pistol to my head and was going to shoot me. I got away from him, and left. A great many came away at the same time, for it wasn't possible for us to stay there."

"Now tell me candidly," I said, "how the colored people themselves behaved."

"Well, just tolerable. They were like a bird let out of a cage. You know how a bird that has been long in a cage will act when the door is opened; he makes a curious fluttering for a little while. It was just so with the colored people. They didn't know at first what to do with themselves. But they got sobered pretty soon, and they are behaving very decent now."

Harpers Ferry affords a striking illustration of the folly of secession. The government works here gave subsistence to several hundred souls, and were the life of the place. The attempt to overturn the government failed; but the government works, together with their own prosperity, the mad fanatics of Harpers Ferry succeeded easily enough in destroying.

"The place never will be anything again," said Mr. B. of the repair shop, "unless the government decides to rebuild the armory — and it is doubtful if that is ever done."

V

Charlestown

ONE MORNING I took the train up the valley to Charlestown, distant from Harpers Ferry eight miles. The railroad was still in the hands of the government. There were military guards on the platforms, and about an equal mixture of Loyalists and Rebels within the cars. Furloughed soldiers, returning to their regiments at Winchester or Staunton, occupied seats with Confederate officers just out of uniform. The strong, dark, defiant, self-satisfied face typical of the second-rate "chivalry" and the good-natured, shrewd, inquisitive physiognomy of the Yankee speculator going to look at Southern lands were to be seen side by side, in curious contrast.

There also rode the well-dressed wealthy planter, who had been to Washington to solicit pardon for his treasonable acts, and the humble freedman returning to the home from which he had been driven by violence, when the war closed and left him free. Mothers and daughters of the first families of Virginia sat serene and uncomplaining in the atmosphere of mothers and daughters of the despised race, late their slaves or their neighbors', but now citizens like themselves, as clearly entitled to places in the train as the proudest dames of the land.

We passed through a region stamped all over by the heel of war. For miles not a fence or cultivated field was visible.

"It is just like this all the way up the Shenandoah Valley," said a gentleman at my side, a Union man from Winchester. "The wealthiest people with us are now the poorest. With hundreds of acres they can't raise a dollar. Their slaves have left them, and they have no money, even if they have the disposition, to hire the freed people."

I suggested that farms, under such circumstances, should be for sale at low rates.

"They should be; but your Southern aristocrat is a mono-maniac on the subject of owning land. He will part with his acres about as willingly as he will part with his life. If the valley had not been the best part of Virginia, it would long ago have been spoiled by the ruinous system of agriculture in use here. Instead of tilling thoroughly a small farm, a man fancies he is doing a wise thing by half tilling a large one. Slave labor is always slovenly and unprofitable.

"But everything is being revolutionized now. Northern men and Northern methods are coming into this valley as sure as water runs downhill. It is the greatest corn, wheat and grass country in the world. There was scarcely anything raised this season except grass; you could see hundreds of acres of that waving breast-high without a fence."

At the end of a long hour's ride we arrived at Charlestown, chiefly interesting to me as the place of John Brown's martyrdom. We alighted from the train on the edge of boundless unfenced fields into whose melancholy solitudes the desolate streets emptied themselves — rivers to that ocean of weeds. The town resembled some unprotected female sitting sorrowful on the wayside, in tattered and faded apparel, with unkempt tresses fallen negligently about features which might once have been attractive.

On the steps of a boardinghouse I found an acquaintance whose countenance gleamed with pleasure "at sight," as he said, "of a single loyal face in that nest of secession." He had been two or three days in the place, waiting for luggage which had been miscarried.

"They are all Rebels here — all Rebels!" he exclaimed, as he took his cane and walked with me. "They are a pitiably poverty-stricken set; there is no money in the place, and scarcely anything to eat. We have for breakfast salt fish, fried potatoes, and treason. Fried potatoes, treason, and salt fish for dinner. At supper the fare is slightly varied, and we have treason, salt fish, fried potatoes, and a little more treason.

"My landlady's daughter is Southern fire incarnate; and she illustrates Southern politeness by abusing Northern people and the government from morning till night, for my especial edification. Sometimes I venture to answer her, when she flies at me, figuratively speaking, like a cat. The women are not the only outspoken Rebels, although they are the worst. The men don't hesitate to declare their sentiments, in season and out of season."

My friend concluded with this figure: "The war feeling here is like a burning bush with a wet blanket wrapped around it. Looked at from the outside, the fire seems quenched. But just peep under the blanket and there it is, all alive, and eating, eating in. The wet blanket is the present government policy; and every act of conciliation shown the Rebels is just letting in so much air to feed the fire."

A short walk into the center of town took us to the scene of Brown's trial. It was a consolation to see that the jail had been laid in ashes, and that the courthouse, where that mockery of justice was performed, was a ruin abandoned to rats and toads, with names of Union soldiers scrawled along the walls. It was also a consolation to know that the courthouse and jail would probably never be rebuilt, the county seat having been removed from Charlestown to Shepherdstown — "forever," say the resolute loyal citizens of Jefferson County, who refuse to vote it back again.

As we were reflecting how unexpectedly at last justice had been done in that courthouse, the townspeople passed on the sidewalk, one of whom, at a question which I put to him, stopped quite willingly and talked with us. I have seldom seen a handsomer young face, a steadier eye, or more decided poise and aplomb; neither have I ever seen the outward garment of courtesy so filled out with the spirit of arrogance. His brief replies, spoken with a pleasant countenance, yet with short, sharp, downward inflections, were like pistol shots. Very evidently the death of John Brown, and the war that came swooping down in the old man's path to avenge him and to accomplish the work wherein he failed, were not pleasing subjects to this young Southern blood. And no wonder.

His coat had an empty sleeve. The arm which should have been there had been lost fighting against his country. His almost savage answers did not move me; but all the while I looked with compassion at his fine young face, and that pendent idle sleeve. He had fought against his country; his country had won; and he was of those who had lost not arms and legs only but all they had been madly fighting for, and more — prosperity, prestige, power. His beautiful South was devastated, and her soil drenched with the best blood of her young men.

Whether regarded as a crime or a virtue, the folly of making war upon the mighty North was now demonstrated, and the despised Yankees had proved conquerors of the chivalry of the

South. "Well may your thoughts be bitter," my heart said, as I thanked him for his information.

To my surprise he appeared mollified, his answers losing their explosive quality. He even seemed inclined to continue the conversation; and as we passed on, we left him on the sidewalk looking after us wistfully, as if the spirit working within him had still some word to say different from any he had yet spoken. What his secret thoughts were, standing there with his dangling sleeve, it would be interesting to know.

Walking on through the town, we came to open fields on the farther side. Here we engaged a bright young colored girl to guide us to the spot where Brown's gallows stood. She led us into a wilderness of weeds, parting them before her with her hands. The country all around us lay utterly desolate, without enclosures, without cultivation. We seemed to be striking out into the rolling prairies of the West, except that these fields of ripening and fading weeds had not the summer freshness of the prairie grass. A few scattering groves skirted them; and here and there a fenceless road drew its winding, dusty line away over the arid hills.

"This is about where it was," said the girl, after searching among the tall weeds. "Nobody knows now just where the gallows stood. There was a tree here, but that has been cut down and carried away, stump and roots and all, by folks that wanted something to remember John Brown by. Every soldier took a piece of it, if 't was only a little chip."

I stood long on the spot, amid the gracefully drooping goldenrod, and looked at the same sky old John Brown looked his last upon, and the same groves, and the distant Blue Ridge, the sight of whose cerulean summits, clad in Sabbath tranquillity and softest light, must have conveyed a sweet assurance to his soul.

Then I turned and looked at the town out of which flocked the curious crowds to witness his death. Over the heads of the spectators, over the heads of the soldiery surrounding him, his eye ranged until arrested by one strangely prominent object. There it still stands on the outskirts of the town, between it and the fields — a church, pointing its silent finger to heaven and recalling to the earnest heart those texts of Scripture from which John Brown drew his inspiration, and for the truth of which he willingly gave his life.

I had the curiosity to stop at this church on our way back to town. The hand of ruin had smitten it. Only the brick walls and zinc-covered spire remained uninjured. The belfry had been broken open, the windows demolished. The doors were gone. Within, you saw a hollow thing, symbolical. Two huge naked beams extended from end to end of the empty walls, which were scribbled over with soldiers' names, and with patriotic mottoes interesting for proud Virginians to read. The floors had been torn up and consumed in cooking soldiers' rations; and the foul and trampled interior showed plainly what use it had served.

The church which overlooked John Brown's martyrdom, and under whose roof his executioners assembled afterwards to worship not the God of the poor and the oppressed but the God of the slaveholder and the aristocrat, had been converted into a stable.

VI

Washington, D.C.

LATE in the evening of August 29, I reached Washington. Nearly every reader, I suppose, is familiar with descriptions of the national capital: its broad streets, the still more spacious avenues crossing them diagonally, and the sweeping undulations of the plain on which it is built, giving to the city its "magnificent distances"; the manner in which the streets are built up, with here and there a fine residence surrounded by buildings of an inferior character, often with mere huts, adjacent; the dust in summer, the mud in winter, the rubbish, the garbage; and the corresponding character of the population, the most heterogeneous to be found in any American city — all this has been too often outlined to be dwelt upon by me.

I noticed one novel feature in the city, however. At the hotel where I stopped, at the attorney general's office, and again at the White House, I met repeatedly throngs of the same or similar strange faces.

It happened to be one of the President's reception days, and the halls of the White House were crowded. Some were walking to and fro, singly or in pairs; some were conversing in groups; others were lounging on chairs, tables, window seats, or whatever offered a support to limbs weary of long waiting. One was

paring his nails; another was fanning himself with his hat; a
third was asleep, with his head resting much cramped in a corner of the walls; a fourth was sitting in a window, spitting tobacco juice at an urn three yards off.

Faces of old men and young men were there — some weary
and anxious, a few persistently jocose, and nearly all betraying
the unmistakable Southern type. It was, on the whole, a well-
dressed crowd, for one so abominably filthy.

"Nineteen out of twenty of all these people," I was told by
the President's secretary, "are pardon-seeking Rebels. The most
of them are twenty-thousand-dollar men, anxious to save their
estates from confiscation."

One gay and jaunty old man was particularly diverting in his
remarks. He laughed at the melancholy ones for their long
faces, pretending that he could tell by each man's looks which
clause of the exceptions, in the President's amnesty proclama-
tion, his case came under.

"You were a civil officer under the Confederate Government.
Am I right? Of course I am. Your face shows it. My other friend
here comes under Number Three — he was an officer in the
army. That sad old gentleman yonder, with a standing collar,
looks to me like one of those who left their homes within the
jurisdiction of the United States to aid the Rebellion. He's a
Number Tenner. And I reckon we are all Thirteeners" — that
is, persons of the thirteenth excepted class, the value of whose
taxable property exceeded twenty thousand dollars.

"Well, which clause do you come under?" asked one.

"I am happy to say I come under three different clauses.
Mine's a particularly beautiful case. I've been here every day
for a week waiting on the President, and I expect to have the
pleasure of standing at this door many a day to come. Take

example by me, and never despair." And the merry old man frisked away, with his cap slightly on one side, covering gray hairs. His gay spirits, in that not very hilarious throng, attracted a good deal of attention: but his was not the mirth of an inwardly happy mind.

"You are not a Southern man?" said one of the crowd, singling me out.

"No," said I. "I am a Yankee. What have you done to be pardoned for?"

"I am worth over twenty thousand dollars; that's my difficulty."

"And you aided the Rebellion?"

"Of course" — laughing. "Look here!" — his manner changed, and his bright dark eye looked at me keenly — "what do you Northerners, you Massachusetts men particularly, expect to do now with the niggers?"

"We intend to make useful and industrious citizens of them."

"You can't!" "You never can do that!" "That's an absurdity!" exclaimed three or four voices; and immediately I found myself surrounded by a group eager to discuss that question.

"The nigger, once he's free, won't work!"

"No," said another. "He'll steal, but he won't work."

"I pity the poor niggers, after what you've done for them," said a third. "They can't take care of themselves; they'll starve before they'll work, unless driven to it; and in a little while they'll be exterminated, just like the Indians."

"I don't think so," I said. "The Negro is very much like the rest of us in many respects. He won't work unless he is obliged to. Neither will you. So don't blame him. But when he finds work a necessity, that will drive him to it more surely than any master."

"You Northerners know nothing of the Negro; you should see him on our plantations!"

"I intend to do so. Meantime, you should see him in our Northern cities, where he takes care of himself very well, supports his family, and proves an average good citizen. You should look into the affairs of the Freedmen's Bureau here in Washington. There are in this city and its vicinity upwards of thirty thousand colored people. The majority have been suddenly swept into the department from their homes by the war. You would consequently expect to find a vast number of paupers among them. But, on the contrary, nearly all are industrious and self-supporting; only about three hundred are receiving partial support from the government. Now take my advice: give your Negroes a chance, and see what they will do."

"We do give them all the chance they can have. And it's for our interest to induce them to work. We are dependent on labor; we are going to ruin as fast as possible for want of it. In the course of eight or ten years, maybe, they will begin to find out that everything in creation don't belong to them now they are free, and that they can't live by stealing. But by that time, where will we be? Where will the Negro be?"

Of these men, one was from Georgia, one from North Carolina, and others from Florida and Virginia; yet they all concurred in the opinion, which no argument could shake, that the freedmen would die, but not work.

Our conversation was interrupted by the opening of the President's room. A strong tide instantly set towards it, resulting in a violent jam at the door. I was carried in by the crowd, but got out of it as soon as possible, and placed myself in a corner where I could observe the proceedings of the reception.

President Johnson was standing behind a barrier which extended the whole length of the room, separating him from the crowd. One by one they were admitted to him, each man presenting his card as he passed the barrier. Those who were without cards were refused admission until they had provided themselves with those little conveniences at a desk in the hall.

I should scarcely have recognized the President from any of his published pictures. He appeared a man rather below medium height, sufficiently stout, with a massy, well-developed head, strong features, dark, iron-gray hair, a thick, dark complexion, deep-sunk eyes with a peculiarly wrinkled, careworn look about them, and a weary expression generally. His voice was mild and subdued, and his manner kindly. He shook hands with none.

To each applicant for pardon he put a question or two, sometimes only one, and dispatched him with a word of promise or advice. No one was permitted to occupy more than a minute or two of his time, while some were disposed of in as many seconds.

On the whole, it was an interesting but sad scene; and I still carry in my memory the President's weary look, and the disappointed faces of the applicants, who, after long waiting, and perhaps going through this same ceremony day after day, received no intimation that the object of their hopes was near its accomplishment.

VII

Bull Run

TAKING the train at Washington, and crossing the long railroad bridge which spans the Potomac, I entered a portion of Virginia rendered desolate by war. Running down to Alexandria, and making a short stop there, we rattled on towards Manassas.

All the names throughout that region are historical, stamped upon the memory of America by the burning brand of war. The brakeman bawls words which start you with a thrill of recollection. The mind goes back through four fiery years of conflict to the campaign of '61 — that first season of disaster and dismay, which associated the names of Fairfax Court House, Centreville, Bull Run, Manassas, with something infinitely horrible and fatal. And now this quiet journey into what was then the "enemy's country," with hot-blooded Virginians (now looking cool enough) sitting upon the seats next us, and conversing tamely and even pleasantly with us when we accost them.

From Alexandria to Manassas Junction is twenty-seven miles. Through all that distance we saw no signs of human industry, save here and there a sickly, half-cultivated cornfield.

"Manassas Junction!" announced the brakeman, and we alighted. A more forbidding locality can scarcely be imagined.

Nearby a new tavern was building, of so fragile and thin a shell that it seemed as if the first high wind must blow it down. All around was a desolate plain, slightly relieved from monotony by two or three Rebel forts overgrown with weeds.

A tall young member of the Western press accompanied me. I went to a stable to secure a conveyance to the battlefield; and returning, found him engaged in lively conversation with a red-faced and excitable young stranger. The latter was speaking boastingly of "our army."

"Which army do you mean? For there were two, you know," said my friend.

"I mean the Confederate Army, the best and bravest army that ever was!"

"It seems to me," remarked my friend, "the best and bravest army that ever was got pretty badly whipped."

"The Confederate Army never was whipped! We were overpowered."

"I see you Southern gentlemen have a new word. With us, when a man goes into a fight and comes out second best, the condition he is in is vulgarly called *whipped*."

"We were overpowered by numbers!" ejaculated the Rebel. "Your army was three times as big as ours."

"That's nothing, for you know one Southerner was equal to five Yankees."

"And so he is, and always will be! But you had to get the niggers to help you."

"What are a few niggers? They would always run, you know, at sight of their masters, while of course such a thing was never known as their masters running from them!"

The unhappy member of the "overpowered" party flushed and fumed a while, not knowing what answer to make, then burst forth: "It was the foreigners! You never would have beaten us if it hadn't been for the foreigners that made up your armies!"

"What!" said my friend. "You, an American, acknowledge yourself beaten by foreigners! I am ashamed of you!"

And the wagon arriving, he jumped into it with a laugh, leaving the Southerner not whipped of course, but decidedly "overpowered" in this little contest of wit.

"That young fellow," said our driver, "was one of Mosby's guerrillas. There are plenty of them around here. They are terrible at talking, but that is about all."

The wagon was an ambulance which had cost the government two hundred and fifty dollars a few months before. The springs proving inferior, it was condemned and sold at auction for twenty-four dollars. "I paid a hundred and twenty-five for it next day," said the driver, "and it's well worth the money. I was down here with my regiment when I got my discharge, and it struck me something might be made by taking visitors out to the battlefields. But I haven't saved a cent yet; passengers are few, and it's mighty hard business, the roads are so awful bad."

Worse roads are not often seen in a civilized country. The original country roads had passed into disuse; and, the fences being destroyed, only the lines of straggling bushes and trees that grew beside them remained to mark their course. Necessity and convenience had struck out new roads winding at will over the fenceless farms. We crossed thinly wooded barrens, skirted old orchards, and passed now and then a standing chimney that marked the site of some ruined homestead; uphill and downhill, rocking, rattling, jolting, and more than once nearly upsetting.

I remember not more than three or four inhabited houses on our route. In a wild field near the shelter of some woods was a village of half-ruined huts, interesting as having served in wartime as Rebel winter quarters. At last, eight miles north from the junction, we reached the scene of the first battle of Bull Run.

This was the plateau from which our almost victorious forces had driven and redriven the enemy, when Johnston's reinforcements, arriving by the railroad which runs obliquely on the west, changed what was so nearly a triumph for our arms into a frightful disaster. Many of the trees had now been cut away. Every fence had disappeared. Where had waved fields of grass and grain, extended one vast, neglected, barren tract of country. The Widow Henry's humble abode had been swept away. The widow herself was killed by a chance shot on the day of battle. A little picket fence surrounding her grave was the only enclosure visible in all that region.

Close by were the foundations of her house, a small square space run up to tallest weeds. Some of the poor woman's hollyhocks still survived, together with a few lonesome-looking peach trees cut with balls. Within a few yards of the spot where her house was, on the summit of the eminence, stands a pyramidal monument of rough red sandstone, bearing this inscription:

In
MEMORY
of the
PATRIOTS
who fell at
BULL RUN
July 21st, 1861

There seems to have been something fatal to our armies in the mere name of Bull Run. The visitor to the scene of the first disaster is already on the field of the second. The battles of the subsequent year, fought on a more stupendous scale, included within their scope the hills on which we were standing.

To reach the scene of the principal contest in 1862, however, an advance of a mile or two had to be made. We rode on to a piece of woods, in the shade of which we halted, surrounded by marks of shot and shell in the timber, and by soldiers' graves lying lonely among the trees, with many a whitened bone scattered protruding. There, it being midday, we partook of luncheon sauced with Widow Henry's peaches.

On the west was a large stony field sloping up to a wood-crowned height — a field strewn thick with dead in '62. We reached the crest, which, strengthened greatly by an unfinished railroad-track cut, afforded the enemy their most formidable position during the second Bull Run battle.

At the summit of the field stands another monument, dedicated to the "Memory of the Patriots who fell at Groveton, August 28th, 29th, and 30th, 1862." This inscription had been mutilated by some Rebel hand and made to read "Confederate Patriots"; but my tall friend, arming himself with a stone, stepped upon the pedestal, amid the black rows of shells surrounding it, and ground the offensive word out of the tablet.

Groveton, which has given the field its name, is a little cluster of three or four buildings lying west of it on the turnpike. There are two or three points of striking resemblance between the first and second battles of Bull Run. At one time almost a victory, this also proved at last a defeat; and again the North was filled with consternation at seeing the barrier of its armies broken, and the country laid open to the foe. After the first

Bull Run, the Rebels might have entered Washington almost without opposition. After the second, they did invade Maryland, getting as far as Antietam. It is also worthy of note that in each fight the victory might have been rendered complete but for the failure of an important command to perform the part assigned it. General Patterson remained inert at Winchester while Johnston, whom it was his business to look after, hastened to reinforce Beauregard and turn the scale of battle. At the second Bull Run, General Porter's neglect to obey the orders of General Pope wrought incalculable mischief, and contributed similarly to change the opening successes into final discomfiture.

Returning, we stopped at the "stone house" near the first battlefield in hopes of getting personal information from the inhabitants. They were present during the fight, and the outer walls show the destructive visits of cannon shot. The house was formerly a tavern, and the man who kept it was one of those two-faced farmers, secessionists at heart but always loyal to the winning side. By working well his political weathercock, he had managed to get his house through the storm, although in somewhat dismantled condition. The barroom was as barren as the intellect of the owner.

The only thing memorable we obtained there was some extraordinary cider. This the proprietor was too proud to sell, or else the pretense that it belonged to the "old nigger" was nearer the truth than my tall friend was willing to admit. At all events, the "old nigger" brought it and received pay for it besides, evidently contrary to his expectations and to the disappointment of the landlord.

"Didn't you think, Uncle, the white folks were great fools to kill each other the way they did?" said my friend.

" 'Twouldn't do for me to say so. Dey was old enough, and ageable enough, to know best. But I couldn't help tink'n, sah!"

Returning to the junction, I saw a very different type of Virginia Negro: an old man of seventy, who conversed intelligently but in a strangely subdued tone, which bespoke long suffering and patience. He had been a free man seven years, he told me; but he had a brother who still served the man he belonged to.

"But he, too, is free now," I said. "Doesn't he receive wages?"

The old man shook his head sadly. "There's nothing said about wages to any of our people in this part of the country. They don't dare to ask for them, and their owners will hold them as they used to as long as they can. They are very sharp with us now. If a man of my color dared to say what he thought, it would be all his life was worth!"

VIII

Fredericksburg

LEAVING Washington on the twelfth of September, a breezy sail of three hours down the Potomac brought us to Acquia Creek. The creek was still there, debouching broad and placid into the river; for luckily, destroying armies cannot consume the everlasting streams. The forests, which densely covered all that region before the war, had been cut away. Not a building of any kind was to be seen; and only the blackened ruins of half-burned wharves, extending out into the river, remained to indicate that here had been an important depot of supplies.

Taking the cars near an extemporized landing, we traversed a country of shaggy hills, and arrived at a hiatus in the railroad. The bridge over the Rappahannock not having been rebuilt since the war, it was necessary to cross to Fredericksburg by another conveyance than the cars. A long line of coaches was waiting for the train. I climbed the topmost seat of the foremost coach, which was soon leading the rumbling, dusty procession over the hills toward the half-ruined city.

Fredericksburg had not yet begun to recover from the effects of Burnside's shells. Scarcely a house in the burned portions had been rebuilt. Many houses were destroyed, and only the solitary chimney stacks remained. High over the city soar the church spires which, standing between two artillery fires on the day of battle, received the ironical compliments of both. The zinc sheathing of one of these steeples is riddled and ripped, and the tipsy vane leans at an angle of forty-five degrees from its original perpendicular.

Sitting next to me on the stage top was a vivacious young expressman who was in the battle and who volunteered to give me some account of it. He spoke only of "our army," without calling it by name, but at last, by inference and indirection, I got at the fact: "our army" was the Rebel army.

"I am a son of Virginia!" he told me with proud satisfaction. "I was opposed to secession at first, but afterwards I went into it with my whole heart and soul. Do you want to know what carried me in? State pride, sir! I'd give more for Virginia than for all the rest of the Union put together; and I was bound to go with my state."

This was spoken with a certain rapture, as a lover might speak of his mistress. I think I never before realized so fully what "state pride" was. In New England and the West, you find very little of it. However deep it may lie in the hearts of people, it is not their habit to rant about it. You never hear a Vermonter or an Indianian exclaim: "I believe my state is worth all the rest of the Union!" Their patriotism is too large and inclusive to be stopped by narrow state boundaries.

In the case of Virginians, I think that the mere name of the state has something to do with their pride in her. To hear one of them enunciate the euphonious syllables is as good as eating a peach. *"V-i-r-g-i-n-i-a,"* he tells you, dwelling with rich intonations on the luscious vowels and consonants, and he seems proudly conscious of having spoken a charm which enwraps him in an atmosphere of romance. But suppose a different

name: instead of Virginia, Stubland, for example. It might indeed be the best state of all, yet, believe me, *Stubland* would
have in all its borders no soil fertile enough to grow the fine
plant of state pride.

"I believe," I said, "there is but one state as proud as Vir-
gina, and that is fiery little South Carolina."

"I have less respect for South Carolina," he said, "than for
any other state in the Union. South Carolina troops were the
worst in the Confederate army. It was South Carolina's self-
conceit and bluster that caused the war."

(State pride in another state than Virginia was only "self-
conceit.")

"Yes," I said, "South Carolina began the war; but Virginia
carried it on. If Virginia had thrown the weight of her very
great power in the Union against secession, resort to arms would
never have been necessary. By seceding, she lost wealth, influence, slavery, and the blood of her bravest sons; and what has
she gained? I wonder, sir, how your state pride can hold out so
well."

"Virginia," he replied, his eyes doing the fine frenzy again,
"Virginia made the gallantest fight that ever was; and I am
prouder of her today than I ever was in my life!"

"But you are glad she is back in the Union again?"

"To tell the truth, I am. I think more of the Union, too,
than I ever did before. It was a square, stand-up fight; we got
beaten, and I suppose it is all for the best. The very hottest
secessionists are now the first to come back and offer support
to the government." He tapped a little tin trunk he carried. "I
have fifty pardons here, which I am carrying from Washington
to Richmond, for men who, a year ago, you would have said
would drown themselves sooner than take the oath of allegiance

to the United States. It was a rich sight to see these very men crowding to take the oath. It was a bitter pill to some, and they made wry faces; but the rest were glad enough to get back into the old Union. It was like going home."

"What astonishes me," I said, "after all the Southern people's violent talk about the last ditch — about carrying on an endless guerrilla warfare after their armies were broken up, and fighting in swamps and mountains till the last man was exterminated — what astonishes me is that they take so sensible a view of their situation and accept it so frankly; and that you, a Rebel, and I, a Yankee, are sitting on this stage talking over the bloody business so good-naturedly!"

"Well, it is astonishing! Southern men and Northern men ride together in the trains, stop at the same hotels, as if we were all one people — as indeed we are. One nation now," he added, "as we never were before, and never could have been without the war. . . ."

Fredericksburg stands upon a ridge on the right bank of the river. Behind the town is a plain, with a still more elevated ridge beyond. From the summit of the last you obtain an excellent view of the battlefield; the plain below the town where Hooker fought: the heights on the opposite side of the river manned by our batteries; the fields on the left; and the plain between the ridge and the town, where the frightfullest slaughter was.

Along by the foot of the crest runs a road with a wall of heavy stones on each side. In this road the Rebels lay concealed when the first attempt was made to storm the heights. The wall on the lower side, towards the town, is the "stone wall" of history. It was a perfect breastwork, of great strength, and in the very best position that could have been chosen. The earth from the fields is banked against it; and this, together with the weeds and bushes which grew there, served to conceal it from our men.

The sudden cruel volley which poured over it into their very faces, scarce a dozen paces distant, as they charged, was the first intimation of any enemy below the crest. No troops could stand that deadly fire. They broke and, leaving the ground strewn with the fallen, retreated to the "ravine" — a deep ditch with a little stream flowing through it, in the midst of the plain.

"Just when they turned to run, that was the worst time for them!" said a young Rebel I met on the heights. "Then our men had nothing to fear; they just rose right up and let 'em have it! You never saw anything look as that plain did after the battle. Saturday morning, before the fight, it was brown; Sunday it was all blue; Monday it was white; and Tuesday it was red."

I asked him to explain this seeming riddle.

"Don't you see? Before the fight there was just the field. Next it was covered all over with your fellows in blue clothes. Saturday night the blue clothes were stripped off, and only their white underclothes left. Monday night these were stripped off, and Tuesday they lay in their naked skins."

"Who stripped the dead?"

"It was mostly done by the North Carolinians. They are the triflin'est set of men!"

"What do you mean by *triflin'est?*"

"They ha'n't got no sense. They'll stoop to anything. They're more like savages than civilized men. They say *we 'uns* and *you 'uns,* and such outlandish phrases."

The young Rebel thought our army might have been easily destroyed after Saturday's battle — at least that portion of it which occupied Fredericksburg. "We had guns on that point that could have cut your pontoon bridge in two; and then our artillery could have blown Burnside to pieces, or have compelled his surrender."

"Why didn't you do it?"

"Because General Lee was too humane. He didn't want to kill so many men."

There is a private cemetery on the crest, surrounded by a brick wall. Burnside's artillery had not spared it. I looked over the wall, badly smashed in places, and saw overthrown monuments and broken tombstones. The heights all around were covered with weeds and scarred by Rebel intrenchments.

On the brow of the hill, overlooking the town, is the Marye estate, one of the finest about Fredericksburg before the blast of battle struck it. The house was large and elegant, occupying a beautiful site, and surrounded by terraces and shady lawns. Now, if you would witness the results of artillery and infantry firing, visit that house. The pillars of the porch, built of brick and covered with cement, were speckled with the marks of bullets. Shells and solid shot had made sad havoc with the walls and woodwork inside. The windows were shivered, the partitions torn to pieces, the doors perforated.

I found a gigantic Negro at work at a carpenter's bench in one of the lower rooms. He seemed glad to receive company, and took me from the basement to the zinc-covered roof, showing me all the more remarkable shot holes.

"De Rebel sharpshooters was in de house; dat's what made de Yankees shell it so."

"Where is your master?" I asked.

"I ha'n't got no master now; Mr. Marye was my master. He's over de mountain. I was sold at auction in Fredericksburg oncet, and he bought me fo' twelve hundred dolla's. Now he pays me wages — thirty dolla's a month. I wo'ked in de mill while de wa' lasted. Men brought me co'n to grind. Some brought a gallon; some brought two qua'ts; it was a big load if anybody brought half a bushel. Dat's de way folks lived. Now he's got anoder man in de mill, and he pays me fo' tak'n' keer o' dis sher place and fitt'n' it up a little."

"Are you a carpenter?"

"I kin do whatever I turns my hand to."

The young Rebel corroborated this statement. Although he did not like niggers generally, and wished they were all out of the country, he said Charles (for that was the giant's name) was an exception; and he gave him high praise for the fidelity and sagacity he had shown in saving his master's property from destruction.

While we were sitting under the portico, a woman came up the hill and began to talk and jest in a familiar manner with Charles. My Rebel acquaintance looked exceedingly disgusted.

"That woman," he said to me, "has got a nigger husband. That's what makes her talk that way. White folks won't associate with her, and she goes with darkies. We used to have lynch law for them cases. Such things wa'n't allowed. A nigger had better have been dead than be caught living with a white woman."

"Are you sure such things were not allowed? Five out of six of your colored population have white blood in their veins. How do you account for it?"

"Oh, that comes from white fathers!"

"And slave mothers," said I. "That I suppose was all right; but to a stranger it doesn't look very consistent. You would lynch a poor black man for living in wedlock with a white woman, and receive into the best society white men who were raising illegitimate slave children by their colored mistresses."

"Yes, that's just what was done; there's no use denying it. I've seen children sold at auction in Fredericksburg by their own fathers. But nobody ever thought it was just right. It always happened when the masters was in debt and their property had to be taken."

The field below the stone wall belonged to this young man's mother. It was now a cornfield: a sturdy crop was growing where the dead had lain in heaps.

"Soon as Richmond fell I came home; and 'Lijah and I went to work and put in that piece of corn. I didn't wait for Lee's surrender. Thousands did the same. We knew that if Richmond fell, the war would be removed from Virginia, and we had no notion of going to fight in other states. The Confederate Army melted away just like frost in the sun, so that only a small part of it remained to be surrendered."

He invited me to go through the cornfield and see where the dead were buried. Near the middle of the piece a strip some fifteen yards long and four wide had been left uncultivated. "There's a thousand of your men buried in this hole; that's the reason we didn't plant here."

Returning to Fredericksburg, I visited the plain northwest of the town, also memorable for much hard fighting. I found a pack of government wagons there, an encampment of teamsters, and a few Yankee soldiers, who told me they were tired of doing nothing, and "three times as fast for going home" as they were before the war closed.

In the midst of this plain stands a brown brick mansion said to have been built by George Washington for his mother's family. Not far off is a monument erected to Mary, mother of Washington, whose mortal remains rest here. It is of marble, measuring some nine feet square and fifteen in height, unfinished, capped with weeds, and bearing no inscription but the names of visitors who should have blushed to desecrate the tomb of the venerated dead. The monument has in other ways been sadly misused, in the first place by balls which nicked and chipped it during the battle; and afterwards by relic hunters, who, in their rage for carrying away some fragment of it, have left scarce a corner of cornice or pilaster unbroken.

IX

Chancellorsville

IN CONVERSATION with my Rebel acquaintance at the Marye house, I had learned that his friend " 'Lijah" sometimes conveyed travelers over the more distant battlefields. So I engaged his horse and buggy for the following day.

Breakfast was scarcely over next morning when I saw a thin-faced countryman drive up to the door in an old one-horse wagon with two seats, and a box half filled with cornstalks. I was inclined to criticize the establishment, which was not altogether what I had been led to expect.

"I allow he a'n't a fust-class hoss," said Elijah. "Only give three dollars for him."

"What are you going to do with those cornstalks?"

"Fodder for the hoss. They're all the fodder he'll git till night; for we're go'n' into a country whar thar's noth'n' mo'e for an animal to eat than thar is on the palm of my hand."

Elijah cracked his whip, the horse frisked his tail and struck into a cow-trot which pleased him. "You see, he'll snake us over the ground right pert!"

Elijah then proceeded to tantalize me by telling what a mule he had at home. He could not say enough in praise of the mule. "Paid eight hundred dollars for him in Confederate money. He earned a living for the whole family last winter. I used to go reg'lar up to Chancellorsville and the Wilderness, buy up a box of clothing, and go down in Essex and trade it off for corn."

"What sort of clothing?"

"Soldiers' clothes from the battlefields. Some was flung away, and some, I suppose, was stripped off the dead. Any number of families jest lived on what they got from the Union armies in that way. They'd pick up what garments they could lay hands on, wash 'em up and sell 'em."

We took the plank road to Chancellorsville, passing through a waste country of weeds or undergrowth, and passed the line of Sedgwick's retreat, a few miles from Fredericksburg.

"Shedrick's men was in line acrost the road hyer, extendin' into the woods on both sides; they had jest butchered their meat, and was beginnin' to cook their suppers when Magruder struck 'em on the left flank." (Elijah was wrong; it was not Magruder, but McLaws. These local guides make many such mistakes, and it is necessary to be on guard against them.) "They jest got right up and skedaddled! The whole line jest faced to the right, and put for Banks's Ford. Thar's the road they went."

Every mile or two we came to a small farmhouse near which there was usually a small crop of corn growing. "Every man after he got home, after the fall of Richmond, put in to raise a little somethin' to eat. Some o' the corn looks poo'ly but it beats no corn at all."

I learned that farms of fine land could be had all through this region for ten dollars an acre. Elijah hoped that men from the North would come in and settle. "But," he said, " 't would be dangerous for any one to take possession of a confiscated farm. He wouldn't live a month.

"The emancipation of slavery," added Elijah, "is wo'kin'

right for the country mo'e ways 'an one. The' a'n't two men in twenty, in middlin' circumstances, but that's beginnin' to see it. I'm no friend to the niggers, though. They ought all to be druv out of the country. They won't wo'k as long as they can steal. I have my little crop o' corn, and wheat, and po'k. When night comes, I must sleep; then the niggers come and steal all I've got."

I pressed him to give an instance of the Negroes' stealing. He could not say that they had taken anything lately, but they "used to" rob his cornfields and hen roosts, and "they would again." Had he ever caught them at it? No, he could not say that he ever had. Then how did he know that the thieves were Negroes? He knew it, because "niggers would steal."

"Won't white folks steal, too, sometimes?"

"Yes," said Elijah. "Some o' the poo' whites are a durned sight wus'n the niggers!"

"Then why not drive them out of the country, too? You see, your charges against the Negroes are vague, and amount to nothing."

"I own," he replied, "thar's now and then one that's ekal to any white man. Thar's about ten in a hundred, honest and smart as anybody."

"That," I said, "is a good many. Do you suppose you could say more of the white race, if it had just come out of slavery?"

"I don't believe," said Elijah, "that ye could say as much!"

We passed the remains of the house "whar Harrow was shot." It had been burned to the ground.

"You've heerd about Harrow? He was Confederate commissary; he stole mo'e hosses f'om the people, and po'ed the money down his own throat, than would have paid fo' fo'ty men like him, if he was black."

A mile or two farther on, we came to another house.

"Hyer's whar the man lives that killed Harrow. He was in the army, and because he objected to some of Harrow's doin's, Harrow had him arrested, and treated him very much amiss. That ground into his feelin's, and he deserted fo' no other pup- pose than to shoot him. He shot Harrow in that house you see burnt to the ground, and then went spang to Washington. Oh, he was sharp!"

(On our return we met the slayer of Harrow riding home from Fredericksburg on a mule — a fine-looking young fellow, of blond complexion, finely chiseled nose and lips, and an eye full of sunshine. "Jest the best-hearted, nicest young fellah in the wo'ld, till ye git him mad. Then look out!" I think it is often the most attractive persons, of fine temperaments, who are capable of the most terrible wrath when roused.)

The plank road was in such ruined condition that nobody thought of driving on it, although the dirt road beside it was in places scarcely better. But by means of much persuasion, en- forced by a whip, Elijah kept the old horse jogging on. Oak trees, loaded with acorns, grew beside the road. Black walnuts, already beginning to lose their leaves, hung their delicate balls in the clear light over our heads. So we approached Chancellors- ville, twelve miles from Fredericksburg.

"Hyer we come to the Chancellorsville farm. Many a poo' soldier's knapsack was emptied of his clothes, after the battle, along this road!" said Elijah, remembering last winter's business with his mule.

The road runs through a large field bounded by woods. The marks of hard fighting were visible from afar off. A growth of saplings edging the woods had been killed by musketry: they looked like thickets of bean poles. The ground everywhere,

in the field and in the woods, was strewn with rotting knapsacks and haversacks, battered canteens and tin cups, and fragments of clothing which Elijah's customers had not deemed
worth while to pick up. On each side of the road were breastworks and rifle pits extending into the woods.

Of Chancellorsville House, formerly a large brick tavern,
only the half-fallen walls and chimney stacks remained. Here
General Hooker had his headquarters until the wave of battle
on Sunday morning rolled so hot and so near that he was compelled to withdraw. The house was soon after fired by a Rebel
shell, when full of wounded men, and burned.

"Every place ye see these big bunches of weeds, that's whar
tha' was hosses or men buried," said Elijah. "These holes are
whar the bones have been dug up for the bone factory at Fredericksburg."

It was easy for the bone seekers to determine where to dig.
The common was comparatively barren, except where grew
those gigantic weeds. I asked Elijah if he thought many human
bones went to the factory.

"Not unless by mistake. But people a'n't always very par-
tic'lar about mistakes if thar's money to be made by."

Seeing a small enclosure midway between the road and the
woods on the south, we found it a burying ground ridged with
unknown graves. Not a headboard, not an inscription, indicated who were the tenants of that little lonely field. And Elijah
knew nothing of its history; it had been set apart, and the scattered dead had been gathered together and buried there since
he passed that way.

We found breastworks thrown up all along the plank road
west of the farm — the old worn planks having been put to good
service in their construction. The tree trunks pierced by balls,

the boughs lopped off by shells, the strips of timber cut to pieces by artillery and musketry fire, showed how desperate the struggle had been. The endeavors of the Confederates to follow up with an overwhelming victory Jackson's swift and telling blows on our right, and the equally determined efforts of our men to retrieve that disaster, rendered this the scene of a furious encounter.

Elijah thought that if Jackson had not been killed by his own men after delivering that thunderstroke, Hooker would have been annihilated. "Stonewall" was undoubtedly the enemy's best fighting general. His death was to them equal to the loss of many brigades. With regard to the manner of his death there can be no longer any doubt. I have conversed with Confederate officers who were in the battle, all of whom agree as to the main fact. General Jackson, after shattering our right wing, posted his pickets at night with directions to fire upon any men that might approach. He afterwards rode forward to reconnoiter, returned inadvertently by the same road, and was shot by his own orders.

X

The Wilderness

SOON we were approaching the scene of Grant's first great
blow aimed at the Rebel capital. On the field of Chancellorsville you already tread the borders of the field of the Wilderness — if that can be called a field which is mere interminable
forest, slashed here and there with roads.

Passing straight along the plank road, we came to a large
farmhouse which had been gutted by soldiers and but recently
reoccupied. It was still in a scarcely habitable condition. However, we managed to obtain a cup of cold water. I observed that
it tasted strongly of iron.

"The reason is, we took twelve camp kettles out of the well,"
said the man of the house, "and nobody knows how many more
there are down there."

In the edge of the forest a little farther on is the Wilderness
Church — a square-framed building which showed marks of
such usage as every uninhabited house receives at the hands of
a wild soldiery.

"Many a time have I been to meet'n' in that shell, and sot
on hard benches, and heard long sermons!" said Elijah. "But
I reckon it'll be a long while befo'e them doors are darkened
by a congregation ag'in. Oncet we'd have met a hundred wagons
on this road go'n' to market; but we ha'n't met mo'e 'na dozen
today."

We kept to the clay road, passed some old fields, and entered the great Wilderness — a high and dry country, overgrown with scrub oaks, pines and cedars. Poles lashed to trees for tent supports indicated where our regiments had encamped; and soon we came upon abundant evidences of a great battle. Heavy breastworks thrown up on Brock's Crossroad, planks from the plank road piled up and lashed against trees to form a shelter for our pickets, knapsacks, clothing, fragments of harness, tin plates, canteens, fragments of shells, straps, buckles, cartridge boxes, socks, old shoes, rotting letters, desolate tracts of perforated and broken trees — all these signs, and others sadder still, remained to tell their silent story of the great fight of the Wilderness.

And what appalling spectacle is this? In the cover of thick woods, the unburied remains of two soldiers — two skeletons side by side, two skulls almost touching each other, like the cheeks of sleepers! I came upon them unawares as I picked my way among scrub oak. I knew that scores of such sights could be seen here a few weeks before; but the United States Government had sent to have its unburied dead collected together in the two national cemeteries of the Wilderness; and I had hoped the work was faithfully done.

"They was No'th Carolinians; that's why they didn't bury 'em," said Elijah, after a careful examination of the buttons fallen from the rotted clothing.

The buttons may have told a true story: North Carolinians they may have been; yet I could not believe this to be the true reason why they had not been decently interred. It must have been that these bodies, and others we found afterwards, were overlooked by the party sent to construct the cemeteries. It was shameful negligence, to say the least.

The cemetery was nearby — a little clearing surrounded by a picket fence and comprising seventy trenches, each containing the remains of I know not how many dead. Each trench was marked with a headboard inscribed: "Unknown United States soldiers, killed May, 1864."

Elijah said that the words *United States soldiers* indicated plainly that it had not been the intention to bury Rebels there. As a grim sarcasm on this neglect, somebody had flung three human skulls over the paling into the cemetery, where they lay blanching among the graves.

Close by a corner of the fence were three or four Rebel graves with old headboards. The words indicated that those buried were North Carolinians. Elijah considered this somehow corroborative of his theory derived from the buttons. The graves were shallow, and the settling of the earth over the bodies had left the feet of one of the poor fellows sticking out.

I followed a woodland path where the ground was level, and singularly free from the twigs, branches and old leaves with which forests usually abound. I noticed, however, many charred sticks and half-burned roots and logs. Then the terrible recollection overtook me: these were the woods that were on fire during the battle. I called Elijah.

"Yes, all this was a flame of fire while the fight was go'n' on. It was full of dead and wounded men. Cook and Stevens, farmers over hyer, men I know, heard the screams of the poor fellahs burnin' up, and come and dragged many a one out of the fire and laid 'em in the road."

XI

Spotsylvania

E LIJAH wished to drive me next day to Spotsylvania Court-house, and, as an inducement, promised to tackle up his best mare. No ingenuity of plan, however, sufficed to cajole me. There was a livery stable in Fredericksburg, and next morning, accordingly, there might have been seen wheeling up to the tavern a shining vehicle — a new buggy with the virgin gloss upon it — drawn by a prancing iron-gray in a splendid new harness. The driver was a youth who wore his cap rakishly over his left eyebrow. That I might have nothing to regret, the stable-keeper had given me a driver who was in the Spotsylvania battle.

"You cannot have seen much service at your age," I said, examining his boyish features.

"I was four year in de army, anyhow," he replied, spitting tobacco juice with an air of old experience. "I enlisted when I was thirteen. I was under de quartermaster at first; but de last two year I was in de artillery."

I observed that he used *de* for *the* almost invariably, with many other peculiarities of expression which betrayed early association with Negroes.

"What is your name?"

"Richard H. Hicks."

"What is your middle name?"

"I ha'n't got no middle name."

"What does the *H* stand for?"

"*H* stands for Hicks: Richard H. Hicks; dat's what dey tell me."

"Can't you read?"

"No. I never went to school, and never had no chance to learn."

Somehow this confession touched me with a sadness I had not felt even at the sight of dead men in the woods. He, young, active, naturally intelligent, was dead to a world without which this world would seem to us a blank — the world of literature. To him the page of a book, the column of a newspaper, were meaningless.

"Do you mean to go through life in such ignorance?" I asked.

"I'd learn to read if I had de chance."

"Find a chance! Make a chance! Even the little Negro boys are getting the start of you."

"I reckon I'll go to school some dis winter," said he. "Dar's go'n' to be a better chance fo' schools now; dat's what dey say."

"Why now?" I asked.

"I don't know; on'y dey say so."

"You think, then, it was a good thing that the Confederacy got used up and slavery abolished?"

"It mought be a good thing. All I know is, it's so, and it can't be ho'ped (helped). It suits me well enough. I've been gitt'n' thirty dollars a month dis summer, and that's twicet mo'e 'n I ever got befo'e."

As we rode over the hills behind Fredericksburg, a young fellow came galloping after us on a mule.

"Whar ye go'n', Dick?" he called to Hicks.

"I'm go'n' to de battlefield wi' dis gentleman."

"He's from the No'th, then," said the young fellow.

"How do you know?" I asked.

"Because no South'n man ever goes to the battlefields: we've seen enough of 'em." He became very sociable as we rode along. "Ye see that apple tree? I got a right good pair o' pants off one o' your soldiers under that tree once. He was one of Sedgwick's men; he was killed when Sedgwick took the heights. Shot through the head. The pants wa'n't hurt none." And putting spurs to his mule, he galloped ahead.

I noticed that he and Richard, like many young men, white and black, I had seen about Fredericksburg, wore United States Army trousers.

"Dey was all we could git one while," said Richard. "I reckon half our boys 'u'd have had to go widout pants if it hadn't been for de Union Army."

Richard expressed great contempt (inspired by envy, I thought) of the young chap riding the mule. "United States Gov'ment give away a hundred and fifty old wore-out mules in Fredericksburg not long ago; so now every lazy fellow can straddle his mule! He a'n't nobody, though he thinks he's a heavy coon-dog!"

"What do you mean by a *heavy coon-dog?*"

"Why, when a man owns a big plantation, and a heap o' darkies, and carries a heavy pocket, or if he's do'n' a big thing, den we call him a heavy coon-dog. Jeff Davis was a heavy coon-dog; but he's a light coon-dog now!"

It is twelve miles from Fredericksburg to Spotsylvania Courthouse. At the end of nine or ten miles we began to meet with signs of skirmish lines, rifle pits, and graves by the roadside. Rising a gentle ascent, we had a view of the courthouse and of the surrounding country — barren, hilly fields, with boundaries of timber beyond. Grant's main line of breastworks, very heavy, crosses the road at nearly right angles and stretches away out of sight on either side. We rode on to the courthouse — a brick building with heavy pillars in front, one of which had been broken off by a shell, leaving a corner of the portico hanging. There were but six other buildings of any importance in the place, all more or less battered by artillery.

Entering the courthouse amid heaps of rubbish which littered the yard, I had the good fortune to find the county clerk at his desk. He received me politely and offered to show me about the building. It had been well riddled by shot and shell; but masons and carpenters were at work repairing damages, so that there was a prospect of the county, in a few months, having a court-house again.

"What is most to be regretted," the clerk said, "is the destruction of documents which can't be restored. All the records and papers of the court were destroyed by the Union soldiers after they got possession." And he showed me a room heaped with the fragments. It looked like a room in a ragman's warehouse.

Returning to his office, he commenced talking freely of the condition and prospects of the county. Many families were destitute. The government had been feeding as many as fifteen hundred persons at one time.

"How many of these were blacks?"

"Perhaps one fifth."

"How large a proportion of the population of the county are blacks?"

"Not quite one half."

"The colored population require proportionately less assistance, then, than the white?" He admitted the fact, and then criticized severely the government's system of feeding the destitute. "Hundreds are obtaining assistance who are not entitled to any. They have only to go to the overseers of the poor appointed by government, put up a poor mug, and ask for a certificate in a weak voice. They get it, and come and draw their rations. Some draw rations both here and at Fredericksburg, thus obtaining a double support, while they are well able to work and earn their living, if left to themselves. The system encourages idleness, and does more harm than good. All these evils could be remedied, and more than half the expense saved the government, if it would entrust the entire management to the hands of the citizens."

"Is it the whites or the blacks who abuse the government's bounty?"

"The whites."

"It appears, then, that they have the same faults you ascribe to the blacks. They are not overhonest, and they will not work unless obliged to."

"Yes, there are shiftless whites to be sure. There's a place eight miles west from here, known as Texas, inhabited by a class of poor whites steeped in vice, ignorance, and crime of every description. They have no comforts, and no energy to work and obtain them. They have no books, no morality, no religion; they go clothed like savages, half sheltered and half fed — except that government is now supporting them."

"Do the whites we are feeding come mostly from that region?"

"Oh, no, they come from all over the county. Some walk as far as twenty miles to draw their rations. A general impression prevails that this support comes from a tax on the county; so every man, whether he needs it or not, rushes in for a share. It is impossible to convince the county people that the United States Government is feeding them. Why, sir, there are men in the back districts who will not yet believe that the war is over, and slavery at an end! . . ."

I walked on to the tavern where Hicks was baiting his horse. The landlord took me to a room where he kept, locked up, a very remarkable curiosity. It was the stump of a tree, eleven inches in diameter, which had been cut off by bullets — not by cannon shot but by leaden bullets — in the Spotsylvania fight. It looked like a colossal scrub broom.

"I had a stump twice as big as this, cut off by bullets in the same way, but some Federal officers took it from me and sent it to the War Department at Washington."

In one of the rooms I found a Union officer lying on a lounge, sick with the prevailing fever. He seemed glad to see a Northern face. "It is fearfully lonesome here; and I have no companion but the ague."

Learning that he had been for some time in command of the post, I inquired why the citizens appeared so eager to save the government expense in feeding their poor.

"It is very simple: they wish to get control of the business in order to cut off the Negroes. They had rather have the assistance the government affords withdrawn altogether than that the freedmen should come in for a share. It is their policy to keep the blacks entirely dependent upon their former masters, and consequently as much slaves as before."

"You hear many complaints that the blacks will not work?"

"Yes, and they are true in certain cases: they will not work for such wages as their late owners are willing to give. In other words, they will not work for less than nothing. But when they have encouragement they work very well in their fashion — which is not the Yankee fashion, certainly, but the fashion which slavery has bred them up to. The masters have not yet learned how to treat their old servants under new conditions. They cannot learn that they are no longer slaves. That is one great source of trouble. On the other hand, where the freedman receives rational, just and kind treatment, he behaves well and works well, almost without exception."

"What do you think would be the effect if our troops were withdrawn?"

"I hardly know; but I should expect one of two things: either that the freedmen would be reduced to a worse condition than before, or that they would rise in insurrection."

Riding west from the courthouse, we passed McCool's house, in a pleasant shady place, and reached the scene where the eight days' fighting culminated. Of the woods, despoiled by the storm of iron and lead, only a ghostly grove of dead trunks and dreary dry limbs remained. Keeping around the western edge of these, we came to a strange medley of intrenchments, which it would have required an engineer to unravel and understand. Here Grant's works had been pushed up against Lee's, swallowing them as one wave swallows another. Nowhere else have I seen evidences of such close and desperate fighting.

Upon a hacked and barkless trunk at the angle of the woods, in the midst of graves, was nailed aloft a board bearing these lines:

> On Fame's eternal camping ground
>   Their silent tents are spread,
> And glory guards with solemn round
>   The bivouac of the dead.

A thick undergrowth had sprung up in the woods. I noticed, stooping among the bushes by the breastworks, an old woman and two young girls.

"Dey're chincapinnin'," said Richard.

But I observed that they gathered the chincapin nuts not from the bushes but from the ground. Curiosity impelled me to follow them. The woman had a haversack slung at her side; one of the girls carried an open pail. They passed along the intrenchments, searching intently and occasionally picking something out of the dirt. Pressing into the bushes, I accosted them. They scarcely deigned to look at me, but continued their strange occupation. I questioned them about the battle; but their answers were as vague and stupid as if they then heard of it for the first time. Meanwhile I obtained a glance at the open mouth of the heavily freighted haversack and the half-filled pail, and saw not chincapins, but several quarts of old bullets.

XII

Richmond

O N THE fifteenth of September, I took the train at Fredericksburg for Richmond, expecting to make in three hours
the journey which our armies were more than as many years in
accomplishing. We passed amid the same desolate scenes which
I had everywhere observed since I set foot upon the soil of
Virginia — old fields and undergrowths, with signs of human
life so feeble and so few that one began to wonder where the
country population of the Old Dominion was to be found. Ash-
land, sixteen miles from Richmond, was the first really civilized-
looking place we passed. Farther on I looked for the suburbs of
the capital. But Richmond has no suburbs. The pleasant villages and market gardens that spread smilingly for miles around
our large Northern towns are altogether wanting here. Suddenly
the melancholy waste of the country disappears, and you enter
the outskirts of the city.

And is this indeed Richmond into which the train glides so
smoothly? Is this the fort-encircled capital whose gates refused
so long to open to our armies? — and have we entered with so
little ado? Now no Rebel guard is at hand to march you through
the streets; but friendly faces throng to welcome you, to offer
you seats in carriages, and to invite you to the hospitalities of
hotels. And these people, meeting or passing you, or seated before their doors in the warm September afternoon, are no longer

enemies, but tamed, complacent citizens of the United States like yourself.

I was surprised to find that the storm of war had left Richmond so beautiful a city, although she appeared to be mourning for her sins at the time in dust and ashes — dust which every wind whirled up from the unwatered streets, and the ashes of the burned district.

Here are no such palatial residences as dazzle the eye in New York, Chicago and other Northern cities; in their place you see handsome rows of houses, mostly of brick, shaded by trees, and with a certain air of comfort and elegance which is very inviting. The streets are sufficiently spacious, and regularly laid out, many of them being thrown up into long, sweeping lines of beauty by the hills on which they are built. The hills indeed are the charm of Richmond, overlooking the falls of the James, on the left bank of which it stands, giving you shining glimpses of the winding river up and down — commanding views of the verdant valley and the hilly country around — and here, at the end of some pleasant street, falling off abruptly into the wild slopes of some romantic ravine.

In size, Richmond strikes one as very insignificant, after all the noise it has made in the world. Although the largest city of Virginia, and ranking among Southern cities of the second magnitude, any of our great Northern towns could swallow it as one pickerel swallows a lesser, and scarcely feel the morsel in its belly. In 1860, it had a population of not quite thirty-eight thousand — less than that of Troy or New Haven.

The morning after my arrival, I visited the burned district. All up and down, as far as the eye could reach, the business portion of the city bordering on the river lay in ruins. Beds of cinders, cellars half filled with bricks and rubbish, broken and blackened walls, impassable streets deluged with debris, here a granite front still standing and there the iron fragments of crushed machinery — such was the scene which extended over thirty entire squares and parts of other squares.

I was reminded of Chambersburg; but here was ruin on a more tremendous scale. Instead of small buildings like those of the modest Pennsylvania town, tall blocks, great factories, flour mills, rolling mills, foundries, machine shops, warehouses, banks, railroad, freight and engine houses, two railroad bridges, and one other bridge spanning on high piers the broad river were destroyed by the desperate Rebel leaders on the morning of evacuation.

"They meant to burn us all out of our homes," said a citizen whom I met on the Petersburg railroad bridge. "It was the wickedest thing that ever was done in this world!"

"But," I said, "what was their object in burning their own city, the city of their friends?"

"The devil only knows, for he set 'em on to do it! It was spite, I reckon. If they couldn't hold the city, they determined nobody else should. They kept us here four years under the worst tyranny under the sun; then when they found they couldn't keep us any longer, they just meant to burn us up. I tell ye, stranger, it was the intention to burn Richmond, and it's a miracle that any part of it was saved. As luck would have it, there was no wind to spread the fire; then the Federals came in, let on the water, went to work with the engines, and put it out."

"Why didn't the citizens do that?"

"I don't know. Everybody was paralyzed. It was a perfect panic. The Yankees coming! the city burning! our army on a retreat! — you've no idea of what it was. Nobody seemed to know what to do. God save us from another such time!"

Subsequently I conversed with citizens of every grade upon this exciting topic, and found opinions as various as the political views of their authors. Those aristocrats who went in for the war but kept out of the fight, and who favored the Davis government because it favored them, had no censure for the incendiaries. "The burning of the city was purely accidental," one blandly informed me.

"No considerable portion of it would have been destroyed if it hadn't been for private marauding parties," said another. "The city was full of such desperate characters. They set fires for the purpose of plundering. It was they, and nobody else, who shut off the water from the reservoirs."

The laboring class, on the other hand, generally denounced the Confederate leaders as sole authors of the calamity. It was true that desperadoes aided in the work, but it was after the fugitive government had set them the example.

Here is the opinion of a Confederate officer, Colonel D——, whom I saw daily at the hotel. "It is not fair to lay the whole blame on the Confederate Government, although, heaven knows, it was bad enough to do anything! The plan of burning the city had been discussed beforehand: Lee and the more humane of his officers opposed it; Early and others favored it; and Breckinridge took the responsibility of putting it into execution."

The work of rebuilding the burned district was progressing in places quite vigorously. Here I had the satisfaction of seeing the Negroes, who "would not work," actually at their tasks. Here, as everywhere else in Richmond, and indeed in every part of Virginia I visited, colored laborers were largely in the majority. They drove the teams, made the mortar, carried the hods, excavated the old cellars or dug new ones, and sitting amid the ruins, broke the mortar from the old bricks and put them up in neat piles ready for use.

There were also colored masons and carpenters employed on the new buildings. I could not see but that these people worked just as industriously as the white laborers. And yet, with this scene before my very eyes, I was once more informed by a cynical citizen that the Negro, now that he was free, would rob, steal or starve before he would work.

Strolling along a street near the river below the burned district, I looked up from the dirty pavements and saw a sign nailed to the corner of a large, gloomy brick building, bearing in great black letters the inscription:

LIBBY PRISON

Passing the sentinel at the door, I entered. The ground floor was partitioned into offices and storerooms, and presented few objects of interest. A large cellar room below, paved with cobblestones, was used as a cookhouse by our soldiers then occupying the building. Ascending a flight of stairs, I found myself in a large, whitewashed, barren room. Two rows of stout wooden posts supported the ceiling. The windows were iron-grated, those of the front looking out upon the street, those of the rear commanding a view of the canal close by.

There was an immense garret above, likewise embracing an entire floor. These were the prison rooms of the infamous Libby. I found them occupied by a regiment of colored troops, some sitting on the floor (for there was not a stool or bench), some resting their backs against the posts or whitewashed walls, others lying at length on the hard planks with their heads pillowed on knapsacks.

But the comfortable colored regiment faded from sight as I ascended and descended the stairs, and walked from end to end of the dreary chambers. A far different picture rose before me — the diseased and haggard men crowded together there, dragging out their weary days, deeming themselves oftentimes forgotten by their country and their friends — men who mounted those dungeon stairs, not as I mounted them, but to enter a den of misery, starvation and death.

On the opposite side of the same street, a little farther up, was Castle Thunder — a very commonplace brick block, considering its formidable name. It was still used as a prison; but it had passed into the hands of the United States military authorities. At the iron-barred windows of the lower story, and behind wooden-barred windows above, could be seen the faces of soldiers and citizens imprisoned for various offenses.

Belle Isle I had already seen from the heights of Richmond — a pleasant hill rising out of the river above the town — and I thought that surely no pleasanter or more healthful spot could have been selected for an encampment of prisoners. But it is unsafe to trust the enchantment of distance; and after seeing Libby and Castle Thunder, I set out to visit Belle Isle.

I crossed over to Manchester by a bridge which had been constructed since the fire. As both the Richmond and Danville and the Richmond and Petersburg railroad bridges were destroyed, an extraordinary amount of business and travel was thrown upon this bridge. It was shaken with omnibuses and freight wagons, and enveloped in clouds of dust. Loads of cotton and tobacco, the former in bales, the latter in hogsheads, were coming into the city; and throngs of pedestrians were passing to and fro.

I passed the great humming mills by the riverside and, turning to the right, reached Belle Isle Bridge after a brisk fifteen minutes' walk. Crossing over, I entered the yard of a nail factory, where men were breaking up heavy old iron, cannons, mortars and car wheels by means of a four-hundred-pound shot dropped from a derrick forty feet high. Beyond the factory rose the pleasant hill I had viewed from the city. I climbed its southern side and found myself in the midst of a scene not less fair than I had anticipated. Behind me was a cornfield, covering the summit; below rushed the river among its green and rocky islands; while Richmond rose beyond, picturesquely beautiful on its hills and rosy in the flush of sunset.

But where had been the prisoners' camp? I saw no trace of it on that slope. Alas, that slope was never trodden by their feet and its air they never breathed. At the foot of it is a flat, spreading out into the stream, and almost level with it at high water. Already night fog was beginning to creep over it. This flat, which was described to me as a marsh in the rainy season and covered with snow and slush and ice in winter, was the "Belle Isle" of our prisoners.

Yet they were not allowed the range even of that. A trench and embankment enclosing an oblong space of less than six acres formed the deadline which it was fatal to pass. Within this as many as twelve thousand men were at times crowded, with no shelter but a few tattered tents.

As I was examining the spot, a throng of begrimed laborers crossed the flat, carrying oars and embarking in boats on the low shore looking towards the city. They were workmen from the nail factory returning to their homes. One of them offered me a place in his boat. I perched myself in the bow while he, standing in the stern, propelled it across with a pole.

"Where were the dead buried?" I asked.

"The dead Yankees? They buried a good many thar in the sand bar. But they might as well have flung 'em into the river. A freshet washed out a hundred and twenty bodies one time."

"Did you see the prisoners when they were here?"

"I wasn't on the island. But from Richmond anybody could see their tents hyer, and see them walking around. I was away most of the time."

"In the army?"

"Yes, sir. I enlisted fo' three months, and they kept me in fou' years," he said, as men speak of unforgiven wrongs. "The war was the cruelest thing and the wust thing fo' the South that could have been. What do you think they'll do with Jeff Davis?"

"I don't know," I replied. "What do you think?"

"I know what I'd like to do with him: I'd hang him as quick as I would a mad dog! Him and about fo'ty others: old Buchanan along with 'em."

"Why, what has Buchanan done?"

"He was in cahoots with 'em, and as bad as the baddest. If we had had an honest President in his place, thar never'd have been war."

From the day I entered Virginia it was a matter of continual astonishment to me to hear the common people denounce the Davis despotism. They were all the more bitter because it had deceived them with lies and false promises so long. Throughout the loyal North, the feeling against the secession leaders was naturally strong; but it was mild as candlelight compared with the fierce furnace-heat of hatred which I found kindled in many a Southern breast.

Avoiding the currents sweeping towards the falls, my man pushed into smooth waters and landed me close under the walls of his own house.

"This yer is Brown's Island," he told me. "You've heerd of the laboratory whar they made ammunition fo' the army?" He showed me the deserted buildings and described an explosion which took place there, blowing up the works and killing, scalding and maiming many of the operatives.

Passing over a bridge to the mainland, I was hastening towards the city when I met, emerging from the somber ruins of the burned district, a man who resembled more a wild creature than a human being. His hands, arms and face were blackened with cinders, his clothes hung in tatters, and his expression was fierce and haggard. With a sweeping gesture of his long lean arm and clawlike fingers, he clutched my shoulder.

"Come back with me," said he, "and I'll tell ye all about it. I'll tell ye all about it, stranger."

"About what?"

"The explosion of the laboratory thar!"

Dragging me towards Brown's Island, he proceeded to jabber incoherently about that dire event.

"Wait till I tell you!" like the Ancient Mariner with skinny hand holding his unwilling auditor. "My daughter was work'n' thar at the time; and she was blowed all to pieces! My God, it was horrible! Come to my house and if you don't believe me, you shall see her! Blowed all to pieces, my God!"

His house was close by, and the daughter, who was "blowed all to pieces," was to be seen standing miraculously at the door in a remarkable state of preservation, considering the circumstances. She came to the wicket to meet us, and then I saw that her hands and face were covered with cruel scars.

"Look!" said he. "All to pieces, as I told you!"

"Don't, Pa!" said the girl coaxingly. "You mustn't mind him," she whispered to me. "He is a little out of his head."

"He has been telling me how you were blown up in the laboratory. You must have suffered fearfully from those wounds!"

"Oh, yes. There was five weeks nobody thought I would live. But I didn't mind it," she added, "for it was in a good cause."

"A good cause!" shrieked the old man, and he burst forth with a stream of execrations against the Confederate Government which made my blood chill.

But the daughter smilingly repeated, "It was a good cause, and I don't regret it. You mustn't mind what he says."

I helped her get him inside the wicket, and made my escape, wondering, as I left them, which was the more insane of the two.

Next morning, as I was passing Castle Thunder, I observed, besieging the doors of the United States Commissary on the opposite side of the street, a hungry-looking, haggard crowd — sickly-faced women, jaundiced old men and children in rags; with here and there a seedy gentleman who had seen better days, or a stately female in faded apparel, which, like her refined manners, betrayed the aristocratic lady whom the war had reduced to want.

These were the destitute of the city, thronging to receive alms from the government. The regular rations, issued at a counter to which each was admitted in turn, consisted of salt fish and hardtack, but I noticed that to some tea and sugar were dealt out. All were provided with tickets previously issued by the Relief Commission. One tall, sallow woman requested me to read her ticket and tell her if it was a "Number Two."

"They told me it was, whar I got it, but I like to be shore."

I assured her that it was truly a "Number Two," and asked why it was preferable to another.

"This is the kind they ishy to sick folks; it allows tea and sugar," she replied, wrapping it around her skinny finger.

Colored people were not permitted to draw "destitute rations" at the same place with the whites. There were a good many colored servants in the crowd, however, drawing for their mistresses who remained at home, too ill or too proud to come in person.

At the place where "destitute rations" were issued to the blacks, business appeared very dull. I inquired the reason and learned this astonishing fact. The colored population crowded into Richmond equaled the white population, being estimated as high as twenty-five thousand. Of the whites, over *two thousand* were receiving support from the government. The number of blacks receiving such support was less than two hundred. How is this discrepancy to be accounted for?

Of the freedmen's willingness to work under right conditions, there can be no question. Where they have a show of a chance for themselves, they manifest commendable pride in supporting themselves and their families. Their feeling for those who have liberated them is unbounded gratitude. They are ashamed to ask alms of the government which has already done so much for them. No case was known in Richmond of their obtaining destitute rations under false pretenses; but in many instances, as I learned, they had preferred to suffer want rather than apply for aid.

The reverse of all this may be said of a large class of whites. Many, despising labor, would not work if they could. Others, reared amid wealth which had now been stripped from them, could not work if they would. Towards the United States Government they entertained no such feeling of gratitude as animated the freedmen. On the contrary, they seemed to think that they were entitled to support from it during the remainder of their lives.

"You ought to do something for us, for you've took away our niggers," whined a well-dressed woman one day in my hearing.

This was the spirit manifested by many, both of the rich and poor. They felt that they had a sacred right to prey upon the government, and any curtailment of that privilege they regarded as a fraud. So notorious was their rapacity that they were satirically represented as saying to the government: "We have done our best to break you up, and now we are doing our best to eat you up."

Where such a spirit existed, it was not possible to prevent hundreds from obtaining aid who were not entitled to it. It was the design of the Relief Commission to feed only indigent women and children. No rations were issued by the commissary except to those presenting tickets; and tickets were issued only to those whose destitute condition was attested by certificates signed by a clergyman or physician. To secure these certificates, however, was not difficult, even for those who stood in no need of charity. Clergymen and physicians were not all honest. Many of them believed with the people that the government was a fit object for good secessionists to prey upon.

Besides the Relief Commission and the Freedmen's Commission, both maintained by the government, I found an agency of the American Union Commission in Richmond. This commission, supported by private benevolence, was organized to aid the people of the South "in the restoration of their civil and social condition, upon the basis of industry, education, freedom, and Christian morality." In Richmond, it was doing a useful work. To the small farmers about the city it issued ploughs, spades, shovels and other implements — for the war had beaten pitchforks into bayonets and cast ploughshares into cannon. Earlier in the season it had distributed many thousand papers of garden seeds to applicants from all parts of the state — a still greater benefit to the impoverished people, with whom it was a common saying that "good seed ran out under the Confederacy."

The Union Commission performed likewise an indispensable part in feeding the poor. Those clergymen and physicians who were so prompt to grant certificates to secessionists not entitled to them were equally prompt to refuse them to persons known as entertaining Union sentiments. To the few genuine Union people of Richmond, therefore, the commission came and was welcomed as an angel of mercy. But it did not confine its favors to them: having divided the city into twelve districts and appointed inspectors for each, it extended its aid to such of the needy as the Relief Commission had been unable to reach.

At the tent of the Union Commission near a fountain on Capitol Square, I met a quiet little man in laborer's clothes whom the agent introduced to me as "Mr. H——," adding, "There were two votes cast against the ordinance of secession in this city. One of those votes was cast by Mr. H——. He is one of the twenty-one Union men of Richmond."

He looked near fifty years of age but told me he was only thirty-two. "I've been through such things as make a man look old!" He showed me his gray hair, which he said was raven black before the war.

"I was four times taken to conscript camp but never sent off to fight. I worked in a foundry, and my employer got out exemption papers for me."

Although poor and uneducated, he had early formed strong

convictions on the subject of slavery. "I was an abolitionist be-fore I ever heard the word abolitionist."

He corroborated the worst accounts I had heard concerning the state of society in Richmond during the war.

"It seemed as though there was nothing but thieving and robbery going on. The worst robbers were Hood's men, set to guard the city. They'd halt a man and shoot him down if he wouldn't stop. They'd ask a man the time, and snatch his watch. They went to steal some chickens of a man I knew, and as he tried to prevent them, they killed him. At last the women got to stealing. We had an insurrection of women here, you know. I never saw such a sight. They looked like flocks of old buz-zards, picked geese and cranes; dressed in all sorts of odd rigs; armed with hatchets, knives, axes — anything they could lay their hands on.

"They collected together on the square and Governor Letcher made 'em a speech from the monument. They hooted him. Then Jeff Davis made a speech; they hooted him, too. They didn't want speeches, they said; they wanted bread. Then they begun to plunder the stores. They'd just go in and carry off what they pleased. I saw three women put a bag of potatoes, a barrel of flour, and a firkin of butter in a dray. Then they ordered the darky to drive off, with two women for a guard."

Another of the faithful twenty-one was Mr. L——, whom I found at a restaurant kept by him near the old market. It was he who carried off Colonel Dahlgren's body after it had been buried by the Rebels at Oak Wood.

"I found a Negro who knew the spot and hired him to go with me one dark night and dig up the body. We carried it to Mr. Rowlett's house [Rowlett was another of the faithful] and afterwards took it through the Confederate lines, in broad daylight, hid under a load of peach trees, and buried it in a metallic case. It lay there until after the evacuation, when it was dug up and sent home to Admiral Dahlgren's family."

Of the labors, perils, sacrifices and anxieties which the Union men of Richmond underwent, no adequate account has ever been published or ever will be published. "I did no other business at the time," one of them told me. "I gave my whole life to it, and all my means. I nearly went crazy.

"Besides Libby and Castle Thunder, there were several smaller prisons in Richmond. There was one next door to us here. There was another on the opposite side, a little farther up the street. We had the prisoners under our very eyes, and couldn't help doing something for them. We could see their haggard faces and imploring eyes looking out at us from the windows — or from behind the windows, for it wasn't safe for them to come too near.

"One day I saw one approach a little nearer than usual — his head was perhaps a foot from the window — when the guard deliberately put up his gun and blew out his brains. He was immediately carried away in a cart; and as a little red stream trickled along the ground, a boy ran after it, shouting: 'Thar's some Yankee blood; bring a cup and ketch it!' The papers next day boasted that in an hour the dead man was under the sod."

"After the war was over and our troops had possession," added Mr. L——, "I saw what I had never expected to see in this world. I saw the very men who had robbed, persecuted and imprisoned me rewarded by our government. I came back to find that under the administration of our own generals, Ord and Patrick, it was in a man's favor to be known as a secessionist and against him to be known as a Union man.

"The Union men were insulted and bullied by them, the

colored people were treated worse under their rule than they had ever been by the Rebels themselves, and the secessionists were coaxed and petted. A Rebel could obtain from government whatever he asked for, but a Union man could obtain nothing.

"When we were feeding and flattering them at a rate that made every loyal man sick at heart, I sent a request in writing for a little hay for my horse. I got a refusal in writing: I couldn't have any hay. At the same time the government was feeding in its stables thirty horses for General Lee and his staff."

A hundred similar instances of partiality shown to the Rebels by the Ord and Patrick administration were related to me by eyewitnesses, coupled with accounts of insults and outrages heaped upon loyal men and freedmen. Happily Ord and Patrick and their proslavery rule had passed away; but there were still complaints that it was not the true Union men who had the ear of the government, but those whose unionism had been put on as a matter of policy and convenience. This was no fault of General Terry, although he was blamed for it. When I told him what I had heard, he said warmly:

"Why don't these men come to me? They are the very men I wish to see."

"The truth is, General, they were snubbed so often by your predecessors that they have not the heart to come."

"But I have not snubbed them. I have not shown partiality to traitors. Everybody knows that I have no love for slavery or treason, and that my heart throbs with sympathy for these men and the cause in which they have suffered."

One evening I met by appointment, at the tent of the Union Commission, a number of the dauntless twenty-one, and accompanied them to a meeting of the Union League. It was a beautiful night, and as we walked by the fountain, one remarked: "Many an evening, when there was as pretty a moon as this, I have wished that I might die and be out of my misery. That was when I was in prison for being loyal to my country."

At the rooms of the league I was surrounded by these men, nearly every one of whom had been exiled or imprisoned for that cause. I witnessed the initiation of newcomers; but in the midst of the impressive solemnities I could not but reflect, "How faint a symbol is this of the *real league* to which the twenty-one were sworn in their hearts! To belong to this is now safe and easy enough; but to have been a true member of that, under the reign of terror — how very different!"

On the corner of Grace Street, opposite my hotel, I looked out every morning upon the columns and pilasters, and spire clean as a stiletto, of St. Paul's Church. This is the church, and (if you enter) yonder is the pew, in which Jeff Davis sat on Sundays and heard the gospel of Christ interpreted from the slave owners' point of view. Here he sat on that memorable Sabbath when Lee's dispatch was handed in to him, saying that Richmond was lost. The same preacher who preached on that day still propounds his doctrines from the desk. The same sexton who handed in the dispatch glances at you, and, if you are well dressed, offers you a seat in a good place. The same white congregation that arose then in confusion and dismay, on seeing the president go out, sit quietly once more in their seats; and the same colored congregation looks down from the gallery. The seats are still bare — the cushions that were carried to the Rebel hospitals to serve as mattresses having not yet been returned.

Within an arrow's shot from St. Paul's, in the State Capitol on Capitol Square, were the halls of the late Confederate Congress. I visited them only once and found them a scene of dust and confusion — emblematical. The desks and seats had been ripped up, and workmen were engaged in sweeping out the last vestiges of Confederate rule. The furniture was already at an auction room on Main Street, selling under the hammer.

I reported the fact to Mr. C——, of the Union Commission, who was looking for furniture to be used in the freedmen's schools, and he made haste to bid for the relics. I hope he got them, for I can fancy no finer poetical justice than the conversion of the seats on which sat the legislators of the great slave empire, and the desks on which they wrote, into seats and desks for little Negro children learning to read.

A short ride from the city are two cemeteries worth visiting. On one side Hollywood, where lie buried President Monroe and his doctrine. On the other side Oak Wood, a wild, uncultivated hill, half covered with timber and brush, shading numerous Confederate soldiers' graves. Here, set apart from the rest by a rude fence, is the "Yankee Cemetery," crowded with the graves of patriot soldiers who fell in battle or died of slow starvation and disease in Richmond prisons. A melancholy field, which I remember as I saw it one gusty September day, when wild winds shook down over it whirling leaves from the reeling and roaring trees.

Lieutenant M——, of the Freedmen's Commission, having invited me to visit Camp Lee, about two miles from the city, came for me one afternoon in a fine large carryall, comfortably covered, cushioned and carpeted.

"Perhaps you will not feel honored," he remarked as we rattled up Broad Street, "but you will be interested to know that this is General Robert E. Lee's headquarters wagon. You are riding on the seat he rode on through the campaigns of the last two years. Your feet are on a piece of carpet which one of the devoted secessionists of Richmond took up from his hall floor expressly to line the general's wagon bottom. After Lee's surrender, this wagon was turned over to the quartermaster's department, and the quartermaster turned it over to us."

Camp Lee, formerly a fairground, was the conscript camp of the Confederacy. I had been told many sad stories of young men and men of middle age, some of them loyal, seized by conscript officers and sent thither, as it were to a reservoir of the people's blood whose stream was necessary to keep the machinery of despotism in motion. I paced the grounds where, with despairing hearts, they took their first lessons in the art by which they were to slay and be slain. I stood by the tree under which deserters were shot. Then I turned to a very different scene.

The old barracks buildings were now the happy homes of a village of freedmen. Groups of barefooted and woollyheaded Negro children were at play before the doors, filling the air with their laughter. The old men took off their caps to me, the wise old aunties welcomed me with dignified smiles, and younger women looked up brightly from their ironing or cooking as I went by.

The young men were all away at their work. It was, with few exceptions, a self-supporting community, only about a dozen old or infirm persons, out of three hundred, receiving aid from the government.

Next to the uncompromising Union men, the most sincerely loyal Virginians I saw in Richmond, or elsewhere, were those who had been lately fighting against us. Only now and then a Confederate soldier had much of the spirit of the Rebellion left in him.

"The truth is," said Colonel D——, "we have had the devil whipped out of us. It is only those who kept out of the fight that are in favor of continuing it. I fought you with all my might until we got whipped; then I gave it up as a bad job; and now there's not a more loyal man in the United States than I am." He had become thoroughly converted from the heresy of secession. "No nation can live that tolerates such a doctrine; and, if we had succeeded, the first thing we should have done would have been to repudiate it."

I became acquainted with several officers of this class, who inspired me with confidence and sympathy. Yet the animus of secessionists who kept out of the war, especially of the women, still manifested itself spitefully on occasions.

"It is amusing," said Mrs. W——, "to see the pains some of them take to avoid walking under the flag we keep flying over our door."

Of Confederate patriotism, I did not hear very favorable accounts. It burst forth in a beautiful tall flame at the beginning of the war. There were soldiers'-aid societies, patronized by ladies whose hands were never before soiled by labor. Stockings were knit, shirts cut and sewed, and carpets converted into blankets by these lovely hands. If a fine fellow appeared among them, more inclined to gallantry in the parlor than to gallantry in the field, these same lovely hands thrust him out and he was told that "only 'the brave deserves the fair.' "

But Southern heat is flashy and intense; it does not hold out like the slow, deep fire of the North. The soldiers'-aid societies soon grew to be an old story, and the lovely ones contented themselves with cheering and waving their handkerchiefs when the "noble defenders of the South" marched through the streets.

The sons and brothers of influential families were kept out of the war by an ingenious system of "details." Every man was conscripted; but, while the poor and friendless were hurried away to fight the battles of slavery, the favored aristocrat would get "detailed" to fill some "bombproof" situation, as it was called.

"These 'bombproofs' finally got to be a very great nuisance," a candid old gentleman told me. "Men were 'detailed' to fill every comfortable berth the government, directly or indirectly, had anything to do with; and as the government usurped, in one way or another, nearly all kinds of business, it soon became difficult for an old or infirm person to get any sort of light employment. A friend of mine, whom the war had ruined, came down from the country, thinking he could get something to do here. He saw able-bodied young men oiling the wheels of the cars. He was old and lame, but he felt himself well able to do that kind of work.

"So he applied for a situation, and found that the young men he saw were 'detailed' from the army. Others were 'detailed' to carry lanterns for them when they had occasion to oil the car wheels at night. It was so with every situation the poor man could have filled."

I took an early opportunity to make the acquaintance of Governor Pierpont, whom I found to be a plain, somewhat burly, exceedingly good-humored and sociable person. The executive mansion occupies pleasant grounds, enclosed from a corner of Capitol Square; and as it was not more than three minutes' walk from my hotel, I found it often very agreeable to go over and spend a leisure hour or two in his library.

Once I remarked to him: "What Virginia needs is an influx

of Northern ideas, Northern energy, Northern capital. What other way of salvation is open to her?"

"None; and she knows it. It is a mistake to suppose that Northern men and Northern capital are not welcome here. They are most heartily welcome; they are invited. Look at this."

He showed me a beautiful piece of white clay, and a handsome pitcher made from it. "Within eighty miles of Richmond, by railroad, there are beds of this clay from which might be manufactured pottery and porcelain sufficient to supply the entire South. Yet they have never been worked; and Virginia has imported all her fine crockeryware. Now Northern energy will come in and coin fortunes out of that clay. Under the old labor system, Virginia never had any enterprise; and now she has no money. The advantages she offers to active businessmen were never surpassed. Richmond is surrounded with iron mines and coal fields, woodlands and farmlands of excellent quality; and is destined from its very position, under the new order of things, to run up a population of two or three hundred thousand within not many years."

I inquired about the state finances.

"The Rebel state debt will, of course, never be paid. The old state debt, amounting to forty millions, will eventually be paid, although the present is a dark day for it. There is no livestock to eat the grass; the mills are destroyed; business is at a standstill; there is no bank stock to tax — nothing to tax, I might almost say, but the bare land. We shall pay no interest on the debt this year; and it will probably be three years before the back interest is paid."

As an illustration of native enterprise, he told me that there was but one village containing fifty inhabitants on the canal between Richmond and Lynchburg, a distance of one hundred

and fifty miles; and land lying upon it was worth no more today than it was before the canal was constructed. "Neither is
there a village of any size on the James River between Richmond and Norfolk. How long would it be before brick villages
and manufacturing towns would spring up on such a canal and
river in one of the free states? Wasn't it about time," he added,
"for the old machine to break to pieces?"

At the hotel I used to meet a prosperous-looking, wide-awake
person, whom I at once set down as a Yankee. I learned that he
was at the head of a company of Northern men who had recently purchased extensive coal fields near the James River,
twelve miles above Richmond.

"The mines," he said, "had been exhausted once and abandoned, so we bought them cheap. These Virginians would dig
a little pit and take out coal until water came in and interfered
with their work; then they would go somewhere else and dig
another little pit. So they worked over the surface of the fields,
but left the great body of the coal undisturbed. They baled
with a mule.

"Now we have come in with a few steam pumps which will
keep the shafts free from water as fast as we sink them; and we
are taking out cargoes of as good anthracite as ever you saw.
Here is some of it now," pointing to a line of loaded carts coming up from the wharf, where the coal was landed.

I asked what labor he employed.

"Negro labor. There is none better. I have worked Negroes
all my life, and prefer them in my business to any other class of
laborers. Treat a Negro like a man, and you make a man of
him."

XIII

Fair Oaks

AT NINE O'CLOCK one fine morning, Major K——, young Judge Advocate of the Department of Virginia, called for me, accompanied by an orderly bringing a tall war horse that General Terry was so kind as to furnish for my use.

I was soon riding out of the city by the major's side — taking the New Market Road. First we came to a circle of detached forts surrounding the city; a few minutes' ride brought us to a heavy line of earthworks surrounding the first line. These were the original fortifications of Richmond. Crossing a desolate undulating country of undergrowth, we reached the works below Laurel Hill, of more recent construction and of more formidable character. The embankments were eighteen feet high from the bottom of the ditch. There were two lines of bristling abatis. These, together with the wooden revetments of the works, had been levied upon by the inhabitants in search of firewood.

Three quarters of a mile beyond we came to the heavy intrenchments of the Army of the James. Between the two lines were the picket lines of the opposing forces, in places no more than three hundred yards apart. Here the two armies lay and watched each other through the last weary autumn and winter of the war. The earth was blotched with "gopher holes" — hasty excavations in which veteran videttes proceeded to intrench themselves on being sent out to a new post.

"It was astonishing," said the major, "to see what a breastwork they would throw up in a few minutes, with no other tools than a bayonet and a tin plate. The moment they were at their station, down they went, scratching and digging."

We rode past the Federal works into the winter quarters of the army — a city of huts with streets regularly laid out, now deserted and in ruins. Here and there I noted an old-fashioned New England well sweep still standing. The line of works was semicircular, both ends resting on the river. Within that oxbow was the encampment of the Army of the James.

We next visited New Market Heights, where Butler's colored regiments formed unflinchingly under fire and made their gallant charge, wiping out with their own blood the insults that had been heaped upon them by white troops. "The army saw that charge, and it never insulted a colored soldier after that," said the major.

We then galloped across country, intending to strike Dutch Gap Canal. More than once we were compelled to dismount and tear our way through abatis and chevaux-de-frise. The result was, we lost our bearings, and after riding several miles quite blindly, struck the James at Deep Bottom. Then up the river we galloped to a yellow elevation of earth across a narrow peninsula, which proved to be Dutch Gap.

The canal was there — a short, deep channel connecting the river with the river again. The James here describes a long loop, seven miles in extent, doubling back upon itself, so that you may stand on this high bank and throw a stone either into the southward-flowing or the northward-returning stream. On the lower side the channel is deep enough for ships. Not so at

the upper end — the head that was blown out having fallen
back and filled up the canal. At high water, however, small
vessels sometimes get through. The tide had just turned, and we
found a considerable body of water pouring through the gap.

Riding up the Richmond Road, we stopped at the first human habitation we had seen since leaving Laurel Hill. The
house had been a goodly mansion in its day, but now everything
about it showed the ruin and dilapidation of war. The windows
were broken, and the garden, outhouses and fences destroyed.
This proved to be Cox's house, and belonged to a plantation of
twenty-three hundred acres which included Dutch Gap.

Looking at the desolation which surrounded it, I could
hardly believe that this had formerly been one of the finest
farms in Virginia, worked by a hundred Negroes and furnished
with reapers, threshers, a gristmill and sawmill — all of which
had been swept away as if they had never been.

We found lying on a bed in a dilapidated room a poor man
sick with chills. He had some bread and milk brought for us,
and gave us some useful hints about avoiding the torpedoes
when we should reach Fort Harrison. He described the depreda-
tions committed on the place by "Old Butler"; and related how
he himself was once taken prisoner by the Yankee marines on
the river.

"They gave me my choice — to be carried before the admiral,
or robbed of my horse and all the money I had about me. I preferred the robbing; so they cleared me out and set me free."

I said, "If you had been taken before the admiral, you would
have got your liberty and saved your property."

His voice became deep and tremulous as he replied: "But I
didn't consider horse nor money; I considered my wife. I'd
sooner anything than that she should be distressed. She knew

I was a prisoner, and all I thought of was to hurry home to her with the news that I was safe."

Taking leave of the sick man, we paid a brief visit to the casements of Fort Harrison, then spurred back to Richmond, which we reached at sunset, having been nine hours in the saddle and ridden upwards of forty miles.

Another morning, with two gentlemen of General Terry's staff and an orderly to take care of our horses, I rode out of the city on the Nine Mile Road, which crosses the Chickahominy at New Bridge, to visit some of the scenes of McClellan's Richmond campaign. Passing the fortifications, and traversing a level, scarcely inhabited country, we reached the line of the Richmond and York River Railroad. But no railroad was there, the iron having been taken up to be used elsewhere.

Near by was Fair Oaks Station, surrounded by old fields, woods, and underbrush. Here was formerly a yard in which stood a group of oaks, the lower trunks of which had been rendered conspicuous, if not beautiful, by whitewash: hence, "*fair oaks.*"

It was a wild, windy, dusty day. A tempest was roaring through the pines over our heads as we rode on to the scene of General Casey's disaster. I asked an inhabitant why the place was called "Seven Pines."

"I don't know, unless it's because there's about seven hundred."

He was living in a little wooden house, close by a Negro hut. "The Yankees took me up and carried me away, and destroyed all I had. My place don't look like it did before, and never will, I reckon. They come again last October, Old Butler's devils; all colors; heap of black troops; they didn't leave me anything."

We rode eastward along the lines of intrenchments thrown up by our troops after the battle; passed through a low, level tract of woods on the borders of the Chickahominy swamps; and, pressing northward, struck the Williamsburg Road. Colonel G——, of our party, was in the Fair Oaks fight. He came up with the victorious columns that turned back the tide of defeat.

"I never saw a handsomer sight than Sickles's brigade advancing up that road Sunday morning, the second day of the battle. The enemy fired upon them from these woods, but never a man flinched. They came up in column, magnificently, to that house yonder; then formed in line of battle across these fields, and went in with flags flying and bayonets shining, and drove the Rebels. After that we might have walked straight into Richmond, but McClellan had to stop and go to digging."

We dismounted in a sheltered spot to examine our maps, then passed through the woods by a crossroad to Savage's Station, coming out upon a large undulating field. Of Savage's house only the foundations were left, surrounded by a grove of locust trees. My companions described to me the scene of McClellan's retreat from this place — the hurry, the confusion, the flames of government property abandoned and destroyed. Sutlers forsook their goods. Even the officers' baggage was devoted to the torch. A single pile of hardtack, measuring forty cubic feet, was set on fire and burned.

Then came the battle of Savage's Station, in which the corps of Franklin and Sumner, by determined fighting, saved our army from being overwhelmed by the entire Rebel force. This was Sunday again, the twenty-ninth of June: so great had been the change wrought by four short weeks! On that other Sunday the Rebels were routed, and the campaign, as some aver, might

have been gloriously ended by the capture of Richmond. Now
nothing was left for us but ignominious retreat and failure,
which proved all the more humiliating, falling so suddenly
upon the hopes with which real or fancied successes had inspired the nation.

XIV

Petersburg

ON SEPTEMBER 27, I left Richmond for Petersburg. The railroad bridge having been burned, I crossed the river in a coach and took the cars at Manchester. A ride of twenty miles through pine barrens and oaken woods, passing occasionally a dreary-looking house and field of "sorry" corn, brought us within sight of the "Cockade City."

Having a letter from Governor Pierpont to a prominent citizen, I sallied out by moonlight from my hotel and picked my way to his house. Judge —— received me in his library, and kept me until a late hour listening to him. He portrayed the ruin of the once proud and prosperous state, and the sufferings of the people. His remarks touching the freedmen were refreshing, after the abundance of cant on the subject to which I had been treated. He thought they were destined to be crowded out of Virginia, which was adapted to white labor, but that they would occupy the more southern states, and become a useful class of citizens.

Many were leaving their homes, with the idea that they must do so in order fully to assert their freedom; but the majority were still at work for their old masters. He was already convinced that the new system would prove more profitable to employers than the old one. Formerly he kept eight family servants; now he had but three, who, stimulated by wages, did the work of all.

The judge told a story of a free Negro to whom he had often loaned money without security before the war. Recently this Negro had come to him again and asked the old question, " Have you plenty of money, master? "

"Ah, James," said the judge, "I used to have plenty, and I always gave you what you wanted, but you must go to somebody else now, for I haven't a dollar."

"That's what I was thinking," said James. "I haven't come to borrow this time, but to lend." And, taking out a fifty-dollar note, with tears in his eyes he entreated the judge to take it.

Returning to the hotel, I missed my way, and seeing a light in a little grocery store, went in to make inquiries. I found two Negroes talking about the bombardment. Finding me a stranger, they invited me to stop and repeated the story for my benefit.

At the time of the evacuation, the Negroes "had to keep right dark" to avoid being carried away by their masters. Some went across the Appomattox and had to swim back, the bridges being burned. They described to me the beauty of the scene when the mortars were playing in the night, and the heavens were spanned with arches of fire.

"It was a right glad day for us when the Rebels went out and the Federals came in; and I don't believe any of the people could say with conscientiousness they were sorry — they had all suffered so much. The Rebels set all the tobacco warehouses afire, and burned up the foundry and commissary stores. That was Sunday. Monday morning they went out, and the Federals came in, without an hour between them."

Early next morning I went out to view the town. In size and importance Petersburg ranks as the second city in the state. In

1860 it had 18,275 inhabitants, with fifty manufacturing establishments in operation. I found the city changed greatly from
its old prosperous condition. Its business was shattered. Its well-
built, pleasant streets, rising upon the south bank of the Appomattox, were dirty and dilapidated.

All the lower part of the town showed the ruinous effect of
the shelling it had received. Tenantless and uninhabitable
houses, with broken walls, roofless, or with roofs smashed and
torn by missiles, bear silent witness to the havoc of war. In the
ends of some buildings I counted more than twenty shot holes.
Many battered houses had been repaired — bright spots of new
bricks in the old walls showing where projectiles had entered.

The city was thronged by a superfluous black population
crowding in from the country. I talked with some, and tried to
persuade them to go back and remain at their old homes. But
they assured me that they could not remain: their very lives had
been in danger; and they told me of several murders perpetrated upon freedmen by the whites in their neighborhoods, besides other atrocities. Yet it was evident many had come to
town in the vague hope of finding happy adventures and bettering their condition.

I remember a gang of men, employed by the government,
waiting for orders with their teams on the sunny side of a
ruined street. Several, sitting on the ground, had spelling books:
one was teaching another his letters; a third was reading aloud
to a wondering little audience; an old man in spectacles, with
gray hair, was slowly and painfully spelling words of two letters,
which he followed closely with his heavy dark finger along the
sunlit page — altogether a singular and affecting sight.

Having letters to General Gibbon commanding the military
district, I obtained a valuable guide to the fortifications in the

person of Colonel E——, of his staff. We drove out the Jerusalem
Plank Road, leaving on our right the reservoir which Kautz's
cavalry in their dash at the city mistook for a fort, and retired
from with commendable discretion.

Leaving the plank road and striking across the open country,
we found, in the midst of weedy fields, the famous "crater" —
scene of one of the most fearful tragedies of the war. It was a
huge, irregular, oblong pit, perhaps a hundred feet in length
and twenty in depth. From this spot, spouting like a vast black
fountain from the earth, rose the garrison, guns and breastworks
of one of the strongest Rebel forts, mined by our troops and
blown into the air on the morning of July 30, 1864.

There was a deep ravine in front, up in the side of which the
mine had been worked. The mouth was still visible, half hidden
by rank weeds. In spots the surface earth had caved, leaving
chasms opening into the mine along its course. The mouth of
the Rebel countermine was also visible — a deep, dark, narrow
cavern supported by framework in the lower side of the crater.
Lying around were relics of the battle — bent and rusted bayonets, canteens and fragments of shells. And all around were
graves.

In the earthworks I saw a Negro man and woman digging out
bullets. They told me they got four cents a pound for them in
Petersburg. It was hard work, but they made a living at it.

Riding southward along the Confederate line, we came to
Fort Damnation, where the Rebels used to set up a flagstaff for
our boys to fire at with a six-pound Parrott gun, making a wild
sport of warfare. Opposite was Fort Hell, built by our troops
and named in compliment to its profane neighbor. The intrenched picket lines between the two were not more than
seventy-five yards apart, each connected with its fort by a cov-

ered way. These works were in an excellent state of preservation. Fort Hell especially, constructed with bombproofs and
galleries which afforded the most ample protection to its garrison, was in as perfect condition as when first completed. With
a lighted torch I explored its magazine, a cave with deep dark
chambers and walls covered with cold sweat.

All along in front of the Rebel defenses extended the Federal
breastworks, and it was interesting to trace the zigzag lines by
which our troops had, slowly and persistently, pushed their position ever nearer and nearer to the enemy's. Running around
all, covered by an embankment, was Grant's army railroad.

A very good corduroy road, built by our army, took us
through deserted villages of huts, where had been its recent
winter quarters; past abandoned plantations and ruined dwellings; over a plain which had been covered with forests before
the war, but where not a tree was now standing; and across the
line of the Norfolk Railroad, of which not a sleeper or rail remained. We passed Fort Morton, confronting the "crater," and
halted on a hill in a pleasant little grove of broken and dismantled oaks. Here were the earthworks and bombproofs of
Fort Stedman, the possession of which had cost more lives than
any other point along the lines, not excepting the "crater." Captured originally from the Rebels, retaken by them, and recap-
tured by us, it was the subject of incessant warfare.

Returning to town by the City Point Road, we set out again in
the afternoon to visit the more distant fortifications. Driving
out the Boydton Plank Road to the Lead Works, we there left
it on our right, and proceeded along a sandy track beside the
Weldon Railroad, where wagonloads of North Carolina cotton,
laboring through the sand, attested that the damage done to this
railroad in December of the previous year by Warren's corps —

which destroyed with conscientious thoroughness fifteen miles of the track — had not yet been repaired.

Passing the winter quarters of the Sixth Corps, we approached one of the most beautiful villages ever seen. It was sheltered by a grove of murmuring pines. An arched gateway admitted us to its silent streets. It was constructed entirely of pine saplings and logs. Even the neat sidewalks were composed of the same material. The huts — if those little dwellings, built in a unique and perfect style of architecture, may be called by that humble name — were furnished with bedrooms and mantelpieces within, and plain columns and fluted pilasters without, all of rough pine. The plain columns were formed of single trunks, the fluted ones of clusters of saplings — all with the bark on, of course. The walls were similarly constructed. The village was deserted with the exception of a safeguard, consisting of half a dozen United States soldiers, stationed there to protect it from vandalism.

The gem of the place was the church. Its walls, pillars, pointed arches and spire, one hundred feet high, were composed entirely of pines selected and arranged with surprising taste and skill. The pulpit was in keeping with the rest. Above it was the following inscription: "Presented to the members of the Poplar Spring Church by the 50th N. Y. V. Engineers. Capt. M. H. McGrath, architect."

XV

Fortress Monroe

A FEW DAYS later, I took the steamer from Richmond down the James to Norfolk and Fortress Monroe. This voyage possesses an interest which can merely be hinted at. You are gliding between shores rich with historical associations old and new. The mind goes back to the time when Captain John Smith, with the expedition of 1607, sailed up this stream, which they named in honor of their king.

But you are diverted from those recollections by the landmarks of recent famous events: the ruins of ironclads below Richmond; the wrecks of gunboats; obstructions in the channel; Fort Darling on a high bluff; every commanding eminence crowned by a redoubt; Dutch Gap Canal; Deep Bottom; Butler's tower of observation; Malvern Hill, where the last battle of McClellan's retreat was fought — a gentle elevation on the north bank, marked by a small house and clumps of trees; Harrison's Landing — a long pier extending out into the river; Jamestown, the first settlement in Virginia — now an island with a few huts only, and two or three chimneystacks of burned houses — looking as desolate as when first destroyed at the time of Bacon's rebellion nearly two hundred years ago; Newport News below, a place with a few shanties and a row of grinning

batteries; Hampton Roads, bristling and animated with shipping — the scene of the fight between the *Merrimac* and the
Monitor, initiating a new era in naval warfare; Hampton away
on the north, with its conspicuous square white hospital; Norfolk on the south, up the Elizabeth River; the Rip-Raps, and
Sewall Point; and, most astonishing of all, that huge finger of
the military power placed here to hold these shores — Fortress
Monroe.

It was a windy day; the anchored ships were tossing on the
white-capped waves; but the fortress presented a beautiful calm
picture as we approached it, with its proud flag whipping in the
breeze, its white lighthouse on the beach, and the afternoon
sunshine on its broad walls and grassy ramparts.

Before the war, there was a large hotel between the fortress
and the wharves, capable of accommodating a thousand persons.
This was torn down because it obstructed the range of the guns;
and a miserable one-and-a-half-story dining saloon had been
erected in its place. Here, after much persuasion, I managed to
secure a lodging under the low, unfinished roof.

Next morning, I obtained admission within the massive walls
of the fortress. I crossed the moat on the drawbridge, and entered the gate opening under the heavy bastions. I found myself
in the midst of a village on a level plain, shaded by trees. A
guard was given me, with orders to show whatever I wished to
see, with one exception — the interior of Jefferson Davis's
private residence. The retired Rebel chief had been removed
from the casemate in which he was originally confined and was
occupying Carroll Hall, a plain, three-story building built for
officers' quarters.

I walked past the doors and looked up at the modest window
curtains, wondering what his thoughts were, sitting there medi-

tating his fallen fortunes, with the flag of the nation he had attempted to overthrow floating above his head, and its cannon frowning on the ramparts around him. Did he enjoy his cigar, and read the morning newspaper with interest?

The strength and vastness of Fortress Monroe astonishes one. I was shown the great magazine which Arnold, one of the Booth conspirators, proposed to blow up. His plan was to get a clerk-ship in the ordnance office, which would afford him facilities for carrying out his scheme. Had this succeeded, the terrible explosion would not only have destroyed the fortress but not a building on the point would have been left standing.

While I was at General Miles's headquarters, an interesting case of pardoned rebellion was developed. Mr. Y——, a noted secessionist of Warwick County, was one of those who had early pledged his life, his fortune and his sacred honor to the Confederate cause. He had commenced his patriotic service by seizing at his wharf on the Warwick River a private vessel which happened to be loading with lumber at the time when the state seceded, and sending her as a prize up to Richmond; and he had crowned his career by assisting Wirz in his official work at Andersonville.

During the war the government against which he was fighting had taken the liberty of cutting a little lumber on this gentleman's abandoned lands. He had since become professedly loyal, paid a visit to the good President at Washington, and returned to his estates with his pardon in his pocket. The first thing he did was to drive off the government contractor's employees with threats of violence. He would not even allow them to take away the government property he found on his place, but threatened to shoot every man who approached for that purpose. An officer came to headquarters when I was there, requesting a guard of

soldiers to protect the lives of the laborers during the removal
of this property.

As it was my intention to visit some of the freedmen's settlements in the vicinity, the general kindly placed a horse at my
disposal. A short gallop brought me to the village of Hampton,
distant from the fortress something over two miles.

On the night of August 7, 1861, the Rebels, under General
Magruder, initiated what has been termed the "warfare against
women and children and private property" which marked the
war of the Rebellion by laying this old aristocratic town in
ashes. It had been mostly abandoned by the secessionist inhabitants on its occupation by our troops, and only a few white
families, with between one and two hundred Negroes, remained. Many of the former residents came back with the Rebel
troops and set fire to their own and their neighbors' houses. Less
than a dozen buildings remained standing, the place being
reduced to a wilderness of naked shells and heaps of ashes.

I found it a thrifty village, occupied chiefly by freedmen. The
former aristocratic residences had been replaced by Negro huts.
These were very generally built of split boards, called pales,
overlapping each other like clapboards. There was an air of
neatness and comfort about them which surprised me no less
than the rapidity with which they were constructed.

Every house had its woodpile, poultry and pigs, and little
garden devoted to corn and vegetables. Many a one had its
stable and cow, and horse and cart. The village was surrounded
by freedmen's farms, occupying the abandoned plantations of
recent Rebels. The crops looked well, though the soil was said
to be poor. Indeed, this was by far the thriftiest portion of Virginia I had seen.

In company with a gentleman who was in search of laborers, I made an extensive tour of these farms, anxious to see with my own eyes what the emancipated blacks were doing for themselves. I found no idleness anywhere. Happiness and industry were the universal rule. I conversed with many of the people, and heard their simple stories. They had but one trouble: the owners of the lands they occupied were coming back with their pardons and demanding the restoration of their estates.

Here they had settled on abandoned Rebel lands, under direction of the government and with the government's pledge, given through its officers and secured by act of Congress, that they should be protected in the use of those lands for three years, each freedman occupying no more than forty acres and paying an annual rent to the government not exceeding six per cent of their value. Here, under the shelter of that promise, they had built their little houses and established their humble homes.

What was to become of them? On one estate of six hundred acres there was a thriving community of eight hundred freedmen. The owner had been pardoned unconditionally by the President, who, in his mercy to one class, seemed to forget what justice was due to another.

The terms which some of these returning Rebels proposed to the freedmen interested me. One man, whose estate was worth sixteen dollars an acre, offered to rent it to families living on it for eight dollars an acre, provided that the houses, which they had themselves built, should revert to him at the end of the year.

My friend broke a bolt in his buggy and we stopped at a blacksmith shop to get another. While the smith, a Negro, was making a new bolt, I questioned him. He had a little lot of half an acre, upon which he had built his own house and shop and shed. He had a family, which he was supporting without any aid from the government. He was doing very well until the owner of the soil appeared, with the President's pardon, and orders to have his property restored to him.

The land was worth twenty dollars an acre. He told the blacksmith that he could remain where he was by paying twenty-four dollars a year rent for his half acre. "I am going to leave," said the poor man quietly, and without uttering a complaint.

I stopped at a little farmhouse beside which was a large pile of wood and a still larger heap of unhusked corn, two farm wagons, a market wagon, and a pair of mules. The occupant of this place also had but twenty acres, and he was "getting rich."

"Has government helped you any this year?" I asked a young fellow we met on the road.

"*Government* helped *me?*" he retorted proudly. "No, I am helping government!"

My friend did not succeed very well in obtaining laborers for his mills. The height of the freedmen's ambition was to have little homes of their own and to work for themselves. And who could blame this simple, strong instinct, since it was not only pointing them the way of their own prosperity, but serving also the needs of the country?

The immediate prospects of Virginia are dismal enough. But beyond this morning darkness I see the new sun rising. With the great barrier, slavery, removed, all the lesser barriers to her prosperity must give way. The current of emigration, of education, of progressive ideas, is surely setting in; and in a few years we shall see this beautiful torpid body rise up, renewed with health and strength, a glory to herself and to the Union.

XVI

East Tennessee

CALLED home from Fortress Monroe by an affair of business, I resumed my Southern tour later in the fall, passing through central and southwestern Virginia. From the grassy hills and vales of southwest Virginia, I went by railroad into east Tennessee.

At first sight, the "Switzerland of America" is apt to disappoint. It is a country of pleasant hills, bounded and broken into by mountains which do not remind you of the Alps. A few first-class farmers have comfortable painted or brick houses, while scattered everywhere over the country are poverty-stricken, weather-blackened little framed dwellings and log huts. The villages are without sidewalks or paved streets. In the rainy season they are wretched. They look like Northern villages that have set out to travel and got stuck in the mud.

Greeneville, county seat of Greene County, is chiefly interesting as being the home of the President. The town, as I saw it one wet morning, was eminently disagreeable. The mud came up to the very doors of its old, dilapidated, unpainted houses. President Johnson's house is on Main Street, a commonplace brick dwelling. The Rebels smashed the windows for him in wartime, but they have been replaced, and the house is now occupied by the county sheriff.

Every man knows "Andy Johnson." He has a good reputation for honesty, but I was told he was "hard on money matters." A prominent citizen who knew him intimately said to me: "Johnson is a man of much greater ability than he has ever had credit for. When he was a tailor, he did his work well — always a good honest job. He has many good traits, and a few bad ones. He is surly and vindictive, a man of strong prejudices, but thoroughly a patriot."

Knoxville, the most considerable town of east Tennessee, is situated on the Holston River, which is navigable by steamers to this point. The place received rough treatment during the war. The Bell House, at which I stopped, was a miserable shell, carpetless and dilapidated, full of broken windows. The landlord apologized for not putting it into repair.

"I don't know how long I shall stop here. Hotel keeping a'n't my business. Nigger dealing is my business. But that's played out. I've bought and sold in my day over six hundred niggers" — spoken with mingled pride and regret. "Now I don't know what I shall turn my hand to. I'm a Georgian; I came up here from Atlanta time it was burned."

At the table of the Bell House, a Southern gentleman called to one of the waiters, a good-looking colored man perhaps thirty years of age — "Here, boy!"

"My name is Dick," said the "boy" respectfully.

"You'll answer to the name I call you, or I'll blow a hole through you!" swore the Southern gentleman.

Dick made no reply, but went about his business. The Southern gentleman proceeded, addressing the company: "Last week in Chattanooga, I said to a nigger I found at the railroad, 'Here, Buck! show me the baggage-room.' He said, 'My name a'n't Buck.' I just put my six-shooter to his head, and, by ——!

he didn't stop to think what his name was, but showed me what
I wanted."

East Tennesseeans, though opposed to slavery and secession,
do not like Negroes. There is more prejudice against color
among the middle and poorer classes — the "Union" men of the
South, who owned few or no slaves — than among planters who
owned them by scores and hundreds.

East Tennessee, owning but a handful of slaves, opposed secession by overwhelming majorities. The secession element
proved a bitter and violent minority. Neighborhood feuds ensued, of a fierce political and personal character. When the Confederate Army came in, the secessionists pointed out their Union
neighbors, and caused them to be robbed and maltreated. They
exposed the retreats of hunted conscripts lying in forests and
caves, and assisted in the pursuit of loyal refugees. When the National forces possessed the country, the Union men retaliated. It
was then the persecutor's turn to be stripped of his property and
driven from his home.

I was sorry to find the fires of these old feuds still burning. At
Strawberry Plains, on the Holston River, a laboring man, whom
I met on the burned railroad bridge, was telling me about Rebel
operations at that place, when a fine fellow came dashing into
the village on horseback.

"There's a dog-goned Rebel now!" said my man, eying
him with baleful glances. "He's a Rebel colonel, just come
back. He'll get warned; and then if he don't leave, he must look
out!"

East Tennesseeans are dressed almost without exception in
coarse, strong "domestic," as the home-manufactured cloth of
the country is called. Domestic is, in fact, an institution not of
Tennessee alone, but of the entire Southern country. In the ab-

sence of manufacturing establishments, the interest in this prim-
itive private industry has not been suffered to decline.

It stood the South in good stead during the war. After impor-
tation of goods was cut off, it clothed the people. All classes
wore it. Even at the time of my visit, I found many proprietors of large estates, the aristocrats of the country, wearing garments which had been spun, colored and woven by their own
slaves.

Tennessee has no system of free schools. There was a common-school fund, derived mainly from public lands given by
the United States; but the war, and waste of the school fund, had
put an end to schools, and I found the new generation growing
up in ignorance. The schoolhouses serve as meetinghouses.
There are few churches besides. Outside of the larger towns,
scarce a spire points its finger towards heaven. This is true not
only of Tennessee, but of the whole South. It is one of the peculiarities of the country which strike the Northern traveler un-
pleasantly.

Yet the east Tennesseans are a church-going people. No especial form of meetinghouse, any more than form of worship, is
necessary to the exercise of that divine faculty by which man
communes with his Maker. The Methodist Church predomi-
nates in east Tennessee. The United Brethren, who admit to
their communion no rum seller, rum drinker, nor slaveholder,
have a powerful influence. They were much persecuted in the
South before the war, as was natural in a country where the
prejudice in favor of rum and slavery was so strong; but of late,
in east Tennessee, they have grown in strength and popularity.

Farming is behind the age. Mowers and reapers, which might
be employed to fine advantage on the beautiful smooth meadows
and grain fields, have scarcely come into use at all. A favorite

method of improving land is to "clover" it; that is, to plough in crops of clover and grass. Farming utensils are nearly all brought from the North; and there is a great need for home manufactures here also.

The further my observations extended, the more strongly I was convinced that mules were an indispensable substitute for horses in the South. Animals there do not receive the cherishing care they get in the North; and the rough, careless treatment which I saw almost universally shown to beasts of burden, not only by the Negroes but also by the whites, can be endured by nothing less hardy than the mule. This valuable creature is also recommended for his brave appetite, which slights no part of the product of a hill of corn, but sturdily masters stalk, cob and shucks.

Farmers told me they were paying the freedmen from eight to fifteen dollars a month, and boarding them. They said: "We can afford to pay more than Virginians can, because we farm it better." They laughed at the Virginians' shiftless methods. Yet a few were beginning to learn that even they were not perfect in the business. One who had visited Iowa, where he saw men plough two rows of corn at a time and mow and reap with machinery, one hand doing the work of four or five men, said he had concluded that they in Tennessee didn't know anything.

XVII
Chattanooga

TWO HUNDRED and fifty miles from Knoxville, lying within a coil of the serpentine Tennessee, surrounded by mountains, is the town of Chattanooga. Here the East Tennessee and Virginia Railroad connects with the Nashville and Chattanooga, and with the Western and Atlantic, making the place an important center of railroad communications. The river is navigable for steamboats eight months of the year. Here are shipped the principal exports of east Tennessee and southern middle Tennessee. Hence the military importance of the place, and its historical interest.

On the east is Missionary Ridge, a range of forest-covered mountains rising from the river. On the southwest is Lookout Mountain, with precipitous front overlooking the river and the town. Rising steeply from the edge of the town is Cameron Hill, a sort of miniature Lookout, its summit flanked by forts and crowned by a battery of a single huge gun.

If you visit Chattanooga, climb, as I did, this hill the first fair morning after your arrival. Away on the south are the mountains of Georgia, on the north, those of Tennessee. Dividing these peaks and ranges with its shining scimitar curves the river, overhung by precipitous crags. Far beneath, as you look from the northern brow, ply the steamboats, puffing white wreaths up into the clear, still air. Opposite, across the river, are clusters of high, wooded hills, with signal stations on their peaks.

In the valley at the foot is Chattanooga, with its multitude of long, low, whitewashed wooden buildings, government store-houses, barracks, shops, rows of huts and corrals such as make haste always to spring up around an army's base of supplies. Surrounding the town are red earthworks and hills of red earth with devious roads and paths winding over them.

I found a strangely mixed population in Chattanooga — traders, adventurers, soldiers, poor whites, refugees and Negroes. There were many Union men from the Cotton States who had escaped into our lines during the war, and either could not or dared not return. Here is a sample of them — a lank, sallow, ragged individual with long black hair and wild beard, whose acquaintance I made in the streets. He was a shoemaker from Georgia. His Rebel neighbors had burned his house and shop, destroyed his tools and forced him to flee for his life. He enlisted in our army and had been fighting his daddy and two brothers.

"My daddy," said he, "is as good a Rebel as you'll find. He has grieved himself nigh-about to death because he didn't gain his independence."

I asked how his father would receive him if he should go back.

"I allow we shouldn't git along together no hack! The first question I'd ask him would be if he'd tuck the oath of allegiance. That would devil him to death. Then I'd ask him if he knowed whar his President Jeff was. Then he'd jest let in to cussin' me. But I can't go back. The men that robbed me are jest as bad Rebels as ever, and they'd burn my house again or give me a bullet from behind some bush."

There was in Chattanooga a school for the children of poor whites and refugees. It numbered one hundred and fifty pupils of various ages — young children, girls of fifteen and sixteen, one married woman, and boys that were almost men, all woefully ignorant. Scarcely any of them knew their letters when they entered school. The big boys chewed tobacco, and the big girls "dipped" snuff. Tobacco was a necessity of life; education wasn't.

The freedmen's schools were not in session at the time of my visit, owing to the smallpox then raging among the Negro population; but I heard an excellent account of them. They numbered six hundred pupils. The teachers were furnished by the Western Freedmen's Aid Society and paid by the freedmen themselves. One dollar a month was charged for each scholar.

"The colored people," said the superintendent, "are far more zealous in the cause of education than the whites. They will starve themselves and go without clothes in order to send their children to school."

Notwithstanding that there were three thousand Negroes in and around Chattanooga, Captain Lucas of the Freedmen's Bureau informed me that he was issuing no rations to them. All were finding some work to do and supporting themselves. He was helping them to make contracts, and sending them away to plantations at the rate of fifty or one hundred a week.

"These people," he said, "have been terribly slandered and abused. They are willing to go anywhere if they are sure of work and kind treatment. Northern men have no difficulty in hiring them, but they have no confidence in their old masters." It was mostly to Northern men, leasing plantations in the Mississippi Valley, that the freedmen were hiring themselves. The usual rate of wages was not less than twelve nor more than sixteen dollars a month, for full hands.

The principal Negro settlement was at Contraband, a village

of huts on the north side of the river. The huts, built by the Negroes themselves, were similar to those I had seen at Hampton, but they lacked the big woodpiles and stacks of corn, and the general air of thrift. I entered several of these houses; in one I found a middle-aged woman patching clothes for her little boy, who was at play before the open door. Although it was a summerlike December day, there was a good fire in the fireplace.

I asked the woman how her people were getting along.

"Some are makin' it right shacklin'," she replied, "there's so many of us here. A heap is workin', and a heap is lazin' around." Her husband was employed whenever he could get a job.

"Are these your chickens?"

"No, I can't raise chickens." It was the fault of her neighbors. "They just pick 'em up and steal 'em in a minute! Heap of our people will pick up, but they're sly. That comes from the way they was raised."

Hearing martial music as I returned across the river, I went up on a hill east of the town and witnessed the dress parade of the Sixteenth Colored Regiment (Tennessee). I never saw a finer military display on a small scale. The drill was perfect. At the order, a thousand muskets came to a thousand shoulders with a single movement, or the butts struck the ground with one sound along the whole line. The contrast of colors was superb — the black faces, the white gloves, the blue uniforms, the bright steel. The music by the colored band was mellow and inspiring, and as a background to the picture, we had a golden sunset behind the mountains.

Next morning General Gillem, in command at Chattanooga, supplied me with a horse and an orderly, and I set out to make the ascent of Lookout Mountain. Riding southward along the eastern side of the mountain, we commenced the ascent by a steep, rough road, winding among trees and huge limestone rocks colored with exquisite tints of brown and gray and green by the moss and lichens that covered them.

A range of crags rose before us and soon hung toppling over us as we continued to climb. A heavy cloud was on the mountain, combed by pine tops a thousand feet above our heads.

As we proceeded, I conversed with the general's orderly. He was a good-looking young fellow, with short curly hair and a sallow complexion. I inquired to what regiment he belonged.

"The Sixth Ohio, colored."

I looked at him with surprise.

"You didn't take me for a colored man, I reckon," he said laughingly. "I was born in bondage near Memphis. My master was my father, and my mother's owner. He made a will that she was to be free, and that I was to learn a trade and have my free dom when I was twenty-one. He died when I was seven years old, and the estate was divided between his mother and two sisters. I don't know what became of the will.

"I was run off into middle Tennessee and sold for three hundred dollars. I was sold again when I was fourteen for sixteen hundred dollars. I was a carpenter; and carpenters was high. When I saw other men no whiter than me working for themselves and enjoying their freedom, I got discontented and made up my mind to put out. The year Buchanan run for President I run for freedom. I got safe over into Ohio, and there I worked at my trade till the war broke out. I went out as an officer's servant."

He met with various adventures, and at length became General Grant's body servant. He described the general as "a short, chunked man, like a Dutchman"; quiet, kind, a great smoker, a heavy drinker, very silent, and seldom excited. "There was only one time when he appeared troubled in his mind. That was on the road to Corinth, after the battle of Shiloh. He used to walk his room all night."

After the government began to make use of colored troops, he went back to Ohio and enlisted. Since the war closed, he had obtained a furlough, returned to his native place and found his mother, who meantime had been held as a slave.

The clouds lifted as we reached the summit of the mountain, fifteen hundred feet above the river. A *lookout* indeed! What cloud shadows were sweeping the mountains and valleys! We left our horses and clambered down over the ledges to the brink of the precipice. Away on the northeast was Chattanooga, with its clusters of roofs resembling sawteeth. Below us was the crooked Tennessee, sweeping up to the base of the mountain in a coil enclosing on the opposite side a foot-shaped peninsula, to which the Indians gave the appropriate name of Moccasin Point. Immediately beneath us, on a shelf of the mountain, was the scene of Hooker's famous "battle in the clouds."

The Rebels occupied a cleared space on that tremendous elevation. Behind them rose the crags; before them gloomed the woods. Along the cleared space, between woods and crags, ran their line of stone breastworks, which still remained. The enemy had heavy guns on the summit of the mountain, but they could not be sufficiently depressed to be of service. Besides, the summit, on the morning of the attack, was immersed in mist, which concealed everything.

The Nashville and Chattanooga Railroad runs around the curve of the river under the mountain. As we sat looking down from the point, a coal train appeared, crawling along the track like a black snake.

A mile and a quarter southeast from town is the National Cemetery of Chattanooga. Seventy-five acres have been set apart by military authorities for the burial of the soldiers who died in hospitals or fell on battlefields in that region. General Thomas, commanding the Division of the Tennessee, was nominally the director of the cemetery works; but he appears to have left all in the hands of Mr. Van Horne, chaplain of the post, who assumed the responsible task of laying out the grounds and supervising the interments.

Copying nothing from the designs of other cemeteries, he has taken nature for his guide. The outline of each section is determined by location. Here, for example, is a shield — the rise of the ground and the natural lines of depression suggesting that form. In the center of each section is a monument, immediately surrounding which are the graves of officers, in positions according to numbers and rank; while around the latter are grouped the graves of private soldiers, in lines adapted to the general shape of the section.

The paths and avenues follow the hollows and curves which sweep from the base in every direction towards the summit. This is surrounded by a single circular avenue, and is to be crowned, according to the chaplain's plan, with a grand central monument, a historic temple overlooking the whole.

The work on the cemetery had thus far been performed by details from the army. The post fund, which amounted to twenty-seven thousand dollars, had defrayed all expenses. But this cannot continue. The time is coming when the people of the states will be called upon to pay the debt they owe to the heroic dead, in liberal contributions towards the completion and adornment of this spot, where probably will be gathered a more numerous host of the slain than in any other national cemetery. From Chickamauga and Missionary Ridge, from Lookout Mountain and Wahatchie, from the scenes of many lesser fights, from the hospitals and possibly also from the fields of Sherman's Atlanta campaign, thousands upon thousands they will come, a silent host, to this "Mecca of American memories."

Nine thousand had already been interred at the time of my visit. No attempt was made to bury the dead by states. "I am tired of state rights," said General Thomas. "Let's have a *national* cemetery."

Out of six thousand interred before the removal of the dead of Chickamauga was begun, only four hundred were unknown. The dead of Chickamauga were being interred while I was there; and the chaplain kindly offered to accompany me to the battlefield, where a regiment of colored soldiers was at work exhuming the buried and gathering together the remains of the unburied dead.

XVIII
Chickamauga

ONE CLOUDY morning the chaplain, accompanied by two ladies of his household, drove us out of Chattanooga on the Rossville Road. Leaving the open valley behind, we crossed a bushy plain and passed through a clump of oaken woods. Before us, on the east, rose Missionary Ridge, forest-covered, its steep sides all russet-hued with fallen leaves, visible through the naked brown trees. The plain was the same which General Hooker's forces swept over in pursuit of the enemy. We passed the Georgia state line, and amid hilly woods, entered the mountain solitudes, crossing Missionary Ridge by Rossville Gap.

Driving southward along the Lafayette Road we soon reached the site of Cloud Spring Hospital, in the rear of the battlefield. A desolate, dreary scene: the day was cold and wet; dead leaves strewed the ground; the wind whistled in the trees. There were indications that the work of disinterment was about to begin. Shovels and picks were ready on the ground; and beside the long, low trenches of the dead waited piles of yellow pine coffins spattered with rain.

A little further on we came to traces of the conflict — boughs broken and trees cut off by shells. We rode southward along the line of battle, with sparse timber on one side and on the other a field of girdled trees. These ghostly groves, called "deadenings," are an especial feature of the Southern landscape. When timbered land is to be put under cultivation, the trees, instead of being cut away, are often merely deadened with the ax, which encircles them with a line severing the bark, and there left to stand and decay slowly through a series of years.

There is something awful and sublime in the aspect of a whole forest of such. The tempest roars among them, but not a limb sways. Spring comes, and all around the woods are green and glad, but not a leaf or tender bud puts forth upon the spectral trunks. It takes from ten to twenty years for these corpses standing over their graves to crumble and disappear beneath them. Sometimes they rot to the roots; or, when all is ready, a hurricane hurls his crashing balls, and the whole grove goes down like tenpins.

Dismal enough looked the "deadening" in the cold and drizzling rain that morning on the battlefield. Scarcely less so seemed the woods beyond, shattered and torn by shot and shell. On the northern side of these was Kelly's house. The Dyer farm was beyond, upon which we found two hundred colored soldiers encamped, in a muddy village of winter huts near the ruins of the burned farmhouse.

The Dyer family were said to be excellent Rebels. Dyer served as a guerrilla; and it was his wife who burned her feather bed in order that it might not be used by our wounded soldiers. After that patriotic act she wandered off in the woods and died. Her husband had since returned, and was now living in a new log hut within sight of the camp.

The camp was a strange spectacle. The men were cooking dinner or drying clothes around outdoor fires of logs which filled the air with smoke. Nearby were piles of coffins — some empty, some containing the remains of soldiers that had just been disinterred. Here and there were scattered trees, hitched at some of which were mules munching their dinners of wet hay.

There were two hundred and seventeen soldiers in camp. At first they had a horror of the work for which they were detailed. All the superstition of the African was roused at sight of the moldering dead. They declared that the skulls moved, and started back with shrieks. An officer, to encourage them, unconcernedly took the bones from a grave and placed them carefully in a coffin. They were induced to imitate his example.

In a few hours they chatted or sang at their work; and in a few days it was common to see them perform their labor and eat their luncheons at the same time — lay bones into the coffin with one hand and hold with the other the hardtack they were nibbling.

More than nine tenths of the bodies taken from Chickamauga were unknown. Some had been buried in trenches, some singly, some laid side by side and covered with a little earth, leaving feet and skull exposed; and many had not been buried at all. Throughout the woods were scattered these lonely graves. The method of finding them was simple.

A hundred men were deployed in a line a yard apart, each examining half a yard of ground on both sides as they proceeded. Thus was swept a space five hundred yards in breadth. Trees were blazed or stakes set along the edge of this space to guide the company on its return. In this manner the entire battlefield had been or was to be searched.

When a grave was found, the entire line was halted until the teams came up and the body was removed. Many graves were marked with stakes, but some were to be discovered only by the disturbed appearance of the ground. Those bodies which had been buried in trenches were but little decomposed, while of those buried singly in boxes, not much was left but bones and dust.

We had diverged from the Lafayette Road in order to ride along the line of battle east of it — passing the positions occupied on Sunday, the second day, by Baird, Johnson and Palmer's divisions, respectively. Next to Palmer was Reynolds; then came Brannan, then Wood, then Davis, then Sheridan, on the extreme right. The line, which on Saturday ran due north and south, east of the road — the left resting at Kelly's house and the right at Gordon's Mills — was on Sunday curved, the right being drawn in and lying diagonally across and behind the road.

In front (on the east) was Chickamauga Creek. Missionary Ridge was in the rear, on a spur of which the right rested. I recapitulate these positions because newspaper accounts of the battle, and historical accounts based upon them, are confused and contradictory; and because an understanding of them is important to what I am about to say.

Quitting the camp, we approached the scene of the great blunder which lost us the battle of Chickamauga. At half-past nine in the morning the attack commenced, the Rebels hurling masses of troops with their accustomed vigor against Rosecrans's left and center. Not a division gave way; the whole line stood firm and unmoved. All was going well when Rosecrans sent the following imperative order to General Wood: *"Close up as fast as possible on General Reynolds, and support him."*

Brannan's division, as you have noticed, was between Wood and Reynolds. How then could Wood close up on Reynolds without taking out his division and marching by the left flank in Brannan's rear? In military parlance, to *close up* may mean two quite different things. It may mean to move by the flank in order to close a gap which occurs between one body of troops and another. Or it may mean to make a similar movement to that by which a rank of soldiers is said to *close up* on the rank in front of it. To *close to the right or left* is one thing; to *close up on,* another.

To Wood, situated as he was, the order could have no other meaning than the latter. He could not *close up* on Reynolds and support him without taking a position in his rear. To McCook, who was present when it was received, he remarked, "This is very singular! What am I to do?" For to take out his division was to make a gap in the army which might prove fatal to it.

"The order is so positive," replied McCook, "that you must obey it at once. Move your division out, and I will move Davis's in to fill the gap. Move quick, or you won't be out of the way before I bring in his division."

Wood saw no alternative but to obey the order. He would have been justified in disobeying it only on the supposition that the commanding general was ignorant of the position of his forces. Had Rosecrans been absent from the field, such a supposition would have been reasonable, and such disobedience duty. But Rosecrans was on the field; and he was supposed to know infinitely more than could be known to any division commander concerning the battle.

Had Wood kept his place, and Reynolds been overwhelmed and the field lost in consequence of that act of insubordination, he would have deserved to be court-martialed and shot. On the contrary, he moved his division out, and in consequence of his strict *obedience* to orders, the field was lost. He had scarcely opened the gap between Brannan and Davis when the Rebels rushed in and cut the army to pieces.

Rosecrans, in his official report, sought to shift responsibility of this fatal movement to Wood. This was manifestly unjust. It

appears to me that the true explanation lies in the fact that
Rosecrans, although a man of brilliant parts, had not the steady
balance of mind necessary to a great general. He could organize
an army or plan a campaign in his tent; but he had no self-
possession on the field of battle. In great emergencies he became
confused and forgetful. It was probably this nervousness and
paralysis of memory which caused the disaster at Chickamauga.

He had forgotten the position of his forces. He intended to
order Wood to close to the left on Brannan; or on Reynolds,
forgetting that Brannan was between them. But the order was
to close up on and *support* Reynolds; whereas Reynolds, like
Brannan, was doing very well, and did not need support.

The routed divisions of the army fled to Chattanooga — the
commanding general among the foremost, where he hastened to
telegraph the War Department and the dismayed nation that all
was lost; while General Garfield, his chief of staff, extricating
himself from the rabble, rode back to the part of the field where
firing was still heard — running the gauntlet of the enemy's
lines — and joined Thomas, who, rallying fragments of corps
on a spur of Missionary Ridge, was stemming the tide of the foe
and saving the army from destruction.

Through woods dotted with the graves of soldiers buried
where they fell, we drove to the scene of that final fight. Bones
of dead horses strewed the ground. At the foot of the wooded
hill were trenches full of Longstreet's slaughtered men. That
was to them a most tragic termination to what had seemed a
victory. Inspired by their recent success, they charged again and
again up those fatal slopes, only to be cut down like ripe grain
by the deadly volleys which poured from a crescent of flame and
smoke, where the heroic remnant of the army had taken up its
position and was not to be dislodged.

XIX

Murfreesboro

O N DECEMBER 14, I bid a joyful farewell to Chattanooga, which is by no means a delightful place to sojourn in, and took the train for Murfreesboro. The weather was cold, and growing colder. Winter had come suddenly. Huge icicles hung from water tanks by the railroad. The rain and mist of the previous night were congealed upon the trees; and the Cumberland Mountains, as we passed them, appeared covered with forests of silver.

The country was uninteresting. Well-built farmhouses were not common; but log huts, many of them without windows, predominated. These were inhabited by Negroes and poor whites. I remember one family living in a box car that had been run off the track. Another occupied a grotesque cabin having for a door the door of a car, set up endwise, marked conspicuously in letters reading "U. S. MILITARY R. R."

Next to me sat a gentleman from Iowa, whose history was a striking illustration of the difference between a slave state and a free state. He had just been to visit a brother living in Georgia. They were natives of North Carolina, from which state they emigrated in early manhood. He chose the Northwest; his brother chose the South; and they had now met for the first time since their separation.

"To me," he said, "it was a very sad meeting. Georgia is a

hundred years behind Iowa. My brother has always been poor, and always will be poor. If I had to live as he does, I should think I had not the bare necessaries of life, not to speak of comforts. His children are growing up in ignorance. When I looked at them, and thought of my own children — intelligent, cultivated, with their schools, their books, magazines and piano — I was so much affected I couldn't speak, and for a minute I'd have given anything if I hadn't seen how he was situated.

"It isn't my merit, nor his fault, that there is so great a difference now between us, who were so much alike when boys. If he had gone to Iowa, he would have done as well as I have. If I had gone to Georgia, I should have done as poorly as he has."

He was the only Northern man in the car besides myself — as was to be seen not only by the countenances of the other passengers but also by the spirit of their conversation. One little boy four years old amused us all. He enjoyed the range of the car and had made several acquaintances, some of whom, to plague him, called him Billy Yank. Great was the little fellow's indignation at this insult.

"I a'n't Billy Yank! I'm Johnny Reb!" he insisted.

As the teasing continued he flew to his mother, who received him in her arms. "Yes, he *is* Johnny Reb! *So he is!*" And his little heart was comforted.

At half-past three we reached Murfreesboro, having been nine hours traveling one hundred and nine miles — about the average rate of speed on Southern roads. Murfreesboro, situated near the center of the state, had in 1860 three thousand inhabitants. It has six churches, and not a decent hotel. Before the war it enjoyed the blessing of a university, a military institute, two female colleges and two high schools, all of which had been discontinued. It was also described to me as "a pretty, shady village before the war." But the trees had been cut away, leaving ugly stump lots; and the country all around was laid desolate.

Knowing the wretched accommodations at the only tavern then open to the public, General Hazen hospitably insisted on my removal to his headquarters on the evening of my arrival. I found him occupying a first-class Tennessee mansion on a hill just outside town. The house was cruciform, with a spacious hall and staircase in the center, opening into lofty wainscoted rooms above and below. The richness of the dark panels and the structural elegance of the apartments were unexceptionable. But the occupants of these could never have known comfort in wintry weather.

The house was built, like all Southern houses, for a climate reputed mild, but liable to surprises of treacherous cold, against which the inhabitants make no provision. The general and I sat that evening talking over war times with a huge fire roaring before us in the chimney. I slept in a particularly airy chamber, with a good fire striving to master the enemy, and found in the morning the contents of the water pitcher fast frozen.

As I breakfasted with the general, he told me of his official intercourse with the inhabitants since he had been in command of the post. "The most I have to do," he said, "is to adjust difficulties between Union men and Rebels. There are many men living in this country who acted as scouts for our army, and who, when they wanted a horse to use in the service of the government, took it without much ceremony. For acts of this kind the law-loving Rebels are now suing them for damages before the civil courts and persecuting them in various ways, so that the military power has to interfere to protect them."

After breakfast we clapped on overcoats and mufflers; then two powerful war horses of the general's came prancing to the

door and we mounted. A vigorous gallop across the outskirts of
the town and out on the Nashville Pike set the sympathetic
blood also on a gallop, and did for us what fire in a Tennessee
mansion could not do. In ten minutes we were thoroughly
warm, with the exception of one thumb in a glove which I wore,
and an ear on the windward side of the general's rosy face.

Riding amid stump fields, where beautiful forests had cast
their broad shades before the war, we entered the area of the
vast fortress constructed by the army of Rosecrans, lying at Murfreesboro after the battle. This is the largest work of the kind
in the United States. A parapet of earth three miles in circumference encloses a number of detached redoubts on commanding eminences. The encircled space is a mile in diameter. It
contained all Rosecrans's storehouses, and was large enough to
take in his entire army. It would require at least ten thousand
troops to man its breastworks.

The converging lines of the railroad and turnpike running to
Nashville pass through it; and across the north front sweeps a
bend of Stones River. We found the stream partly frozen, chaf-
ing between rocky shores sheathed in ice.

A mile beyond, the converging lines mentioned above cut
each other at a sharp angle, the railroad, which goes out of Mur-
freesboro on the left, shifting over to the right of the turnpike.
Crossing them at nearly right angles, a short distance on the
Murfreesboro side of their point of intersection, was the Rebel
line of battle on the morning of the thirty-first of December.
Half a mile beyond this point, on the Nashville side, was the
Union line.

The railroad here runs through a cut with a considerable embankment — a circumstance of vital importance to our army,
saving it probably from utter rout and destruction on that first

day of disaster. The right wing, thrown out two miles and more to the west of the railroad, rested on nothing. An attack was expected, yet no precautions were taken. General Wood, who had posted scouts in trees to observe the Rebels, reported to the commanding general that they were rapidly massing on their left. Rosecrans says he sent the information to McCook; McCook says he never received it.

When the attack came, it was a perfect surprise. It was made with the suddenness and impetuosity for which the enemy was distinguished, and everything gave way before it. Division after division was pushed back, until that providential cut afforded an opportune cover for the rallying and re-forming of the troops.

Another feature of the field is eminently noticeable. The bold riverbanks, curving in and out by the east side of the railroad, made a strong position for the Union left to rest upon. Here, in a little grove called by the Rebels the "Round Forest," between the river and the railroad, was General Wood's division, planted like a post. On his right, like a bolt of iron in that post, was Hazen's brigade, serving as a pivot on which the whole army line swung round like a gate.

The pivot itself was immovable. In vain the enemy concentrated his utmost efforts against it. Terribly smitten and battered, but seemingly insensible as iron itself, there it stuck.

It was extremely interesting to visit this portion of the field in company with one who played so important a part in the events enacted there. We rode through a cotton field of black leafy stalks, with little white bunches clinging to them like feathers or snow. It was across that field, between Round Forest and the railroad, that Hazen's line was formed. On the edge of it, by the forest, still lay the bones of a horse shot under him during the battle.

Nearby was a little cemetery, where the dead of Hazen's brigade were buried. A well-built stone wall encloses an oblong space one hundred feet in length by forty in breadth. Within are thirty-one limestone tablets marking the graves of common soldiers. In the midst of these stands a monument, on which are inscribed the names of officers whose remains are beneath it. It is interesting as being the only monument of importance and durability erected by soldiers during the war. On the south side is the following legend:

HAZEN'S BRIGADE
to
THE MEMORY OF ITS SOLDIERS
WHO FELL AT
STONES RIVER, DEC. 31, 1862
'Their faces toward heaven, their feet to the foe.'

From the soldiers' cemetery at Round Forest we rode on to the new National Cemetery of Stones River, then in process of construction. A stone wall encloses a space of modest size, covered with neatly heaped mounds side by side, in such precise order that one might imagine the dead who sleep beneath them to have formed their ghostly ranks there after the battle, and carefully laid themselves down to rest beneath those small green tents. The tents were not green when I visited the spot, but I trust they are green today, and that birds are singing over them.

XX
Nashville

HAVING spent the remainder of the forenoon in riding over other portions of the field, we returned to Murfreesboro and at three o'clock I took the train for Nashville. At Nashville I remained four days — four eminently disagreeable days of snow, rain, fog, slush and mud. Yet I formed a not unfavorable impression of the city. I could feel the influence of Northern ideas and enterprise pulsating through it.

Its population, which was less than twenty-four thousand at last census, nearly doubled during the war. Its position gives it activity and importance. It is a nostril through which the state has long breathed the Northern air of free institutions. It is a port of entry on the Cumberland, which affords steamboat communication with the great rivers. It is a node from which radiate five important railroads connecting with the South and North. The turnpikes leading out in every direction are the best system of roads I met with anywhere in the South.

The prospects of middle Tennessee for the present year seemed favorable. The freedmen were making contracts and going to work. Returned Rebels were generally settling down to a quiet life and turning their attention to business. The people were much disposed to plant cotton, and every effort was being made to put their desolated farms into tillable condition.

I found considerable business doing with an article which

never before had any value. Cotton seed, which used to be cast
out from the gin houses and left to rot in heaps, was now in
great demand, prices varying from one to three dollars a bushel.
In some portions of the Rebel states it had nearly run out during the war, and those sections which, like Tennessee, had continued culture of the plant were supplying the deficiency. The
seed resembles, after the fiber is removed by the gin, a small pea
covered with fine white wool. It is very oily, and is considered
the best fertilizer for cotton lands.

Nashville is built on the slopes of a hill rising from the south
bank of the Cumberland. Near the summit, one hundred and
seventy-five feet above the river, stands the State Capitol, said
to be the finest in the United States. The site is a lofty crest of
rock which was fortified during the war, converting the capitol
into a citadel. The parapets thrown up around the edifice still
remain.

My visit happened on the first anniversary of the battle of
Nashville, which took place on the fifteenth and sixteenth of
December, 1864 — a battle which, occurring after many great
conflicts, has not yet had ample justice done it. It is to be distinguished as the only immediately decisive battle of the war —
the only one in which an army was destroyed. By it the army of
Hood was annihilated, and a period put to Rebel power in the
states which Sherman had left behind him on his great march.

The scene of the battle is distinctly visible from the housetops
of the city and especially from the capitol. The fight took place
under the eyes of the citizens. Patriots and Rebel sympathizers
were commingled, with friends and relatives of both armies
crowding together to witness the deadly struggle.

The wife of a general officer who was in the thickest of the
fight told me of her experience, watching from the capitol with

a glass the movements of his troops, the swift gallop of couriers, the charge, the repulse, the successful assault, the ground dotted with the slain, and the awful battle cloud, rolling over all, enfolding, as she at one time believed, his dead form with the rest. But he lived; he was present when she told me the story; and I shall never forget the emotion with which he listened to the recital.

The state legislature adjourned for the Christmas holidays on the morning of my visit to the capitol; but I was in time to converse with Mr. Frierson, Speaker of the Senate. He was from Maury County, and a liberal-minded, progressive man for that intensely proslavery and Rebel district. "My freedmen," he said, "are far more intelligent and better prepared to vote than the white population around us." Yet as a class he did not think the Negroes were prepared to exercise the right of suffrage, and he was in favor of granting it only to such as had served in the Union Army. To the Negroes' loyalty and good behavior, he gave the highest praise.

"It is said they would have fought for the Confederacy if the opportunity had been given them. But I know the Negro, and I know that his heart was true to the Union from the first, and I do not believe he would have fought for the Rebellion even on the promise of liberty." He thought the blacks competent to give testimony in the courts; but for this step, society in Tennessee was not prepared. Both the right of voting and of testifying must be given them before long, however.

I was also in time to catch Governor Brownlow as he was going home for the holidays. As an outspoken convert from the proslavery doctrines he used to advocate to the radical ideas which the agitations of the times had shaken to the surface of society, he was interesting to me. He believed a Rebel had no rights except to be hanged, and damned after death. But this and other similar expressions did not proceed so much from a vindictive nature as from that tendency to a strong, extravagant style of statement for which Southern people are noted.

"The Rebels," he said, "are as rebellious as ever. If Thomas and his bayonets were withdrawn, in ten days a Rebel mob would drive this legislature out. Congress," he added, "will have to legislate for all the Rebel states, Tennessee with the rest."

From the governor's I went to division headquarters to call on Major General Thomas — a very different type of native Southern man. Born and bred a Virginian, his patriotism was national, knowing no state boundaries. In appearance, he is the most lionlike of all the Union generals I have seen.

The military division which Thomas commands, called the "Division of the Tennessee," comprises the states of Kentucky, Tennessee, Georgia, Alabama and Mississippi. He did not think that in any of those states there was any love for the Union, except in the hearts of a small minority. Tennessee was perhaps an exception. It was the only one of the Southern states that had reorganized on a strictly Union basis. It had disfranchised the Rebels. East Tennessee could take care of itself; but in middle and west Tennessee, where Rebel sentiment predominated, partisan animosities were so strong that Union men must for some time have the protection of the government.

The general was in receipt of information from reliable sources concerning secret organizations in the Southern states, the design of which was to embarrass the Federal Government and destroy its credit, to keep alive the fires of Rebel animosity, and to revive the cause of the Confederacy whenever there should occur a favorable opportunity, such as a political division of the North, or a war with some foreign power.

He had great faith in the Negro. "I may be supposed to know something about him, for I was raised in a slave state; and I have certainly seen enough of him during and since the war. There is no doubt about his disposition to work and take care of himself, now that he is free." When I spoke of the great difference existing between different African races, he replied: "There is more ability and fidelity in these apish-looking Negroes than you suppose."

Speaking of the laziness with which the Negroes were charged, he said: "They are more industrious than the whites. You see young men standing on street corners with cigars in their mouths and hands in their pockets, swearing the Negroes won't work, while they themselves are supported by their own mothers, who keep boardinghouses. The idle colored families complained of are usually the wives and children of soldiers serving in the Federal Army; and they have as good a right to be idle as the wives and children of any other men who are able and willing to support their families.

"In this city, it is the Negroes who do the hard work. They handle goods on the levee and at the railroad, drive drays and hacks, lay gas pipes and work on new buildings. In the country they are leasing farms; some are buying farms; others work for wages. Able-bodied plantation hands earn fifteen and twenty dollars a month; women, ten and twelve dollars; the oldest boy and girl in a family, five and nine dollars. Hundreds of colored families are earning forty dollars a month, besides their rations, quarters, medical attendance and the support of the younger children."

XXI
Corinth

I LEFT NASHVILLE for Decatur on a morning of dismal rain. The cars were crowded and uncomfortable, with many passengers standing. The railroad owned but three first-class cars, only one of which we had with us. The rest of the train was composed of boxcars supplied with rude seats.

We passed the forts of the city; passed the battleground of Franklin, marked by intrenchments; and speeding on through a well-wooded section of country, entered northern Alabama. As my observations of that portion of the state will be of a general character, I postpone them until I shall come to speak of the state at large.

It was raining again when I left Decatur, ferried across the Tennessee in a barge manned by Negroes. Of the railroad bridge burned by General Mitchell, only the high stone piers remained; and freight and passengers had to be conveyed over the river in that way. I remember a black ferryman whose stalwart form and honest speech interested me, and whose testimony I thought worth noting down.

"I works for my old master. He raised me. He's a right kind master. I gits twenty dollars a month, and he feeds me. Some of the masters about hyer is right tight on our people. Then thar's a heap of us that won't work, and that steal from the rest.

They're my own color, but I can't help saying what's true. They just set right down, thinking they're free, and waiting for luck to come to 'em." But he assured me that the most of his people were at work and doing well.

From the miserable little ferryboat we were landed on the other side in drenching rain. To reach the cars there was a steep muddy bank to climb. The baggage was brought up in wagons and pitched down into mud several inches deep, where passengers had to stand in the pouring shower and see to getting their checks.

On the road to Tuscumbia I made the acquaintance of a young South Carolinian, whose candid conversation offers some points worth heeding. "I think it was in the decrees of God Almighty that slavery was to be abolished in this way; and I don't murmur. We have lost our property, and we have been subjugated, but we brought it all on ourselves. Nobody that hasn't experienced it knows anything about our suffering. We are discouraged; we have nothing left to begin new with. I never did a day's work in my life, and don't know how to begin. You see me in these coarse old clothes; well, I never wore coarse clothes in my life before the war."

Speaking of the Negroes: "We can't feel towards them as you do; I suppose we ought to, but it isn't possible for us. They've always been our owned servants, and we've been used to having them mind us without a word of objection. If that's wrong, we're to be pitied sooner than blamed, for it's something we can't help. I was always kind to my slaves. I never whipped but two boys in my life, and one of them I whipped three weeks ago."

"When he was a free man?"

"Yes; for I tell you that makes no difference in our feeling towards them. I sent a boy across country for some goods. He came back with half the goods he ought to have got for the money. I may as well be frank — it was a gallon of whiskey. There were five gentlemen at the house, and I wanted the whiskey for them. I told Bob he stole it. Afterwards he came into the room and stood by the door — a big, strong fellow, twenty-three years old. I said, 'Bob, what do you want?' He said, 'I want satisfaction about the whiskey.'

"He told me afterwards he meant that he wasn't satisfied I should think he had stolen it, but I thought he wanted satisfaction gentlemen's fashion. I rushed for my gun. I'd have shot him dead on the spot if my friends hadn't held me. They said I'd best not kill him, but that he ought to be whipped. I sent to the stable for a trace and gave him a hundred and thirty with it, hard as I could lay on. I confess I did whip him unmercifully."

"Did he make no resistance?"

"Oh, he knew better than that; my friends stood by to see me through. I was wrong, I know, but I was in a passion. That's the way we treat our servants, and shall treat them until we can get used to the new order of things — if we ever can."

"Meanwhile, according to your own showing, it would seem that some restraint is necessary for you, and some protection for the Negroes. On the whole, the Freedmen's Bureau is a good thing, isn't it?"

He smiled. "Yes, if the nigger is to be free, I reckon it is; but it's a mighty bitter thing for us."

Then, speaking of secession: "I had never thought much about politics, though I believed our state was right when she went out. But when the bells were ringing and everybody was rejoicing that she had seceded, a solemn feeling came over me like I had never had in my life, and I couldn't help feeling there was something wrong. I went through the war; there were thousands like me. In our hearts we thought more of the Stars and Stripes than we did of the old rag we were fighting under."

He was going to Mississippi to look after some property left there before the war. But what he wished to do was to go North. "Only I know I wouldn't be tolerated — I know a man couldn't succeed in business there who was pointed out as a Rebel."

The same wish, qualified by the same apprehension, was frequently expressed to me by the better class of young Southern men; and I always took pains to convince them that they would be welcomed and encouraged by all enlightened communities in the Northern states.

It was a dismal night in the cars. The weather changed, and it grew very cold. Now the stove was red hot; and now the fire was out, with both car doors wide open at some stopping place.

At two in the morning we reached Corinth. A driver put me into his hack and drove about town through the freezing mud to find a lodging. The hotels were full. The boardinghouses were full — all but one, in which I was fortunate enough to find a room. It was a large, lofty room, the door fifteen feet high from the floor. It had been an elegant apartment once, but now the windows were broken, the plastering smashed. The walls were covered with devices, showing that Federal soldiers had been at home here — such as a shield, admirably executed, bearing the motto: "The Union, it must be preserved"; "Heaven Bless our Native Land"; "God of Battles, Speed the Right," and so forth.

The beds were tumbled, some travelers having just got out of them to take the train. A black woman came in to make them. The lady of the house also came in — a fashionably bred Southern woman who had been reduced, by the fortunes of the Rebellion, from the condition of a helpless mistress of many servants to that of a boardinghouse keeper. I asked for more bedclothes — for the walls of the room offered little protection. She said, "I reckon you're mighty particular!"

In the morning, I went to breakfast in a room that showed no chimney and no place for a stove. The outer door was open much of the time, and when it was shut, the wind came in through a great round hole cut for the accommodation of cats and dogs. This, be it understood, was a fashionable Southern residence; and this had always been the dining room, in winter as in summer, though no fire had ever been built in it.

The evening before, the lady had said to me, "The Yankees are the cause that we have no better accommodations to offer you," and I had cheerfully forgiven her. But the Yankees were not the cause of our breakfasting in such a bleak apartment.

Everybody at table was pinched and blue. The lady, white and delicate, sat wrapped in shawls. She was very bitter against the Yankees, until I smilingly informed her that I was a Yankee myself.

"From what state, sir?"

"From Massachusetts."

"Oh!" — with a shudder — "they're bad Yankees!"

"Bad enough, heaven knows," I pleasantly replied, "though, in truth, madam, I have seen almost as bad people in other parts of the world."

The family consisted of three persons — Mr. M——, his wife and their little boy. Notwithstanding their poverty, they kept four black servants to wait upon them. They were paying a man fifteen dollars a month, a cook the same, another woman six, and a girl six: total, forty-two dollars. It was mainly to obtain money to pay and feed these people that they had been compelled to take in lodgers. The possibility of getting along with fewer servants seemed never to have occurred to them.

The freedmen, I was told, were behaving very well. But the citizens were bitterly hostile to the Negro garrison which occupied Corinth. A respectable white man had recently been killed by a colored soldier, and the excitement was intense. It was called "a cold-blooded murder."

Visiting headquarters, I took pains to ascertain the facts in the case. They are as follows:

The said respectable citizen was drunk. Going down the street he staggered against a colored orderly. Cursing him, he said, "Why don't you get out of the way when you see a white man coming?" The orderly replied, "There's room for you to pass." The respectable citizen then drew his revolver, threatening to "shoot his damned black heart out." This occasioned an order for his arrest. He drew his revolver with a similar threat upon another soldier sent to take him, and was promptly shot down. Exit respectable citizen.

Corinth is a bruised and battered village surrounded by forts, earthworks and graves. There is nothing about the town especially worth visiting; and my object in stopping there was to visit the battlefield of Shiloh. I went to a livery stable to engage a horse. I was told of frequent robberies on that road, and urged by the stablekeeper to take a man with me; but I wished to make the acquaintance of the country people and thought I could do better without a companion.

Mounting a sober little iron-gray, I cantered out of Corinth, past the angles of an old fort overgrown with weeds, and entered the wooded country beyond.

A short ride brought me to a broken bridge, hanging its

shaky rim over a stream breast-high to my horse. I paused on
its brink, dubious, until I saw two ladies coming to town on
horseback to do their shopping (the fashion of the country)
rein boldly down the muddy bank, gather their skirts together,
hold up their heels and take like ducks to the water. I held up
my heels and did likewise. This was the route of the great
armies, and anyone who follows will find many a ruined bridge
and muddy stream to ford.

It was a clear, crisp winter's morning. The road wound among
lofty oak, poplar, hickory and gum, striped and gilded with the
slanting early sunshine. Quail flew up from the wayside; turtle-
doves flitted from the limbs above my head; cattle were grazing
on the wild grass of the woods.

Two miles from town I came to a steam sawmill, about which
the forest resounded with the noise of axes, the voices of Negroes shouting to their teams, and the vehement buzz of the saw.
This mill had but recently gone into operation, being one of
hundreds that had been brought from the North and set to
work repairing the damages of war.

Nearby was a new house of rough logs with the usual great
opening through it. It was situated in the midst of ruins which
told too plain a story. Tying my horse, I entered and found one
division of the house occupied by Negro servants, the other by
two lonely white women. One of these was young, the other
aged and bent with grief and years. She sat by the fire, knitting,
wrapped in an ancient shawl and having a white handkerchief
tied over her head. The walls and roof were full of chinks, the
wind blew through the room, and she crouched shivering over
the hearth.

She offered me a chair, and a Negro woman brought in wood,
which she heaped in the great fireplace.

"Sit up, stranger," said the old lady. "I haven't the accommodations for guests I had once; but you're welcome to what I have. I owned a beautiful place here before the war — a fine house, Negro quarters, an orchard and garden, and everything comfortable. The Yankees came and destroyed it. They didn't leave me a fence — not a rail nor a pale. If I had stayed here, they wouldn't have injured me, and I should have saved my house; but I was advised to leave. I have come back here to spend my days in this cabin. I lost everything, even my clothes, and I'm too old to begin life again."

Myself a Yankee, what could I say to console her?

A mile farther on, I came to another log house and stopped to inquire my way of an old man by the gate. His countenance was hard and stern, and he eyed me, I thought, with a sinister expression. "I allow you're from the North?"

"Yes," I replied. "I am from New England."

"I'm glad to see ye. Alight. It's a right cool morning: come into the house and warm."

I confess to a strong feeling of distrust as I looked at him. I resolved, however, to accept his invitation. He showed me into a room which appeared to be the kitchen and sleeping room of a large family. Two young women and several children were crowded around the fireplace. The old man, as he sat and talked with me, spat his tobacco juice (not always with accuracy) at the backlog. I remarked that the country appeared very quiet.

"Quiet to what it was," said the old man, with a wicked twinkle. "You've probably heard of some of the murders and robberies through here. I've been robbed time and again. I've had nine horses and mules stole."

"By whom?"

"The bushwhackers. They've been here to kill me three or

four times; but, as it happened, the killing was on t' other side. They come to my house of a Tuesday night, last Feb'uary. They rode up to the house and surrounded it, a dozen or fifteen of 'em. 'Old Lee!' they shouted, 'we want ye!' As I looked out through the chinks in the logs, I could see 'em moving around.

" 'You've no honest business this hour o' the night.' I says.

" 'Come out, or we'll fire your house.'

" 'Stand back, then,' I says, 'while I open the door.'

"I opened it a crack, but instead of going out, I just put out the muzzle of my gun and let have at the fust man.

" 'Boys! I'm shot!' he says. I'd sent a slug plumb through his body. Whilst the others was getting him away, I loaded up again. In a little while they come back, mad as devils. I didn't wait for 'em to order me out, but fired as they come up to the door. I hit one of 'em in the thigh. After that they went off and I didn't hear any more of 'em that night."

"What became of the wounded men?"

"The one I shot through the body got well. The other died."

"How did you learn?"

"They was all neighbors of mine. They lived only a few miles from here, over the Tennessy line."

"Why did those men wish to murder you?"

"They had a spite again me, because they said I was a Union man."

"But you are not a Yankee."

"I was born in Tennessy, and have lived either in Tennessy or Mississippi all my days. But I never was a secessioner; I went agin the war; and I had two son-in-laws in the Federal Army. Both these girls' husbands was fighting the Rebels, and that's what made 'em hate me. They was determined to kill me; and after that last attempt on my life, I refugeed. I went to the

Yankees, and didn't come back till the war wound up. There's scoundrels watching for a chance to bushwhack me now."

"Old Lee'd go up mighty quick, if they wa'n't afeared," remarked one of the daughters.

"I'm on hand for 'em," said the old man — and now I understood that wicked sparkle of his eye. "Killing is good for 'em. A lead bullet is better for getting rid of 'em than any amount of silver or gold, and a heap cheaper!"

Two miles north of old Lee's I came to the state boundary and saw, just over the line in Tennessee, a wild figure of a man riding before me. He was mounted on a rawboned mule, and wore a flapping gray blanket which gave him a fantastic appearance. The old hero's story had set me thinking of bushwhackers, and I half fancied this solitary horseman — or rather muleman — to be one of that amiable gentry.

He had pursued me from Corinth and passed me unwittingly while I was sitting in old Lee's kitchen. He was riding fast to overtake me. Or perhaps he was only an innocent country fellow returning from town. I switched on, and soon came near enough to notice that the mule's tail was fancifully clipped to resemble a rope with a tassel at the end of it; also that the rider's face was mysteriously muffled in a red handkerchief.

I was almost at his side when, hearing voices in the woods behind, I looked around and saw two more mounted men coming after us at a gallop. The thought flashed through my mind that these were the fellow's accomplices. One to one had not seemed very formidable; but three to one would not be so pleasant.

I pressed my iron-gray alongside the tassel-tailed mule and accosted the rider, determined to learn what manner of man he was before the others arrived. The startled look he gave me, and the blue nose that peered out of the sanguinary handkerchief, showed me that he was as harmless a traveler as myself. He was a lad about eighteen years of age. He had tied up his ears to defend them from the cold, and the bandage over them had prevented him from hearing my approach until I was close.

"It's a cule day," he remarked with numb lips, as he reined his mule aside to let me pass at a respectful distance — for it was evident he regarded me with quite as much distrust as I had him.

At the same time the other two mounted men came rushing upon us, through half-frozen puddles, with splash and clatter and loud oaths; and one of them drew from his pocket something so like a pistol that I half expected a shot.

"How are ye?" said he, halting his horse and spattering me with muddy water. "Right cold morning! Hello, Zeek!" to the rider of the tassel-tailed mule. "I didn't know ye, with yer face tied up that fashion. Take a drink?" Zeek declined. "Take a drink, stranger?" And he offered me the pistol, which proved to be a flask of whiskey. I declined also. Upon which the fellow held the flask unsteadily to his own lips for some seconds, then passed it to his companion. After drinking freely, they spurred on again with splash and laughter and oaths, leaving Zeek and me riding alone together.

Zeek told me he lived on the edge of the battlefield; and I engaged him to guide me to it. He thought I must be going to search for the body of some friend who fell there. When I told him I was from the North, and that my object was simply to visit the battlefield, he looked at me with amazement.

"I should think you'd be afraid to be riding alone in this country! If it was known you was a Yankee, and had money about you, I allow you'd get a shot from behind some bush."

Flocks of sparrows flew up from the bushes or hopped along the ground. There were bluebirds also; and I noticed one or two robins. "We never see robins hyer only in winter," said Zeek.

Green bunches of mistletoe grew on the leafless brown trees — a striking feature of Southern woods in winter. "It just grows on the tops of trees, without no rute nor nothing. It's a rare chance you find it on the hills; it grows mostly on the bottoms whur thar's mo'e moisture in the air." It was a beautiful sight to me, riding under its verdant tufts, sometimes so low that by rising in the stirrups I could pluck sprigs of it, with translucent pearly berries, as I passed.

We passed but few farmhouses, and those were mostly built of logs. We crossed heavy lines of Beauregard's breastworks, and could have traced the route of the great armies by the bones of horses, cattle and mules whitening by the roadside. A crest of hilly fields showed us a magnificent sweep of level wooded country on the west and south, like a brown wavy sea, with tossed treetops for breakers.

"Mighty pore soil along hyer," observed Zeek.

When I told him that it was as good as much of the soil of New England, which farmers never thought of cultivating without using manures, he said, "When our land gits as pore as that, we just turn it right out, and cle'r again. We don't allow we can afford to manure. But No'th Car'linians come in hyer and take up the land turned out so, and go to manuring it, and raise right smart truck on it."

It was after two o'clock when we came to a hilly field covered with rotting clothes. "Beauregard's troops come plumb up this road, and slept hyer the night befo'e the battle. They left their blankets and knapsacks, and after they got brushed out by the Yankees the second day, they didn't wait to pick 'em up again."

We entered the woods beyond and, after riding some distance, forded Owl Creek — a narrow but deep and muddy stream. Zeek's home was in view from the farther bank, a log house with the usual great opening through the middle, situated on the edge of a pleasant oak grove strewn with rustling leaves, and enclosed, with yard and outhouses, by a Virginia rail fence.

We were met inside the gate by a sister of the young man's, a girl of fifteen in a native bloomer dress that fell just below the knees. Zeek took me into the sitting room and introduced me to his mother. She went to see about getting dinner; and his father came in from the woods where he had been chopping and sat in the chimney corner and talked with me: a lean, bent, good-humored, sensible sort of man. He told me he had five hundred acres of land, but only thirty-six under cultivation. He and Zeek did the work; they had never owned Negroes.

"Three or four niggers is too much money for a pore man to invest in that way. They may lie down and die, and then whur's yer money? Thar was five niggers owned in middle Tennessy," he added, "to one in this part of the state."

Zeek's mother came to announce our dinner. I crossed the open space, pausing only to wash my hands and face in a tin basin half filled with water and pieces of ice, and entered the kitchen. The table was neatly set with a goodly variety of dishes. I remember a plate of fried pork, fricasseed gray squirrel (cold), boiled "back of hog" (warmed up), a pitcher of milk, cold biscuit, cold corn bread, and "sweet bread" (a name given to a plain sort of cake).

We could have dined very comfortably but for the open

doors. Blowing in at one and out at the other, and circulating through numberless cracks between the logs, the gale frisked about our legs and made our hands numb and noses cold while we ate. The fire was of no more use than one built out of doors. Zeek had not yet recovered from the chill of his long ride; and his lank, shivering frame and puckered face under its thin thatch of tow (combed straight down and cut square and short across his forehead from ear to ear) presented a picture at once astonishing and ludicrous.

"Have you got warm yet, Zeek?" I cheerfully inquired.

"No!" — shuddering. "I'm so cule I cain't eat."

"I should think you would be more comfortable with that door closed," I mildly suggested.

He slowly turned his head and as slowly turned it back again with another shiver. The possibility of actually shutting the door seemed scarcely to penetrate the tow thatch. I suppose such an act would have been unprecedented in that country — one which all conservative persons would have shaken their heads at as a dangerous innovation.

Zeek begged to be excused, he was so cule; and taking a piece of squirrel in one hand a biscuit in the other, went and stood by the fire. I found that he was averse to going out again that day: it was now late in the afternoon, and our poor animals had not yet been fed or even taken in from where they stood curled up with the cold by the gate. I accordingly proposed to the old folks to spend the night with them, and to take Zeek with me over the battlefield in the morning.

Mr. —— took me first outdoors, to a stoop on the side of the house opposite the great opening. Thence a door opened into a little framed box of a room built up against the log house as an addition. The walls consisted of naked, rough boards, There was not even a latch to the door, which opened into the universal night and which the wind kept pushing in.

Mr. —— advised me to place the chair against it, which I did. I set the candle in the chair and blew it out after I had got into bed. Then, looking up, I saw with calm joy a star through the roof.

The bed was deep and comfortable and I did not suffer from cold, although I could feel the fingers of the wind toying with my hair. The night was full of noises, like the reports of pistols. It was the old house cracking its joints.

XXII

Shiloh

THE MORNING was very cold. The earth was covered with white frost, like snow. At breakfast (both doors open and everybody shivering) Mrs. —— remarked that if it was any colder in my country, she would not like to live there. I said to her:

"We should call this cold weather, though we have some much colder. But I have suffered more from the cold in Tennessee than I have for ten years in the North. There we know how to make ourselves comfortable in our houses. Here your houses are open. The wind comes in through the cracks, and you do not even think of shutting the doors. My people at home would think they would perish if they had to breakfast with the wind blowing on them." In short, I said so much that I got one of the doors closed, which I considered a great triumph.

Zeek brought our animals to the gate and we set out for the battlefield. Fording Owl Creek at a safe place, we came to an army road made by Wallace's division moving on toward Corinth after the battle. Soon we came upon evidences of a vast encampment. Here our right wing had intrenched itself after the battle. In this place I may remark that the astonishing fact about this field is that our army did not intrench *before* the battle. Three weeks it lay at Shiloh, menaced by the enemy; Grant himself pronounced an attack probable, and the sagacious Sherman expected it; yet when it came it proved a perfect surprise; it found our lines badly arranged, weak and undefended by a single breastwork.

Beyond was a magnificent field, swept of its fences but stuck all over with abandoned tent supports, showing where our finally victorious legions had lain. "This field was just like a city after the fight," said Zeek. I noticed that the trees in the surrounding groves were killed. "The Yankees skinned 'em for bark to lay on," Zeek explained.

Crossing Shiloh Branch, a sluggish little stream, we ascended a woody hill, along the crest of which a row of graves showed where Hildebrand's picket line was attacked on that disastrous Sunday morning. Each soldier had been buried where he fell. Fires in the woods had burned the bottoms of headboards. I stopped at one grave within a rude log-rail enclosure. "In memory of L. G. Miller," said the tablet; but the remainder of the inscription had been obliterated by fire.

We rode on to Shiloh Church, formerly a mere log cabin in the woods and by no means the neat white-steepled structure which the name of country church suggests. There Beauregard had his headquarters after Sunday's battle. It was afterwards torn down for its timbers, and now nothing remained but half-burned logs and rubbish.

Below the hill, a few rods south of the church, Zeek showed me some Rebel graves. There many a poor fellow's bones lay scattered about, rooted up by swine. I saw an old half-rotted shoe containing a skeleton foot. But the most hideous sight of all was a grinning skull pushed out of a hole in the ground, exposing the neck bone with a silk cravat still tied about it in a fashionable knot.

A short distance southeast we visited the ruins of the Widow Ray house, burned to the ground in the midst of its blasted orchard and desolated fields. "A girl that lived hyer fell mightily in love with a Yankee soldier. Saturday night, he allowed there was going to be a battle, and come to bid her good-by. He got killed; and she went plumb distracted. She's married now to a mighty clever feller."

Zeek had another romantic story to tell as we returned to the church. "Hyer's whur the bale of hay was. When the Rebs was brushing out the Yankees, an old Reb found a Yankee soldier nigh about this spot that had been wounded and was perishing for a drink of water. He just took him and got him behind a bale of hay that was hyer, and give him drink out of his canteen, just like he'd been his own brother. Some of the time he'd be nussing him behind the hay and the rest he'd be shooting the Yankees over it. Some one asked him why he took such a heap of pains to save one Yankee life, while he was killing as many mo'e as he could. 'They're fighting enemies,' he said, 'but a wounded man is no longer an enemy, he's a feller being.' "

Cantering over the hills, we came to the scene of a severe infantry fight in the woods. There was a wild burial place containing some fifty patriot graves, originally surrounded by a fence of stakes wattled with saplings. Both the fence and the headboards had been broken down and partly burned. All around us were sheep feeding in the open woods; and withdrawn to the seclusion of the little burial ground was a solitary ewe and a pair of newborn lambs.

Not far away was a fence surrounding the resting places of "two officers and seventeen private Rebels," as an inscription cut in the side of a blackjack informed us. There was a story connected with these graves. A Federal soldier found on the dead body of one of the officers a watch, his likeness, his wife's likeness, a letter from his wife, and a letter written by himself requesting that in case he should fall, these relics might be sent to her. The soldier faithfully fulfilled this duty; and at the close of the war the wife, following the directions he forwarded to her, came and found his grave.

We rode on to the spot which has given the battle its Northern name. Under high bluffs stood the two log huts, a dwelling and a grocery which constituted the town of "Pittsburgh." There was not so much as a wharf there, but steamers made their landing against the natural bank. There was absolutely nothing there now, the two huts having been burned. Wild ducks sat afloat on the broad smooth river. It was not easy, looking down from those heights upon the tranquil picture, to call up that other scene of battle panic and dismay — the routed Federal troops pouring through the woods, disorganized, beaten, seeking the shelter of the bluffs and the protection of the gunboats, the great conflict roaring behind them; the victorious Rebels in wild pursuit; a solemn Sabbath changed to a horrible carnival of mad passions and bloodshed.

"The Rebels just fanned 'em out," said Zeek. "The Yankees put up white flags under the bluff, but the Rebels didn't come near enough to see 'em; they tuke a skeer — the Federals fell back so easy they was afraid of some trick. Thar was such a vast amount of 'em they couldn't all get to the landing. Some got drowned trying to swim Snake Creek. Numbers and numbers tried to swim the river. A Federal officer told me he saw his men swim out a little ways, get cold, then wind up together and go to hugging each other, and sink." Such are the traditions of the fight which have passed into the memory of the country people; but they should be taken with considerable allowance.

On the level river bottom opposite the landing we found an extensive cornfield, bounded by heavy timber beyond. Under that shore the gunboats shelled the advancing Rebels. It was there, emerging from the timber into the open field, that our defeated army saw, that Sunday evening, first the advanced cavalry, then a whole division of Buell's army coming to the rescue — banners flying and bayonets glittering among the trees. Glad sight! No wonder the runaways under the bluffs made the air ring with cheers! If Buell did not arrive in time to save that day, he was in time to save the next, and turn defeat into victory.

Taking the Hamburg Road up the river, we reached the scene of General Prentiss's disaster. The Rebels were in our camps that Sunday morning almost before the alarm of attack was given. The houses all along the road were burned. In Prentiss's front was a farm laid waste, the orchard shot to pieces and destroyed by balls. The woods all around were killed, perforated with countless holes as by the bills of woodpeckers.

Striking the Hamburg and Purdy Road, we went west to the spot where the Rebel General Albert Sidney Johnston fell, pierced by a mortal wound. Zeek then piloted me through the woods to the Corinth Road, where, time pressing, I took leave of him, sorry I could not accept his invitation to go home with him to dinner. It was five miles to his father's house, it was twenty miles to Corinth, and the day was already half spent.

Stopping occasionally to talk with people along the road, I did not reach Corinth until sunset. I returned to Mr. M——'s house and was welcomed by Mrs. M——, who seemed almost to have forgotten that I was not only a Yankee but a "bad Yankee" from Massachusetts. And here I may remark that, whatever hostility was shown me by the Southern people on account of my Northern origin, it usually wore off on short acquaintance.

Mrs. M—— had a private room for me this time; and she caused a great, glowing fire to be made for my comfort. After supper she invited me into her sitting room, where we talked freely about the bad Yankees, the war, and emancipation.

Mrs. M——: "Slavery was bad economy, I know; but oh, it was glorious!" — spoken with a kind of romantic enthusiasm. "I'd give a mint of money right now for servants like I once had — to have one all my own!"

She bemoaned the loss of a girl she formerly owned — a bright mulattress, pretty and intelligent. "She could read and write as well as I could. There was no kind of work that girl couldn't do. And so faithful! I trusted everything to her, and was never deceived."

I asked if she could feel in her heart that it was right to own such a creature.

"I believed in it as much as I believed in the Bible. We were taught it from our infancy, we were taught it with our religion. I still think it was right; but I think it was because we abused slavery that it was taken from us. Emancipation is a worse thing for our servants than for us. They can't take care of themselves."

As an illustration of a practice Southern ladies too commonly indulge in, I may state that while we were conversing, she sat in the chimney corner chewing a dainty little quid and spitting into the fire something that looked marvelously like tobacco juice.

As I was to take the train for Memphis at two o'clock in the morning, I engaged a hackman to come for me at one. Relying upon his fidelity, I went to bed, slept soundly, and awoke pro-

videntially at a quarter past the hour agreed upon. I waited
half an hour for him, and he did not appear. Opening the door
to listen for coming wheels, I heard the train whistle. Catching
up my luggage, I rushed out to search, at dead of night, in a
strange town, lampless and fast asleep, for a railroad depot
which I should scarce have thought of finding even by daylight
without inquiring my way.

Not a living creature was abroad; not a light was visible in
any house; I could not see the ground I was treading upon. Fortunately I knew the general direction in which the railroad lay;
I struck it at last; then I saw a light which guided me to the
depot.

But where was the train? It was already overdue. I could hear
it whistling occasionally down the track, where some accident
had happened to it. The depot consisted of a little framed box
just large enough for a ticket office. You stood outside and
bought your ticket through a hole. This box contained a stove,
a railroad lantern, and two men.

The door, contrary to the custom of the country, was kept
scrupulously shut. In vain were my appeals to the two men
within to open it. They were talking and laughing by their comfortable fire, while the waiting passengers outside were freezing.
Two hours we waited, that cold winter's night, for the train
which did not come.

Seeing a flame a short distance up the railroad track, I went
stumbling through the darkness towards it. I found an encampment of Negroes. Twelve men, women and children were
grouped in gypsy fashion about a smoky fire. They were in miserable condition, wretchedly clad, hungry, weary and sleepy,
but unable to sleep. Yet these suffering and oppressed creatures
did for me what men of my own color had refused to do — they

made room for me at their fire, and hospitably invited me to
share such poor comforts as they had. The incident was humiliating and touching.

They told me their story. They had been working all summer
for a planter in Tishomingo County who had refused to pay
them, and now they were hunting for new homes. Two or three
had a little money; the rest had none. It made my heart sick to
look at them and feel that it was out of my power to do them any
real, permanent service. But they were not discouraged. Said the
spokesman of the party, an old gray-haired man in tatters: "I'll
drap my feet into de road in de mornin'; I'll go till I find
somefin'!"

Hearing the train again, whistling in earnest this time, I took
leave of them and reached the depot just as it arrived.

XXIII

Memphis

A T DAYLIGHT we were running through the level lower counties of west Tennessee, by far the most fertile division of the state. Its soil is a rich black mold adapted to the culture of cotton, tobacco and grains, which are produced in great abundance.

Occasionally we passed outdoor fires about which homeless Negroes had passed the night, and around which they still sat or stood in wretched plight, but picturesque and cheerful, watching with vacant curiosity the train as it shot by.

"That's freedom! That's what the Yankees have done for 'em!" was the frequent exclamation from the lips of Southern ladies and gentlemen looking out the car windows.

"They'll all be dead before spring."

"Niggers can't take care of themselves. How much better off they were when they were slaves!"

But there was another side to the picture. At every stopping place, throngs of well-dressed blacks crowded upon the train. They were going to Memphis to "buy Christmas" — as the purchase of gifts for that gay season is termed. Happier faces I have never seen. They were all comfortably clad — many of them elegantly — in clothes they had purchased with money earned out of bondage. They paid with pride the full fares exacted of free people, instead of the half fares formerly demanded for slaves. They occupied cars by themselves which they filled with cheerful conversation and laughter. And nobody said of *them*, "That is freedom! That is what the Yankees have done for them!"

Past cotton fields and handsome mansions we ran into Memphis — a city which surprised me by its beautiful situation and commercial activity. The view of the commerce of Memphis from the esplanade overlooking the landing is one of the most animated imaginable. You stand on the brow of the bluff, with the city behind you and the river below — its broad, sweeping current severing the states. From the foot of the bluff projects an extensive shelving bank, forming a natural landing commonly called a "levee," although no levee is here — the celebrated levee at New Orleans having impressed its name upon all landings of any importance up the river.

You look down upon a superb array of steamers, lying along the shore, their elegantly ornamented pilothouses and lofty tiers of decks supported by slender pillars fully entitling them to be named floating palaces. The levee is crowded with casks and cotton bales, covering acres of ground. Up and down the steep way cut through the brow of the bluff, affording access to the landing from the town, a stream of drays is passing and repassing. Freights are going aboard or coming ashore. Bales of cotton and hay, casks, boxes, sacks of grain, lumber, household furniture, supplies for plantations, mules, ploughs, wagons are tumbled, rolled, carried, tossed, driven, pushed and dragged by an army of laborers from the levee along the broad stages to the steamers' decks.

The movement, the seeming confusion, the rattling of drays, the ringing of boats' bells, the horrible snort of the steam whistle, the singing calls of the deck hands heaving at a rope or lifting some heavy weight, the wild, fantastic gesticulations of gangs of Negroes driving on board a drove of frightened mules, the voices of the teamsters, the arriving and departing packets — the whole forms an astonishing scene. Then, over the immense brown sand bar of the Arkansas shore, the sun goes down in a tranquil sea of fire, reflected in the river — a wonderfully contrasting picture.

Evening comes, and adds picturesque effect to the scene. The levee is lighted by great smoking and flaring flambeaux. The far-illuminating flame shoots up in the night, while the ignited oil falls in little streams of dripping blue fire into the river. Until late at night, and often all night, amid darkness and fog and rain, the loading of freight goes on by this lurid illumination.

The laborers are chiefly Negroes, whose ebon tawny faces, lithe attitudes and sublime carelessness of attire heighten the pictorial effect. Bale after bale is tumbled from the drays and rolled down the levee — a Negro at each end of it holding and guiding it with cotton hooks. At the foot of the landing it is seized by two other Negroes, who roll it along the plank to its place on the deck of the boat. Here are fifty men rolling barrels aboard, each at the other's heels; and yonder is a long straggling file of blacks crossing the stage from the levee to the steamer, each carrying a box on his shoulder.

By a census taken in June, 1865, there were 16,509 freedmen in Memphis. Of this number, two hundred and twenty were indigent persons, maintained not by the city or the bureau but by the freed people themselves. During the past three years, colored benevolent societies in Memphis had contributed five thousand dollars towards the support of their own poor.

There were three thousand pupils in the freedmen's schools. The teachers for these were furnished, here as elsewhere, chiefly by benevolent societies in the North. Visiting these schools in nearly all the Southern states, I did not hear of white people taking any interest in them. With the exception of here and there a man or woman inspired by Northern principles, I never saw or heard of a Southern citizen, male or female, entering one of those humble schoolrooms.

How often, thinking of this indifference and watching the earnest, Christian labors of that little band of refined and sensitive men and women and girls, who had left cheerful homes in the North and voluntarily exposed themselves to privation and opprobrium, devoting their energies to the work of educating and elevating the despised race — how often the stereotyped phrase occurred to me, "The Southern people were always their best friends!"

The wonder was, how these "best friends" could be so utterly careless of the intellectual and moral interests of the freedmen. For my own part, I could never enter one of those schools without emotion. They were often held in old buildings and sheds good for little else. There was not a schoolroom in Tennessee furnished with appropriate seats and desks. I found a similar condition in all the states. The pews of colored churches, or plain benches in the vestries, or old chairs with boards laid across them in some loft over a shop, or out of doors on the grass in summer — such was the usual scene of the freedmen's schools.

In those studies which appeal to the imagination and memory, the colored pupil excels. In those which exercise reflective and reasoning faculties, he is less proficient. But it is in the contrasts of age and of personal appearance which they present that the colored schools differ from all others. I never visited one of any size in which there were not two or three or half a dozen children so nearly white that no one would have suspected the Negro taint. From these, the complexion ranges through all the mixed hues to the shining black of a few pure-blooded Africans, perhaps not more in number than the seemingly pure-blooded whites. The younger the generation, the lighter the average skin; by which curious fact one perceives how fast the race was bleaching under the "peculiar" system of slavery.

The difference in ages is even more striking. Six years and sixty may be seen side by side, learning to read from the same chart or book. Perhaps a bright little Negro boy or girl is teaching a white-haired old man, or bent old woman in spectacles, their letters. There are few more affecting sights than these aged people beginning the child's task so late in life, often after their eyesight has failed.

At Memphis, as at Nashville and other points in Tennessee, I saw much of the operations of the Freedmen's Bureau. General Fisk appeared peculiarly fitted for his position, although, like all the assistant commissioners I saw, he complained that the law establishing the bureau did not permit him to choose his own agents. He had to take such army officers as were given him, some of whom were always incompetent, or neglectful of their duties, or so prejudiced for or against the blacks that they were incapable of administering justice.

A few were in sympathy with slavery. Others, meaning to do right, were seduced from a straightforward course by the dinners to which they were invited by planters who had favors to ask. With such, the rights of the freedmen were sure to suffer when into the opposite scale were thrown the aristocratic Rebel's flattering attentions and the smiles of his fair daughters.

It was the practice of bureau agents to make frequent tours of their counties, and Fisk himself was in the habit of running off every few days to visit some important point where his organizing and conciliatory influence was necessary. Sometimes dramatic scenes occurred at these meetings.

"Not long ago," said Fisk, "I addressed a mixed audience of three thousand persons at Spring Hill. The meeting was presided over by a black man. Rebel generals and Federal generals sat together on the platform. I made a short speech and afterwards answered questions for anybody, white or black, that chose to ask them. I had said that the intention of the bureau was to do justice to all, without respect to color, when there rose up in the audience a tall, well-dressed, fine-looking woman, sallow, very pale, and much agitated, who wished to know if *she* could have justice.

"Said she, 'I was owned by a respectable planter in this neighborhood who kept me as his wife for many years. I have borne him five children. Two of them are dead. A short time ago he married another woman, and drove me and my three children off.' The man was in the audience. Everybody present knew him, and there were a hundred witnesses that could vouch for the woman's story. I told her justice should certainly be done in her case. The respectable planter now supports her and her three children."

The freedmen's courts were designed to adjudicate cases which could not be safely intrusted to the civil courts. They are in reality military courts, and the law by which they are governed is martial law. I found them particularly efficient in Tennessee. The annoying technicalities and quibbles by which in ordinary courts the truth is so often embarrassed here were swept aside, and justice reached with admirable directness. I have watched carefully scores of cases decided by these tribunals, and do not remember one in which substantial justice was not done.

The freedmen's court is no respecter of persons. The proudest aristocrat and the humblest Negro stand on equal footing. I remember a case in which a member of the Tennessee Legislature was the defendant, and upwards of twenty freedmen hired by him were the plaintiffs. He had voted against the Negro Testimony Bill which, if it had passed, would have placed his case in a civil court; and now he had the satisfaction of seeing eight of these blacks stand up and testify against him. He admitted that they were faithful and truthful men; and their testimony was so straightforward, I was astonished that he should have waited to have his accounts with them adjusted by the bureau.

A great variety of business is brought before the bureau. Here is a Negro who has printed a reward offering fifty dollars for information to assist him in finding his wife and children, sold away in times of slavery. Here is a free mulattress who was stolen by a guerrilla during the war and sold into slavery in Arkansas, and she has come to enter a claim for wages earned during two years of enforced servitude. Yonder is a white woman who has been warned by the police that she must not live with her husband because he is black, and who has come to claim protection in her marriage relation, bringing proof that she is in reality a colored woman. That poor old crippled Negro was maimed for life when a slave by a cruel master, who will now be compelled to pension him.

Yonder comes an old farmer with a stout colored boy, to get the bureau's sanction to a contract they wish to make. "Pull off your hat, Bob," says the old man. "You was raised to that"

— for he was formerly the lad's owner. He claims to have been a Union man. "I was opposed to secession till I was swep' plumb away." He is very grateful for what the officers do for him, and especially for the good advice they give the boy. "I'll do well by him and larn him to read, if he'll do well by me."

As they go out, in comes a powerful, short-limbed black in tattered overcoat, with a red handkerchief on his head and with a lordly countenance, looking like a barbarian chief. He has made a crop; found everything — mules, feed, implements; hired his own help — fifteen men and women; managed everything; by agreement he was to have one half; but, owing to an attempt to swindle him, he has had the cotton attached; and now it is not on his own account he has come. He owes his men wages, and they want something for Christmas, which he thinks reasonable, and he desires the bureau's assistance to raise three hundred dollars on the said cotton. "For I'm bound," he says, "to be liberal with my men."

Here is a boy who was formerly a slave, to whom his father, a free man, willed a sum of money which the boy's owner borrowed, giving his note for it, but never repaid — for did not the boy and all that he had belong to his master? The worn and soiled bit of paper is produced; and now the owner will have that money to restore, with interest. Lucky for the boy that he kept that torn and dirty scrap carefully hidden all these years! Such documents are now serving to right many an ancient wrong.

XXIV

Vicksburg

AT MEMPHIS I took passage in a first-class Mississippi packet for Vicksburg. It was evening when I went on board. The extensive saloon, with its long array of staterooms on each side, its ornamental gilt ceiling and series of dazzling chandeliers, was a brilliant spectacle. A corps of swift-handed colored waiters was setting the tables — bringing in baskets of tablecloths and spreading them, immense baskets of crockery and distributing it, and trays of silver, which added to the other noises a jingling accompaniment. Above the stove and bar and captain's office was an astonishing crowd of passengers, mostly standing, talking, drinking, buying tickets, playing cards, swearing, reading, laughing, chewing, spitting and filling the saloon, even to the ladies' cabin at the opposite end, with a thick blue cloud which issued from countless bad pipes and cigars, enveloped the supper tables, and bedimmed the glitter of the chandeliers. In that cloud, supper was to be eaten.

At a signal known only to the initiated, a mighty rush began. Two lines of battle were formed, confronting each other, with the table between them, each dauntless hero standing with foot advanced and invincible right hand laid upon the back of a chair. In this way every place was secured at least five minutes before the thundering signal was given for the beginning of the conflict. At last the gong-bearing steward, anxiously watched by the hostile hosts till the ladies were seated, beat the terrible roll and instantly, every chair was jerked back with a simultaneous clash and clatter, every soldier plunged forward, every coattail was spread, and every pair of trousers was in its seat. Then, rallied by the gong from deck and stateroom and stove, came the crowd of uninitiated ones, hungry, rueful-faced, dismayed, finding themselves compelled to wait until the rest had fed.

After supper there were music and dancing in the afterpart of the saloon, and gambling and clicking glasses and everlasting talk about Yankees and niggers and cotton in the other part. There were a few Federal officers in uniform, and a good many Rebel officers in civil dress. I recognized a thin sprinkling of Northern capitalists and businessmen. But the majority were Mississippi and Arkansas planters going down-river to their estates: a strongly marked, unrefined, rather picturesque class — hard swearers, hard drinkers, inveterate smokers and chewers, wearing sad-colored linen for the most part and clad in coarse "domestic," slouching in their dress and manners, loose of tongue, free-hearted, good-humored and sociable.

They had been to Memphis to purchase supplies for their plantations, or to lease their plantations, or to hire freedmen, or to "buy Christmas" for their freedmen at home. They appeared to have plenty of money, if the frequency with which they patronized the bar was any criterion. Liquors on board the Mississippi steamers were twenty-five cents a glass, and the average cost of such drinking as I witnessed could not have been less than three or four dollars a day for each man.

How shall I describe the conversation of these men? Never a word did I hear concerning literature or the higher interests of life; but their talk was of mules, cotton, niggers, money, Yankees, politics and the Freedmen's Bureau — thickly studded with oaths and garnished with joke and story. Once only I heard the subject of education indirectly alluded to. Said a young fellow, formerly the owner of fifty slaves, "I've gone to schoolkeeping."

"Oh Lord!" said his companion, "you ha'n't come down to that!"

There were a few Tennesseeans aboard who envied the Mississippians their Rebel state government, organized militia and power over the freedmen. "We might make a pile if we could only regulate the labor system. But that can't be done in this dog-goned Brownlow State. In Mississippi, if they can only carry out the laws they've enacted, there'll be a chance."

After a night of fog, Christmas morning dawned. In the cabin the generous steward gave each passenger a glass of eggnog before breakfast, not because it was Christmas, but because passengers were human, and eggnog was one of the necessities of life.

The morning was warm and beautiful. We were running down the broad current between high banks covered with forests on one side, and sand bars extending their broad yellow shelves out into the river on the other. We were making landings at every plantation where passengers or freight were to be put off, or a signal was shown from the shore. Sometimes a newspaper or piece of cloth was fluttered by Negroes on the bank; or a man who wished to come on board stood on some exposed point and waved his handkerchief or hat. There was never a wharf, but the steamer, rounding to in the current and heading upstream, went butting its broad nose against the steep, yielding bank. The planks were pushed out, the passengers stepped aboard or ashore, and the deckhands landed the freight.

Wooding-up was always an interesting sight. A long woodpile lines the summit of the bank, perhaps forty feet above the river. The steamer lands; a couple of stages are hauled out; fifty men rush ashore and climb the bank; the clerk accompanies them with pencil and paper and measuring rod, to take account of the number of cords; then suddenly down comes the wood in an amazing shower, rattling, sliding, bounding, and sometimes turning somersaults into the river. The bottom and side of the bank are soon covered by the deluge; and the work of loading begins in equally lively fashion.

The two stages are occupied by two files of men, one going ashore at a dog-trot, empty-handed, and another coming aboard with the wood. Each man catches up from two to four sticks, according to their size or his own inclination, shoulders them, falls into the current, not of water but of men, crosses the plank and deposits his burden where the corded wood that stood so lately on the top of the bank is once more taking shape, divided into two equally balanced piles on each side of the boiler deck.

The men are mostly Negroes, and the treatment they receive from the mate is about the same as that which they received when slaves. He stands on the shore between the ends of the two stages, within convenient reach of both. Not a laggard escapes his eye or foot. Often he brandishes a billet of wood, with which he threatens and sometimes strikes; and now he flings it at the head of some artful dodger who has eluded his blow. And all the while you hear his hoarse, harsh voice iterating with horrible crescendo: "Get along, *get along!* Out o' the way 'th that wood! Out o' the way! Git on, *git on,* GIT ON!"

Planters got off at every landing by day and night; and although a few came aboard, the company was gradually thinning out. At one plantation a colony of sixty Negroes landed. They had a "heap of plunder." Beds and bedding, trunks, tubs, hen coops, old chests, old chairs, spinning wheels, pots and kettles were put off under the mate's directions without much ceremony. The dogs were caught and pitched into the river, much to the distress of the women and children, who appeared to care more for the animals than for any other property.

These people had been hired for an adjoining plantation. The plantation at which we landed had been laid waste, and the mansion and Negro quarters burned, leaving a grove of fifty naked chimneys standing — "monuments of Yankee vandalism," said my Southern friends.

At one place a fashionably dressed couple came on board and the gentleman asked for a stateroom. Terrible was the captain's wrath. "God damn your soul," he said, "get off this boat!" The gentleman and lady were colored, and they had been guilty of unpardonable impudence in asking for a stateroom.

"Kick the nigger!" "He ought to have his neck broke!" "He ought to be hung!" said the indignant passengers, by whom the captain's prompt action was strongly commended.

The unwelcome couple went quietly ashore and one of the hands pitched their trunk after them. They were in a dilemma: their clothes were too fine for deck passage, and their skins were too dark for a cabin passage. So they sat down on the shore to wait for the next steamer.

"They won't find a boat that'll take 'em," said the grim captain. "Anyhow, they can't force their damned nigger equality on to me!"

Afterwards I heard the virtuous passengers talking over the affair. "How would you feel," said one with solemn emphasis, "to know that *your wife was sleeping in the next room to a nigger and his wife?*"

I had heard much about anticipated Negro insurrections at Christmastime. But the only act of violence that came to my knowledge on that day was a little affair that occurred at Skipwith's Landing on the Mississippi shore, a few miles below the Arkansas and Louisiana line. Four mounted guerrillas, wearing Confederate uniforms and carrying Spencer rifles, rode into the place, robbed a store kept by a Northern man, robbed and murdered a Negro, and rode off unmolested.

Very little was said of this operation. If such a deed, however, had been perpetrated by freedmen, the whole South would have rung with it, and the cry of "Kill the niggers!" would have been heard from the Rio Grande to the Atlantic.

On the afternoon of the third day we came in sight of Vicksburg — four hundred miles from Memphis by water although not more than half that distance in a straight line, so voluminous are the coils of the Great River.

The town, situated on a high bluff with the sunlight on its hills and roofs and fortifications, was a fine sight. It slopes up rapidly from the landing, and is built of brick and wood, not beautiful on a nearer view. The hills are cut through, and their sides sliced off by the deeply indented streets of the upper portion of the city. Here and there are crests completely cut around, isolated, and left standing like yellowish square sugarloaves with irregular tops. These excavations afforded the inhabitants fine facilities for burrowing during the siege.

The base of the hills and the clifflike banks of the dug streets present a most curious appearance, being honeycombed with caves, which still remain a source of astonishment to the stranger. The majority of the caves were mere "gopher holes," as the soldiers call them. Others were quite spacious and aristocratic. Every family had its cave. But only a few of the more extensive ones were permanently occupied.

"Ours" (said a lady resident) "was very large and comfortable. There was first the entrance, under a pointed arch; then a long cross-gallery. Boards were laid down the whole length and covered with carpets. Berths were put up at the sides, where we slept very well. At first we did not take off our dresses when we lay down; but in a little while we grew accustomed to undressing and retiring regularly.

"In the morning we found our clothes quite wet from the natural dampness of the cave. Over the entrance there was built a little arbor, where our cooking was done and where we talked with our neighbors in the daytime, when there were no shells dropping. In the night the cave was lighted up. We lived this sort of life six weeks."

Few buildings were destroyed by shells. Those that were partially injured had generally been patched up. After the twenty-sixth of May, when the bombardment became almost incessant, night and day, it was estimated that six thousand shells were thrown into the city by the mortars on the riverside every twenty-four hours. Grant's siege guns, in the rear of the bluffs, dropped daily four thousand more along the Rebel lines. The little damage done by so great a bombardment is a matter of surprise. Of the women and children in the town, only three were killed and twelve injured.

Both citizens and troops suffered more from the scarcity of provisions than from shells. On both the river and land sides, the city was cut off from supplies. The garrison was put upon fourteen-and-a-half-ounce rations; and in the town, mulemeat and even dogmeat became luxuries.

The day after my arrival I joined a small equestrian party and rode out to visit the fortifications. Three miles northeast we passed Fort Hill, in the "crater" of which, after the Rebel bastions had been successfully mined and blown up, occurred one of the most desperate fights that marked the siege. Pushed up dangerously near to the Rebel position is the advanced Federal line. Between the two, a little way down the slope from Fort Hill, is the spot rendered historic by the interview which terminated the long struggle for the key to the Mississippi. There, in full view of the confronting armies, the two commanding generals met under an oak tree and had their little talk.

Every vestige of the tree, root and branch, had long since disappeared — cut up, broken up, dug up and scattered over the country in the form of relics; and we found on the spot a monument which bids fair to have a similar fate. This was originally a neat granite shaft, erected by private subscription among officers and soldiers of the National Army, and dedicated on July 4, 1864, first anniversary of the surrender. It bears the inscription:

SITE OF
INTERVIEW BETWEEN
MAJOR–GENERAL GRANT, U.S.A.,
AND
LIEUTENANT–GENERAL PEMBERTON,
JULY 4, 1863

Nothing could be more simple and modest. Not a syllable is there to wound the sensibilities of a fallen foe. Yet, since the close of the war, when returning Confederates first obtained access to this monument, it had been shamefully mutilated. The fact that the eagle and shield surmounting the inscription had been obliterated by persistent battering showed that no mere relic hunters had been here, but that the mischief had been done by some enemy's hand.

Next day, in company with Major General Wood, in command of the Department of Mississippi, I visited the fortifications below Vicksburg. For a mile and a half we rode along beside banks perforated with "gopher holes" dug by Rebel soldiers, and lines of rifle pits, which consisted often of a mere trench cut across the edge of a crest. There were the riverside defenses. The real fortifications commenced with a strong fort constructed on a commanding bluff. Standing upon the first redan, we saw a mile or two of low land and shaggy cypress swamps intervening between us and glimpses of shining light which indicated the southward course of the Mississippi.

In this excursion, as in that of the previous day, I noticed on every side practical answers to the question, "Will the freedmen work?" In every broken field, in every available spot on the rugged crests, was the Negro's little cotton patch.

Riding through the freedmen's quarter below the town, the general and I called at a dozen cabins, putting to every person the inquiry — how large a proportion of the colored people he knew were shiftless characters? We got very candid replies, the common opinion being that about five out of twenty still had a notion of living without work. Yet, curiously enough, not one would admit that *he* was one of the five — every man and woman acknowledging that labor was a universal duty and necessity.

Dr. Warren, Superintendent of Freedmen's Schools in Mississippi, spoke of the great eagerness of the blacks to buy or lease land and have homes of their own. This he said accounted in great measure for their backwardness in making contracts. He said to one intelligent freedman: "The whites intend to compel you to hire out to them."

The latter replied: "What if we should compel them to lease us lands?"

There were other reasons why the blacks would not contract. At Vicksburg, a gentleman who had been fifty miles up the valley looking for a plantation said to me: "The Negroes everywhere I went have been shamefully abused. They had been promised that if they would remain and work the plantations, they should have a share of the crops; and now the planters refuse to give them anything. They have no confidence in Southern men, and will not hire out to them; but they are very eager to engage with Northern men."

Mr. C——, a Northern man who had taken a plantation at —— (I omit names, for he told me that not only his property but his life depended upon the goodwill of his neighbors), related to me his experience. He hired his plantation of a gentleman noted for his honesty: "He goes by the name of 'Honest M——' all through the country. But honesty appeared to be a virtue to be exercised only towards white people: it was too good to be thrown away on niggers. This M—— has four hundred sheep, seventy cows, fifteen horses, ten mules and forty hogs, all of which were saved from the Yankees when they raided through the country by an old Negro who ran them off across a swamp. Honest M—— has never given that Negro five cents.

"Another of his slaves had a cow of his own from which he raised a fine pair of oxen: Honest M—— lays claim to those

oxen and sells them. A slave-woman that belonged to him had
a cow she had raised from a calf: Honest M—— takes that, and
adds it to his herd. He promised his niggers a share of the crops
this year; but he has sold the cotton and locked up the corn,
and never given one of them a dollar. And all this time he
thinks he is honest: he thinks Northern capitalists treat free
laborers in this way. You can't get it through the heads of these
Southern planters that the laboring class has any rights."

I met with many planters in the situation of Honest M——.
Having made arrangements to run their plantations, and got in
the necessary supplies, they had discovered that "the niggers
wouldn't contract." They were then trying to lease their lands
to Northern capitalists.

I have seldom met a more anxious, panic-stricken set than
the planters I saw on the steamer going down to Vicksburg to
hire freedmen. Observing the success of Northern men, they
had suddenly awakened to the great fact that, although slavery
was lost, all was not lost, and that there was still a chance to
make something out of the Negro. They could not hire their
own freedmen, and were going to see what could be effected
with freedmen to whom they were not known. Each seemed to
fear lest his neighbor should get the start of him.

"They're just crazy about the niggers," said one, a Mississippian, who was about the craziest of the set. "Crazy to get hold
of 'em."

"But," I remarked, "they say the freedmen won't work."

"Well, they won't," said my Mississippi friend unflinchingly.

"Then what do you want of them?"

"Well, I found everybody else was going in for hiring 'em,
and if anything was to be made, I didn't want to be left out in
the cold." Adding with great candor and earnestness: "*If every-*

body else would have refused to hire 'em anyhow, that would have just suited me: I'd have been willing to let my plantation go to the devil for one year, just to see the free niggers starve."

I saw this gentleman afterwards in Vicksburg, and was not grieved to learn that he had failed to engage a single freedman. "They are hiring to Northern men," said he bitterly, "but they won't hire to Southern men anyhow, if they can help it."

"How do you account for this singular fact?" I asked.

"I don't know. They've no confidence in us; but they imagine the Yankees will do wonders by 'em. The Southern people are really their best friends." At which stereotyped bit of cant I could not forbear a smile.

Meanwhile, the Christmas holidays were effecting a change in the prospects of free labor for the coming year. I never witnessed in so short a time so complete a revolution in public feeling. One day it seemed that everybody was in despair, complaining that niggers wouldn't work; the next, everybody was rushing to employ them. And the freedmen, who before Christmas had refused to make contracts, vaguely hoping that lands would be given them by the government, or leased to them by their owners, now came forward to make the best terms they could.

The presence of the bureau at this time was an incalculable benefit to both parties. It inspired the freedmen with confidence and persuaded them, with the promise of protection, to hire out once more to Southern planters. The trouble was, there was not labor enough in the state to supply the demand. Many Negroes had enlisted in the war; others had wandered back to the slave-breeding states from which they had been sold; others had become small proprietors; and others had died, in consequence of the great and sudden change in their circumstances which the war had brought about.

I have already alluded to the organizing of state militia — an abuse that unfortunately received the sanction of the administration. The only possible excuse for it was the cry raised regarding anticipated Negro insurrections. To guard against danger from a class whose loyalty and good behavior during the war challenged the admiration of the world, arms were put into the hands of Confederate soldiers who had returned to their homes. Power was taken from the friends of the government and put into the hands of its enemies. The latter immediately set to work disarming the former.

They plundered their houses, under the pretense of searching for weapons, committing robberies, murders and other atrocities, with authentic reports of which pages might be filled. Neither were white men known to sympathize with the Union safe from their violence. Governor Humphreys himself, startled by the magnitude of the evil that had been called into existence, had been obliged to disband several militia companies already organized "on learning that they were sworn to kill Negroes asserting their independence, and to drive off Northern men."

There were no doubt serious apprehensions in the minds of people on the subject of Negro insurrections. But a great deal that was said about them was mere cant, with which I have not seen fit to load these pages. There was not, while I was in the South, the slightest danger from a rising of the blacks, nor will there be, unless they are driven to desperation by wrongs.

I remember two very good specimens of formidable Negro

insurrections. One was reported in northern Mississippi and investigated personally by General Fisk, who took pains to visit the spot and learn all the facts. According to his account, "a colored man hunting squirrels was magnified into a thousand vicious Negroes marching upon their old masters with bloody intent."

The other case was reported at the hotel in Vicksburg, where I was stopped by a gentleman who had just arrived from New Orleans. He related an exciting story of a rising of the blacks in Jefferson Parish, and a great slaughter of the white population. He also stated that General Sheridan had sent troops to quell the insurrection.

Afterwards, when at New Orleans, I made inquiry of Sheridan concerning the rumor and learned that it was utterly without foundation. The most noticeable phase of it was the effect it had upon guests at the hotel table. Everybody had been predicting Negro insurrections at Christmastime; now everybody's prophecy had come true, and everybody was delighted. A good deal of horror was expressed, but the real feeling, ill concealed under all, was exultation.

"What will Sumner and Company say now?" cried one.

"The only way is to kill the niggers off, and drive 'em out of the country," said another.

An unrelenting spirit of persecution, shown towards Union men in Mississippi, was fostered by the reconstructed civil courts. Union scouts were prosecuted for arson and stealing. A horse which had been taken by the government, and afterwards condemned and sold, was claimed by the original owner and recovered — the quartermaster's bill of sale, produced in court by the purchaser, being pronounced void. The government had leased to a Northern man an abandoned plantation, with the

privilege of cutting wood upon it at forty cents a cord: the
Rebel owner returns with his pardon and sues the lessee for
alleged damages done to his property by the removal of wood,
to the amount of five thousand dollars; a writ of attachment is
issued under the local court, and the defendant is compelled to
give bond to the amount of ten thousand dollars, or lie in jail.
Such cases were occurring every day.

There was great opposition to the freedmen's schools. Dr.
Warren told me that "if the bureau was withdrawn, not a
school would be publicly allowed." There were combinations
formed to prevent the leasing of rooms for schools; and those
who would have been willing to let buildings for this purpose
were deterred by threats from neighbors. In Vicksburg, schoolhouses had been erected on confiscated land which had lately
been restored to the Rebel owners, and from which they were
ordered, with other government buildings, to be removed.

XXV

Natchez

LEAVING Vicksburg by south-bound steamer, the first point of interest you pass is Davis's Bend, former home of the President of the Confederacy. A curve of the river encircles a pear-shaped peninsula twenty-eight miles in circumference, with a cut-off across the neck, converting it into an island.

About a mile from the river stands the Jeff Davis Mansion, with wide verandas and pleasant shade trees. The plantation comprises a thousand acres of tillable land, now used as a home farm for colored paupers, under a subcommissioner of the bureau. Here are congregated the old, the orphaned, the infirm, and many whose energies were prematurely worn out under the system which the Confederacy was designed to glorify and perpetuate.

Here you find the incompetent and thriftless. Some have little garden spots, on which they worked last season until their vegetables were ripe, when they stopped work and went to eating the vegetables. The government cultivates cotton with their labor; and once, at a critical period, it was necessary to commence ejecting them from their quarters in order to compel them to work to keep the grass down.

The freedmen on other plantations of the island represent other qualities of the race. Besides the home farm, there are five thousand acres divided into farms and homesteads, cultivated by the Negroes on their own account and paying a large rent to the government. There were about three thousand people at the bend. Some worked a few acres, others took large farms and hired laborers. Fifty had accumulated five thousand dollars each during the past two years; and one hundred others had accumulated from one to four thousand dollars. Some of these rising capitalists had engaged Northern men to rent plantations for the coming year and to take them in as partners — the new black code of Mississippi prohibiting the leasing of lands to freedmen.

The colony is self-governing, under supervision of the subcommissioner. There are three courts, each having its colored judge and sheriff. Some sound sense often falls from the lips of these black Solomons. Here is a sample. A colored man and his mother are brought up for stealing a bag of corn.

JUDGE: "Do you choose to be tried by a jury?"

CULPRIT (not versed in the technicalities of the court): "What's dat?"

JUDGE: "Do you want twelve men to come in and help me?"

CULPRIT, emphatically: "No, sah!" — for he thinks one man will probably be too much for him.

JUDGE, sternly: "Now listen, you! You and your mother are a couple of low-down darkies, trying to get a living without work. You are the cause that respectable colored people are slandered, and called thieving and lazy niggers. Now this is what I'll do with you. If you and your mother will hire out today, and go to work like honest people, I'll let you off on good behavior. If you won't, I'll send you to Captain Norton. That means you'll go up with a sentence. And I'll tell you what your sentence will be: three months' hard labor on the home farm, and the ball and chain in case you attempt to run away. Now which will you do?"

CULPRIT, eagerly: "I'll hire out, sah!" And a contract is made for him and his mother on the spot.

The next point of interest is Grand Gulf, the only place that offered any resistance to our gunboats between Vicksburg and Port Hudson. It had before the war a thousand inhabitants, three churches and several steam mills. Water and fire appeared to have conspired against it. The Yankees burned every vestige of the village, and the river has torn away a large section of the bank on which it stood. A number of cheap whitewashed wooden buildings have taken its place on the shore, above and behind which rises a steep rocky bluff, covered with sparse timber, sedge and cane brakes, and crowned by Rebel batteries.

A hundred and twenty miles below Vicksburg is Natchez, one of the most romantically and beautifully situated cities in the United States. It is built on an almost precipitous bluff one hundred and fifty feet above the river, which is overlooked by a delightful park and promenade along the city front. The landing is under the bluff.

The *Quitman* (in which I had taken passage) stopped several hours at Natchez, getting on board a quantity of cotton. Above Vicksburg, I noticed that nearly all the cotton was going northward: below, it was going the other way, toward New Orleans. At every town and at nearly every plantation landing, we took on board sometimes a hundred bales and more, sometimes but two or three, until the *Quitman* showed two high white walls of cotton all round her guards, which were sunk to the water's edge.

On the levee at Natchez I made the acquaintance of an old
plantation overseer. He knew all about cotton raising. "I've
overseed in the swamps, and I've overseed on the hills. You can
make a bale to the acre in the swamps, and about one bale to
two acres on the hills. I used to get ten to fifteen hundred dollars a year. I'm hiring now to a Northern man who gives me
three thousand. A Northern man will want to get more out of
the niggers than we do. Mine said to me last night, 'I want you
to get the last drop of sweat and the last pound of cotton out
of my niggers'; and I shall do it. I can if anybody can."

As we were talking, the mate of the *Quitman* took up an
oyster shell and threw it at the head of one of the deck hands
who did not handle the cotton to suit him. It did not hurt the
Negro's head much, but it hurt his feelings.

"Out on the plantations," observed the overseer, "it would
cost him fifty dollars to hit a nigger that way. It cost me a hundred and fifty dollars just for knocking down three niggers
lately — fifty dollars apiece, by ——!"

He thought the Negroes were going to be crowded out by
the Germans, and went on to say, with true Southern consistency: "The Germans want twenty dollars a month, and we can
hire the niggers for ten and fifteen. The Germans will die in
our swamps. Then as soon as they get money enough to buy a
cart and mule, and an acre of land somewhar, whar they can
plant a grapevine, they'll go in for themselves."

We were nearly all night at Natchez loading cotton. The
Quitman was a fine boat, and passengers, if not deck hands,
fared sumptuously on board of her. The table was equal to that
of the best hotels. An excellent quality of claret was furnished
as part of the regular dinner fare, after the French fashion,
which appears to have been introduced into this country by the

Creoles, and which is to be met with, I believe, only on steamboats on the lower Mississippi.

On the *Quitman,* as on the boat from Memphis to Vicksburg,
I made the acquaintance of all sorts of Southern people. The
conversation of some of them is worth recording.

One, a Mississippi planter, learning that I was a Northern
man, took me aside and with much emotion asked if I thought
there was "any chance of the government paying us for our
niggers."

"What niggers?"

"The niggers you've set free by this abolition war."

"This abolition war you brought upon yourselves; and paying you for your slaves would be like paying a burglar for a
pistol lost on your premises. No, my friend, believe me, you
will never get the first cent as long as this government lasts!"

A Louisiana planter from Lake Providence — and a very intelligent, well-bred gentleman — said: "Negroes do best when
they have a share of the crop; the idea of working for themselves stimulates them. Planters are afraid to trust them to manage, but it's a great mistake. I know an old Negro who, with
three children, made twenty-five bales of cotton this year
on abandoned land. Another, with two women and a blind
mule, made twenty-seven bales. A gang of fifty made three hundred bales — all without any advice or assistance from white
men.

"I was always in favor of educating and elevating the black
race. The laws were against it, but I taught all my slaves to read
the Bible. Each race has its peculiarities: the Negro has his, and
it remains to be seen what can be done with him. Men talk
about his stealing: no doubt he'll steal, but circumstances have
cultivated that habit. Some of my neighbors couldn't have a pig

but their niggers would steal it. But mine never stole from me because they had enough without stealing. Giving them the elective franchise just now is absurd; but when they are prepared for it, and they will be some day, I shall advocate it."

I did not neglect the deck passengers. These were all Negroes with the remnants of their possessions, going to seek their fortunes elsewhere — ill-clad, starved-looking, sleeping on deck in the rain, coiled around the smoke pipe, and covered with ragged bedclothes. The talk of the Negroes was always entertaining. Here is a sample, from the lips of a stout old black woman:

"De best t'ing de Yankees done was to break de slavery chain. I shouldn't be here today if dey hadn't. I'm going to see my mother."

"Your mother must be very old."

"You may know she's dat, for I'm one of her baby chil'n, and I's got 'leven of my own. I've a heap better time now 'n I had when I was in bondage. I had to nus' my chil'n four times a day and pick two hundred pounds cotton besides. My third husband went off to de Yankees. My first was sold away from me. Now I have my second husband again; I was sold away from him, but I found him again after I'd lived with my third husband thirteen years."

I asked if he was willing to take her back.

"He was willing to have me again *on any terms*" — emphatically — "for he knowed I was number one!"

Several native French inhabitants took passage at various points along the river below the Mississippi line. The villages and plantation dwellings along here, with their low roofs and sunny verandas, had a peculiarly foreign and tropical appearance. Another remarkable feature of Louisiana scenery is its forests of cypress growing out of the water, heavy, somber and shaggy with moss.

The complexion of the river is a light mud color, which it derives from the turbid Missouri — the upper Mississippi being a clear stream. Pour off a glass of it after it has been standing a short time, and a sediment of dark mud appears at the bottom. Notwithstanding this unpleasant peculiarity, it is used altogether for cooking and drinking on board the steamboats, and I found New Orleans supplied with it.

XXVI

New Orleans

ON THE morning of January 1, I arrived at New Orleans. It was midwinter, but the mild sunny weather that followed the first chill days of rain made me fancy it May. The gardens of the city were verdant with tropical plants. There were orange trees whose golden fruit could be picked from the balconies which they half concealed. Magnolias, gray oaks and live oaks, some heavily hung with moss that swung in the breeze like waving hair, shaded the yards and streets. Many of the houses are very ancient, with low roofs projecting over the first story, like slouched hatbrims over quaint old faces.

The broad levee, lined with wharves on one side and belted by busy streets on the other, crowded with merchandise and thronged with merchants, boatmen and laborers, presents always a lively and entertaining spectacle. Steam and sailing crafts of every description, arriving, departing, loading, unloading and fringing the city with their long array of smoke pipes and masts, give you some idea of the commerce of New Orleans, the great cotton market of the world.

I put up at the St. Charles, famous before the war as a hotel, and during the war as the headquarters of General Butler. It is a conspicuous edifice, with white-pillared porticoes and a spacious rotunda, thronged nightly with a crowd which strikes a stranger with astonishment. It is a sort of social evening exchange, where merchants, planters, travelers, river men, army men (principally Rebels), manufacturing and jobbing agents, showmen, overseers, idlers, sharpers, gamblers, foreigners, Yankees, Southern men, the well dressed and the prosperous, the rough and the seedy, congregate together, some leaning against the pillars and a few sitting about the stoves, which are almost hidden from sight by the concourse of people standing or moving about in the great central space.

Numbers of citizens regularly spend their evenings here, as at a clubroom. One, an old plantation overseer of the better class, told me that for years he had not missed going to the rotunda a single night. The character he gave the crowd was not complimentary.

"They are all trying to get money without earning it. Each is doing his best to shave the rest. If they ever make anything, I don't know it. I've been here two thousand nights, and never made a cent yet."

What he was thinking of now was a fortune to be made out of labor-saving machinery to be used on the plantations. "I wish I could get hold of a half-crazy feller to fix up a cotton planter, cotton picker, cane cutter, and a thing to hill up some."

He talked cynically of the planters. "They're a helpless set. They're all confused. They don't know what they're going to do. They never did know much else but to get drunk. If a man has a plantation to rent or sell, he can't tell you anything about it; you can't get any proposition out of him."

Among the earliest acquaintances I made at New Orleans was General Phil Sheridan, perhaps the most brilliant and popular fighting man of the war. I found him in command of the Military Division of the Gulf, comprising Louisiana, Texas and Florida. In Florida he had at that time seven thousand troops; in Louisiana, nine thousand; and in Texas, twenty thousand, embracing ten thousand colored troops at Corpus Christi and on the Rio Grande, watching the French movements.

It was Sheridan's opinion that the Rebellion would never be ended until Maximilian was driven from Mexico. Such a government on our borders cherished the seeds of ambition and discontent in the minds of the late Confederates. Many were emigrating to Mexico, and there was danger of their uniting either with the Liberals or the Imperialists, and forming a government inimical to the United States. To prevent such a possibility, he had used military and diplomatic strategy.

Three thousand Rebels having collected in Monterey, he induced the Liberals to arrest and disarm them. Then, in order that they should not be received by the Imperialists, he made hostile demonstrations, sending a pontoon train to Brownsville and six thousand cavalry to San Antonio, establishing military posts, and making extensive inquiries for forage. Under such circumstances, Maximilian did not feel inclined to welcome the Rebel refugees. It is even probable that, had our government at that time required the withdrawal of the French from Mexico, the demand, emphasized by these and similar demonstrations, would have been complied with.

Maximilian is very weak in his position. Nineteen twentieths of the people are opposed to him. There is no legitimate taxation for the support of his government, but he levies contributions upon merchants for a small part of the funds he requires, and draws upon France for the rest. His "government" consists merely of an armed occupation of the country, with long lines of communication between military posts which could be easily cut off one after another by a comparatively small force.

The Southern country, in the general's opinion, was fast becoming "Northernized." It was very poor, and going to be poorer. The planters had no enterprise, no recuperative energy: they were entirely dependent upon Northern capital and Northern spirit. He thought the freedmen's affairs required no legislation, but that the state should leave them to be regulated by the natural law of supply and demand.

Sheridan is a man of small stature, compactly built, with great toughness of constitutional fiber and an alert countenance, expressive of remarkable energy and force. I inquired if he experienced no reaction after the long strain upon his mental and bodily powers occasioned by the war.

"Only a pleasant one," he replied. "During my Western campaigns, when I was continually in the saddle, I weighed but a hundred and fifteen pounds. My flesh was hard as iron. Now my weight is a hundred and forty-five."

He went with me to City Hall, to which the executive department of the state had been removed, and introduced me to Governor Wells, a plain, elderly man, affable and loyal in his speech. I remember his saying that the action of the President in pardoning Governor Humphreys of Mississippi, after he had been elected by the people on account of his services in the Confederate cause, was doing great harm throughout the South, encouraging Rebels and discouraging Union men. "Everything is being conceded to traitors," he said, "before they have been made to feel the Federal power."

He spoke of the strong Rebel element in the legislature which he was combating, and gave me copies of two veto messages which he had returned to it with bills passed for the especial merit of traitors. The new serf code, similar to that of Mississippi, engineered through the legislature by a member of the late Confederate Congress, he had also disapproved.

After this, I was surprised to hear from other sources how faithfully he had been carrying out the very policy he professed to condemn — even going beyond the President in removing from office Union men and appointing secessionists in their place; and advocating the Southern doctrine that the government must pay for the slaves it had emancipated. Such discrepancies between deeds and professions require no comment.

Through the courtesy of Mayor Kennedy, I became acquainted with some of the radical Union men of New Orleans. Like the same class in Richmond and elsewhere, I found them extremely dissatisfied with the political situation.

"The President is trying to help the nation out of its difficulty by restoring to power the very men who created the difficulty," they said. "To have been a good Rebel is now in a man's favor; and to have stood by the government through all its trials is against him. If an original secessionist, or a time-serving, half-and-half Union man, ready to make any concession for the convenience of the moment, goes to Washington, he gets the ear of the administration and comes away full of encouragement for the worst enemies the government ever had. If a man of principle goes to Washington, he gets nothing but plausible words which amount to nothing, if he isn't actually insulted for his trouble."

I called on General T. W. Sherman, in command of the Eastern District of Louisiana, who told me that in order to please the people, our troops had been withdrawn from the interior, and that the militia, consisting mostly of Rebel soldiers, many of whom still wore Rebel uniforms, had been organized to fill their place. The Negroes, whom they treated tyrannically, had been made to believe that it was the United States, and not the state government, that had thus set their enemies to keep guard over them.

From the Freedmen's Bureau I obtained official information regarding the condition of free labor in Louisiana. A detailed account of it would be but a recapitulation, with slight variations, of what I have said of free labor in other states. The whites were as ignorant of the true nature of the system as the blacks. Capitalists did not understand how they could secure labor without owning it, or how men could be induced to work without the whip. It was thought necessary to make a serf of him who was no longer a slave. To this end the legislature had passed a code of black laws even more objectionable than that enacted by Mississippi.

It was estimated that there were at least fifty thousand Northern men in Louisiana. Some were in the lumber business, which had been stimulated to great activity throughout the South. Many were working cotton plantations with every prospect of success; a few had purchased, others were paying a fixed rent, while some were furnishing capital to be refunded by the crop, of which they were to have a third or a half.

Occasionally I heard of one who had taken a sugar plantation. Mr. ——, a merchant of New York, told me he had for two years been working the Buena Vista plantation in Saint James Parish. He employed an agent, and visited the place himself once a year. There were twelve hundred acres under cultivation, for which he paid an annual rent of sixteen thousand dollars. There was one hundred thousand dollars' worth of machinery on the plantation. He employed sixty freedmen. They worked faithfully and well, but needed careful management. During the past year but one had deserted, while two had been discharged.

They received one third of their wages monthly, and the remainder at the end of the year. "If they were paid in full as fast as their work was done, when sugar-making season comes they would be apt to quit, the labor is so hard — though we pay them then fifty cents a night extra."

I inquired concerning profits. "The first year we lost money. This year we have made it up, and more. Next year we shall be in full blast."

I was desirous of seeing a sugar mill in operation, but could hear of none within convenient visiting distance. The scene is thus described in a letter written by a Northern lady whose husband was last year working a Louisiana plantation:

"I am sitting in the gallery of a building two hundred and fifty feet long. This gallery was made expressly for the white overseer, and overlooks all that is going on in the main building. There is a sleeping room in each end of it, and a large open space in the middle which serves as a dining room. In the opposite end of the building I can see the engine which carries all the machinery; just this side of it are the great rollers that crush the cane, and the apron or feed carrier that carries the cane from the shed outside to the crushers.

"Just this side of the crushers are four large vats that receive the juice. From these it is carried into two large kettles, where the lime is put in and the juice is raised to the boiling point, and then skimmed. From these kettles the juice is transferred by means of a bucket attached to a long pole to the next kettle, where it is worked to the right consistency for clarifying.

"This done, it is conveyed by means of a steam pump to the filtering room, where it is passed into large vats filled with burned bones, called bone black, through which it is filtered and thus freed from all impurities. From these filters it is run off into a large cistern, and pumped up by the same steam-pump into tanks, where, by means of faucets, it is drawn into the sugaring-off pan. In this pan it is heated by means of a coil of pipe that winds round and round till it fills the bottom of the pans and carries the steam which, in from fifteen to twenty minutes, finishes the boiling process. From this pan it is let off into a box car, set on a railroad track which runs up and down between the coolers, which are ranged along each side of this end of the building like pews in a church.

"The Creoles along the coast have looked with amazement all summer upon our success with free black laborers, and have been obliged to acknowledge that they never saw a more cheerful, industrious set of laborers. 'But wait till sugar-making comes,' they have said, 'and then see if you can get off your crop without the old system of compulsion. Your niggers will flare up when you get off your ten-hour system. They are not going to work night and day, and you cannot get off the crop unless they do.'

"White sugar makers presented themselves, telling us in all sobriety, 'Niggers cannot be trusted to make sugar,' and offering, with great magnanimity, to oversee the matter for five hundred dollars. J—— declined all such friendly offers, and last Monday morning commenced grinding cane. The colored men and women went to work with a will — no shirking or flinching. The cutters pushed the handlers, the handlers pushed the haulers, and so on, night and day, each gang taking their respective watches, and all moving on with the regularity of clockwork.

"And so the business went on with black engineers, black crushers, black filterers, black sugar makers — all black throughout — but the sugar came out splendid in quantity and quality. Sixty hogsheads of sugar finished by Saturday night, and things in readiness for the Sabbath's rest, is acknowledged by old planters to be the largest run ever made in this sugarhouse for the first week of the sugar season. So they gape and stare, and wonder that humanity and justice can bring forth more profitable results than the driver's whip."

XXVII

Mobile

LEAVING New Orleans for Mobile, I reached Lake Pont-chartrain by railroad in time to take the steamer and be off at sunset. The lake, with its low, dark-wooded shores and its placid, glassy waters, outspread under the evening sky, was a scene of tranquil beauty. I walked the deck with the mate, who had been a good Rebel and taken part in the capture of the United States steamer *Water Witch*.

"I had command of one of the boats," he said. "There was a consultation of officers, and it was proposed to make the attack that night at eleven o'clock; we would have the tide with us then. 'For that very reason,' I said, 'I would postpone it until two. Then we shall have the tide against us. It will be harder pulling down to her, but we can board better, and if we miss grappling the first time, we shan't drift by and get fired upon; and if we fail, we can come back on the tide.' "

The steamer was surprised, and the boarding was a success. "The officer in command of our party was killed, and the command devolved upon me. I got three wounds, but I laid out a man for each wound. I got to the cabin and had my sword at the captain's throat and would have run him through, if he hadn't been mighty glib in his speech: 'I surrender! I surrender!' He didn't stammer a bit! And in a minute I stopped the fighting."

This is the style of story one hears while traveling anywhere in the South. Lying in my berth in the cabin, I was kept awake half the night by Rebel soldiers relating similar adventures.

Next morning we were in the Gulf of Mexico. On the south was the open gulf; on our left, a series of low, barren, sandy islands — Ship Island among them, reminding one of Butler's expedition. We passed the curious well-defined line where the yellowish river water from the bay and the pure liquid crystal of the gulf met and mingled. On our left, the long, smooth swells burst into white breakers on Pelican Island. On the point of Dauphin Island beyond was Fort Gaines, while close upon our right, as we passed up, was Fort Morgan — its brick walls built upon a sheet of sand white as snow.

Having kept the outside passage, instead of the usual route of the New Orleans steamers, our course lay between these forts, up the main channel past the scene of Farragut's famous fight. Above the forts the merchant fleet lies at anchor, twenty-five miles from Mobile — the shallowness of the bay preventing vessels drawing more than ten feet of water from going up to the city. Steamers were plying between the ships and the city, receiving and delivering cargoes.

Four miles below the city we came in sight of the Rebel defenses. The water approaches to the city were strewn with torpedoes, by which four or five vessels of our fleet were blown up. Then we passed a line of obstructions, consisting of piles and sunken wrecks thrown across the channel; and Mobile, a smoking, sunlit city, lay before us on the low shore.

Mobile is a level, shady town, regularly laid out and built on a dry, sandy plain. It is the principal city of Alabama, and the second city in importance in the Gulf states, its commerce ranking next to that of New Orleans. It endured a four years' blockade, falling into Federal hands only at the end of the war. But its great catastrophe did not occur until some time after the termination of hostilities.

The explosion of the captured Confederate ammunition was one of the most terrible disasters of the kind ever known. It was stored in a large three-story warehouse one street back from the river. The last of Dick Taylor's shells were going in when, it is supposed, one of them accidentally ignited. Twenty brick blocks, and portions of other blocks, were instantly blown to atoms. Four or five hundred persons were killed — it was never known how many. A black volcanic cloud of smoke and fragments went up into the sky: "It was big as a mountain," said one. It was succeeded by a fearful conflagration sweeping over the ruins. Ten thousand bales of cotton were burned. The loss of property was so immense that nobody ventured to estimate it.

In the vicinity of the explosion, citizens were thrown off their feet, chimneys knocked down, and windows and doors demolished. Lights of glass were broken all over the city, a mile or more from the scene of the explosion. "I was lifted from the ground, and my hat thrown off," said one man. "Then I looked up, and there were great black blocks of something in the air, high as I could see, and shells exploding."

Said another: "I was riding out a mile from the city. I heard a sound, and at the same time my head and shoulders were thrown forward on my horse's neck. 'That's the first time I've dodged a cannon,' I said, 'and that's after the war is over.' I looked around, and saw the strangest cloud going up slowly over the city. Then I knew it was the shock that had thrown me down."

The town had neither the means nor the material to rebuild: "We made no bricks during the war." I found the scene of the disaster a vast field of ruins. Where had stood the warehouse in which the ammunition was stored, there was a pit twenty feet deep, half filled with water and surrounded by fragments of iron and bricks, and unexploded shells. A large brick block, containing a cotton press, which stood between the magazine and the river, had disappeared. "The bricks were all blown into the water, and we never saw them any more."

Business was brisk. "There are more goods on Dauphin Street today," an old merchant told me, "than I have ever before seen in the whole of Mobile." And the captain of the Mobile steamer which took me up the Alabama to Selma said: "There was never such a trade on this river before. Nobody ever expected such a freight on this boat: her guards are all under water." Her upward-bound lading consisted mostly of supplies for plantations and provincial stores — barrels of Western flour and whiskey that had come down the Mississippi, and boxes of fine liquors, soap, starch and case goods from North Atlantic ports. Her downward freight was chiefly cotton.

XXVIII
Alabama

THE ALABAMA RIVER steamers resemble those of the Mississippi, although inferior in size and style. But one meets a very different class of passengers on board. The Alabamians are a plain, rough set of men, not so fast as the Mississippi Valley planters but more sober, solid, loyal. They like their glass of grog, however, and some of them are very sincere in their hatred of the government. I found the most contradictory characters among them.

Here is one of the despairing class. "The country is ruined; not only the Southern country but the Northern country, too. The prosperity of our people passed away with the institution of slavery. I shall never try to make another fortune. I made one, and lost it in a minute. I had a hundred and fifty thousand dollars in niggers. I am now sixty years old. I'll bet a suit of clothes against a dime, there'll be no cotton crop raised this year. If there's a crop grown, the hands won't pick it. A nigger drayman came to me the other day and asked me to buy him. He said, 'I want a master. When I had a master, I had nothing to do but to eat and drink and sleep, besides my work. Now I have to work and think too.' When I said the law wouldn't allow me to buy him, he looked very much discouraged."

Mr. J——, of Marengo County, also an old man, talked in a different spirit. "The trouble with the freedmen is, they have not yet learned that living is expensive. They never before had any idea where their clothes came from, except that 'Master gave 'em to me.' In my county, I find them generally better disposed than the whites. I don't know of a case where they have been treated kindly and justly and have deserted their masters. A few restless ones are exceptions. I noticed one of my boys that I had asked to make a contract for the coming year packing his things; and I said to him, 'Warren, what are you doing?' He replied, 'Master, they say if we make contracts now, we'll be branded and made slaves again.' "

Mr. G——, one of the bitterest Yankee haters I met, became nevertheless one of my most intimate steamboat acquaintances. I cull the following from many talks I had with him.

"I owned a cotton factory in Dallas County, above Selma. I had two plantations besides, and an interest in a tanyard. Wilson's thieves came in and stripped me of everything. They burned eight hundred bales of cotton. That was because I happened to be running my mill for the Confederate Government. I was making Osnaburgs for the government for a dollar a yard, when citizens would have paid me four dollars; and do you imagine I'd have done that except under compulsion? But the Yankee rascals didn't stop to consider that fact. They skipped my neighbors' cotton and burned mine.

"They robbed our houses of everything they could carry away. I shouldn't have had a thing left if it hadn't been for my niggers. Some of 'em run off my mules and saved 'em. I gave all my gold and silver to an old woman who kept it hid from the raiders. On one of my plantations a colored carpenter and his wife barreled up three barrels of fine table crockery and buried it. An old Negro saved the tannery by pleading with the vandals, and lying to 'em a little bit.

"Three hundred and fifty thousand dollars gold wouldn't cover my losses. I never can feel towards this government like I once did. I started to leave the country; I swore I wouldn't live under a government that had treated me this way. I made up my mind to go to Brazil. I got as far as Mobile, and changed my mind. Now I've concluded to remain here, like any alien. I'm a foreigner. I scorn to be called a citizen of the United States. I shall take no oath, so help me God! Unless," he added immediately, "it is to enable me to vote. I want to vote to give the suffrage to the Negro."

As I expressed my surprise at this extraordinary wish, he went on: "Because I think that will finish the job. I think then we'll have enough of the nigger, North and South, and all will combine to put him out of the country.

"I want this country filled up with white men. I want the large plantations cut up, and manufactories established. We never had any manufactories for this reason: Southern capitalists all jammed their money into niggers and land. As their capital increased, it was a few more niggers, a little more land. The few factories we had were consequently one-horse concerns that couldn't compete with those in the North. They were patronized by men who wanted to buy on credit. If a man had cash, he went to the North to buy goods; if he was short, he bought here. Consequently, to carry on a business of a hundred thousand dollars, a capital of three hundred thousand dollars was necessary. Two thirds of it was sunk — below the water, like the guards of this boat.

"Now I want the old system played out. But," continued G——, "if the Freedmen's Bureau is withdrawn, things will

work back again into their old grooves. The nigger is going to
be made a serf, sure as you live. It won't need any law for that.
Planters will have an understanding among themselves: 'You
won't hire my niggers, and I won't hire yours'; then what's left
for them? They're attached to the soil, and we're as much their
masters as ever. I'll stake my life, this is the way it will work.
The country will be no better off than it ever was.

"To make a farming and manufacturing country, like you
have at the North, we must put the nigger out of the way. For
this reason, I hope the cotton crop this year will be a failure.
And I not only hope, but I know it will. There a'n't labor
enough in the country; the planters are going to bid against
each other, and make contracts they won't be able to keep, and
that's going to put the old Harry into the freedmen."

Mr. H——, of Lowndes County, joined in our conversation.
"I don't believe my friend G—— believes half he says. I am sure
the South is going to make this year a million bales — probably
much more. One thing planters have got to learn: the old system is gone and we must begin new. It won't do to employ the
old overseers; they can't learn to treat the freedmen like human
beings. I told my overseer the old style wouldn't do — the niggers wouldn't stand it — and he promised better fashions; but
it wasn't two days before he fell from grace, and went to whipping again. That just raised the old scratch with them; and I
don't blame 'em."

H—— went on to say that it was necessary now to treat the
Negroes like men. "We must deal justly with them. We must
reason with them — for they are reasonable beings."

Mr. B——, of Monroe County, was a good sample of the hopeful class. "We're brushed out, and must begin new. I've lost as
much as any other man, but it's foolish to sit down and com-

plain of that. I believe if Southern men will only take courage and do their best, in five years the country will be more prosperous than ever. When you hear it said the country is ruined, and the niggers won't work, the trouble is in them that make the complaint and not in the niggers. My niggers say to me, 'Massa Joe, we ought to work mo'e 'n we ever did befo'e; for once, we just worked for our victuals and clothes, and now we're getting wages besides.' And they'll do it — they *are* doing it. If you want a freedman to do what he promises, you've only to set him the example, and do by him just what you promise."

We had lovely weather sailing up the Alabama River. The shores were low, and covered with canebrakes or trees, with here and there dark swamps. Then plantations began to appear, each with its ginhouse and cotton press, planter's house, corncribs and Negro quarters, on the river's bank.

Nearly all the planters I met had been down to Mobile to purchase supplies for the season. Freight went ashore at every landing. Seeing some heavy bars of iron going ashore at one place, I asked an old gentleman to what use they were put on the plantation.

"They are to make ploughs of, sir."

"Does every plantation make its own ploughs?"

"Do we make our own ploughs?" he repeated, regarding me with astonishment. "Why, sir, it wouldn't be a civilized country if we didn't. How do you think, sir, we should get our ploughs?"

"Buy them, or have them made for you."

"Buy our ploughs! It would impoverish us, sir, if we had to buy our ploughs."

"On the contrary, I should think a plough factory could furnish them for less than they now cost you — that, like boots and shoes, it would be cheaper to buy them than to make them."

"No, sir! I've a black man on my plantation who can make as good a plough, at as little cost, as can be made anywhere in the world."

After that I had nothing to say, having already sufficiently exposed my ignorance.

On the third day we reached Selma, three hundred miles above Mobile — a pleasantly situated town looking down from a bluff. I found it a scene of "Yankee vandalism" and ruin. The Confederate arsenal, foundries and rolling mills — the most important works of the kind in the South, furnished with coal and iron by the surrounding country — together with extensive warehouses containing ammunition and military stores, were burned when Wilson captured the place. A number of private stores and dwellings were likewise destroyed; and the work of rebuilding was not yet half completed.

Climbing the steps from the landing to the town, the first object which attracted my attention was a chain gang of Negroes at work on the street, while a number of white persons stood looking on, evidently enjoying the sight and saying to one another, "That's the beauty of freedom! That's what free niggers come to!"

On inquiring what the chain gang had done to be punished in this ignominious manner, I got a list of misdemeanors, one of the gravest of which was "using abusive language towards a white man." Some had transgressed certain municipal regulations, of which, coming in from the country, they were very likely ignorant. One had sold farm produce within the town limits, contrary to an ordinance which prohibits market men from selling so much as an egg before they have reached the market and the bell has rung. For this offense he had been fined twenty dollars, which being unable to pay, he had been put upon the chain. Others had been guilty of disorderly conduct, vagrancy and petty theft, which it was of course necessary to punish. But it was a singular fact that no white men were ever sentenced to the chain gang — being, I suppose, all virtuous.

The battle of Selma was not a favorite topic with the citizens, most of whom were within the stockade or behind the breastworks, captured by an inferior force of the Yankee invaders. But on the subject of the burning and pillaging they were eloquent.

A gray-haired old gentleman said to me: "I was in the trenches when Wilson came. Everybody was. I just watched both ways, and when I saw how the cat was jumping, I threw my musket as far as I could, dropped down as if I was killed and walked into town atter the Yankees. I stood by my own gate when four drunken fellows came up, slapped me on the shoulder and said, 'This old man was in the stockade — he's a Rebel!' 'Of course I'm a Rebel,' I said, 'if I'm ketched in a Rebel trap.'

"They was taking me away when an officer rode up. 'Old man,' says he, 'can you show me where the corn depot is?' 'I reckon I kin, if these gentlemen will let me,' I says. So I got off; and when I had showed him the corn he let me go.

"The fire was first set by our own men: that was in the cotton yards. They blazed up so quick the Yankees couldn't have got thar without they went on wires. The next was the post office; that they burned. The next was a drugstore; the other drugstore they didn't burn, but they smashed everything in it. The arsenal was owing me and my family fifteen hundred dollars when they destroyed it.

"They just ruined me. They took from me six cows, four mules, fifteen hogs, fifteen hundred pounds of bacon, eight barrels of flour and fifty-five sacks of corn. They took my wife's and daughters' clothing to carry flour in. I saw a man take my wife's best dress, empty into it all the flour he could tote, tie it up, clap it on his shoulder and march off. Another went off with an embroidered petticoat full of flour swung on his arm. Another would take a pair of ladies' drawers, fill the legs with flour, and trot off with 'em riding straddle on his neck. It made me feel like if I had 'em down in the squirrel woods, I could shoot a right smart passel of 'em with a will!"

Charles Mencer, a well-known and respectable colored man, related the following: "I worked in a saddle shop at the time of Wilson's raid. I hired my time of my master, and had laid up two hundred dollars in gold and silver: I had invested my earnings in specie and in two watches, because I knew Confederacy couldn't last. The Yankees came Sunday evening; they robbed my house and stole my gold and silver, and one of my watches. Four of them stopped me in the street and took my other watch and my pocketbook, with all my Confederate money in it."

The rest of this man's story possesses a semihistorical interest. "The next Tuesday General Wilson sent for me; he wanted somebody he could trust to carry dispatches down the river to General Canby, and I had been recommended by some colored people. I said I would take them; and I sewed them in my vest collar. Then I went to my master and told him there was no chance for work since the Yankees had come, and got a pass from him to go down to Mobile and find work. Tuesday night I started in a canoe, and paddled down the river. I dodged the Rebel guard when I could, but I was taken and searched twice, and got off by showing my master's pass.

"I paddled night and day, and got to Montgomery Hill on Sunday. There I saw Federal troops and went ashore, and delivered myself to the captain. He took me to General Lucas, who sent me with a cavalry escort to General Canby at Blakely."

For this service Mencer was paid three hundred dollars in greenbacks, which he had invested in a freedmen's newspaper, the *Constitutionalist,* just started in Mobile.

The Negroes everywhere sympathized with the Federal cause and served it when they could; but they would seldom betray a master who had been kind to them. Many stories were told me by the planters, illustrating this fidelity. Here is one, related by a gentleman of Lowndes County:

"The Yankees, when they left Selma, passed through this side of the river on their way to Montgomery. I got the start of 'em and run off my horses and mules. I gave a valise full of valuable papers to my Negro boy Arthur, and told him to hide it. He put it in his trunk — threw out his own clothes to hide my property, for he didn't suppose the Yankees would be mean enough to rob niggers. But they did: after they robbed my house, they went to the Negro quarters and pilfered them. They found my valise, took out my old love letters, and had a good time reading 'em for about an hour. Then they said to Arthur:

" 'You are your master's confidential servant, a'n't you?'

" 'Yes, sir,' says Arthur, proud of the distinction.

" 'You know where he has gone with his mules and horses?'

" 'Yes, sir, I know all about it.'

" 'Jump on to this horse, and go and show us where he is, and we'll give you five dollars.'

" 'I don't betray my master for no five dollars,' says Arthur.

" 'Then,' says they, 'we'll shoot you if you won't show us!' And they put carbines to his head.

"He never flinched. 'You can shoot me if you like,' he says, 'but I sha'n't betray my master!'

"They were so struck with his courage and fidelity that they just let him go. So I saved my horses. He don't know it, but I'm going to give that boy a little farm and stock it for him."

The route of Wilson's cavalry can be traced all the way by the burned ginhouses with which they dotted the country. At Montgomery they destroyed valuable foundries and machine shops, after causing the fugitive Rebels to burn a hundred thousand bales of cotton, with the warehouses which contained it. I followed their track through the eastern counties of Alabama and afterwards recrossed it in Georgia, where the close of hostilities terminated this the most extensive and destructive raid of the war.

Montgomery, capital of Alabama and originally the capital of the Confederacy, is a town of broad streets and pleasant prospects, built on the rolling summits of high bluffs on the left bank of the Alabama, one hundred miles above Selma.

Walking up the long slope of the principal street, I came to the capitol, a sightly edifice on a fine eminence. On a near view, the walls, which are probably of brick, disguised to imitate granite, had a cheap look; and the interior, especially the Chamber of Representatives, in which the Confederate egg was hatched, appeared mean and shabby. This was a plain room with semicircular rows of old desks, covered with green baize exceedingly worn and foul. The floor carpet was faded and ragged. The glaring whitewashed walls were offensive to the eye. The Corinthian pillars supporting the gallery were a cheap imitation of bronze. Over the speaker's chair hung a sad-looking portrait of George Washington.

I remained two days at Montgomery, saw General Swayne and other officers of the bureau, visited plantations in the vicinity.

In Alabama, as in all the Southern states, the original seces-

sionists were generally Democrats and the Union men old-line
Whigs. The latter opposed the revolution until it swept them
away; then they often went into the war with a zeal which
shamed many who were very hot in bringing it on, and very cool
in keeping out of it. I found them now the most hopeful men
of the South. If a planter said to me, "I'm going to raise a big
crop of cotton this year — my Negroes are working finely," I
needed no other test that he belonged to this class.

Concerning the loyalty of the people, I give the testimony of
a very intelligent young man of Chambers County:

"I enlisted in the Confederate Army for one year; and before
my time was up I was conscripted for two years; then, before
these expired, I was conscripted for two more. I was made prisoner in Virginia, and taken to Harrisburg, Pennsylvania. At the
end of the war I was paroled. I knew that my people were
ruined and all my property gone. That consisted in twelve
slaves; their labor supported me before the war, but now I had
nothing but my own hands to depend upon. I made up my mind
to stay where I was and go to work. I hired out to a farmer
for six dollars a month. I had never done a stroke of labor in
my life, and it came hard to me at first. But I soon got used
to it.

"One day a merchant of Harrisburg was riding by and asked
me some questions. A few days after he came that way again and
proposed to me to go into his store. He offered me eighteen
dollars a month. I said to him, 'You are very kind, sir, but you
probably do not know who I am: I am a Rebel soldier, just out
of prison.' He said he believed I was an honest fellow and would
like to try me. I went into his store, and after the first month he
raised my wages to thirty dollars. After the second month, he
gave me forty, and after the third month he gave me fifty.

"I had been a wild boy before the war; I had plenty of money with no restrictions upon my spending it. But I tell you I was never so happy in my life as when I was at work for my living in that store. My employer liked me and trusted me, and I liked the people.

"I have now come home on a visit. My relations and neighbors are incensed because I tell them plainly what I think of the Yankees. I know now that we were all in the wrong, and that the North was right, about the war; and I tell them so. They feel the bitterest animosity against the government, and denounce and abuse the Yankees, and call me a Yankee, the worst name they can give."

"How large a proportion of your people express such sentiments?"

"Well, sir, there are fifteen hundred voting men in the county; and all but about a hundred and eighty feel and talk the way I tell you. They can't be reconciled to living under the old government, and those who are able are preparing to emigrate. A fund has already been raised to send agents to select lands in Mexico."

"Did you find in the North any such animosity towards the people of the South?"

"Very little; and there was this difference: In the North it is only a few ignorant people of the poorer class who hate the South; I believe the mass of Northern people, while they hate treason and rebellion, have only kind feelings towards the Southern people. But with us it is the wealthy and influential class that hates the North, while only the poor whites and Negroes have any loyalty at heart. I wish," he added, "that for every Northern man now settling in the South, a Southern man would go into business in the North, and see for himself, as I

have done, just what sort of people and institutions we have all
our lives been taught to misunderstand and slander."

There is a wide difference between the people of northern
and southern Alabama. The inhabitants of many of the upper
counties were as loyal as those of east Tennessee. In some it was
necessary for the Davis government to maintain a cavalry force
in order to keep the people in subjection. Such a county was
Randolph, whose inhabitants were as strongly opposed to secession as those of Chambers County, its next neighbor on the
south, were in favor of it.

In 1863, the shortness of crops, depreciation of the currency
and the consequent high prices of provisions produced a famine
among the poorer classes. The families of soldiers, fighting the
battles of a Confederacy which paid them in worthless paper,
were left to suffer want, while many who helped to bring on the
war were growing rich by speculating. In Mobile there were insurrections of women, driven by starvation to acts of public violence. The state was finally awakened to the necessity of amelio-
rating these sufferings, and during the last year of the war it fed
with meal and salt one hundred and forty thousand white
paupers.

Everywhere I heard complaints of demoralization occasioned
by the war. There were throughout the South organized bands
of thieves. In Alabama, cotton stealing had become a safe and
profitable business. I was told of men, formerly respectable and
who still held their heads high in society, who were known to
have made large fortunes by it. These men employ Negroes to
do the work, because Negroes cannot give legal evidence against
a white man. During the last three months of 1865, it was estimated that on the line of the Mobile and Ohio Railroad, ten
thousand bales of cotton had been stolen.

There was every prospect of a good cotton crop the present year. Since the invention of the spinning jenny by Arkwright, and of the gin by Whitney, the culture of this great staple has received no such impulse as the recent high prices have given it. The planters were taking courage, the freedmen were at work, and a large amount of Northern capital was finding investment in the state. Even the poor whites, who never before would consent to degrade themselves by labor in the field, seemed inspired by the general activity; and many of them, for the first time in their lives, were preparing to raise a few bales of cotton.

Labor was not abundant. "Our best young men went off with the Yankee army; and our best girls followed the officers." Men of sense and reputation had not much difficulty, however, in securing laborers. "When I got ready to hire," said one, "I just turned about four hundred hogs into a field near the road. Every freedman that came that way stopped; and in a week I had as many as I wanted. They all like to hire out where there is plenty of pork." Others, to fill their quota of hands, were paying the fines of stout Negroes on the chain gangs, and bailing those who were lying in jail.

The hilly northern part of Alabama falls off gradually through rolling prairies and alluvial bottoms of the central, to the low, flat southern portion of the state. All through the lower half the long tree moss grows with luxuriance. It flourishes in a warm, moist climate; and the forests of the entire Southern county below thirty-three degrees are festooned by it. In favorable localities it grows to great length, till its long-fibered masses appear dripping from the trees. One can imagine the effect when the great winds move through the woods, and to their solemn roaring is added the weird, unearthly aspect of a myriad gloomy banners, waving and beckoning from every limb.

Gathered by means of hooks attached to long poles, and seasoned by a simple process, this moss becomes a valuable article of merchandise, principally used in the manufacture of mattresses. I saw many bales of it going down the rivers to New Orleans, Mobile and Savannah. Its color on the boughs is a dull greenish gray; but when prepared for market, it resembles black, crinkled horsehair.

The common-school system of Alabama is very imperfect. The wealthy planters send their children to private schools, and object to taxation for the education of the children of the poor. The poor, on the other hand, take no interest in schools, to which they will not send their children as long as money is to be paid for tuition, or as long as there is cotton to pick and wood to cut at home. The isolation of the inhabitants on plantations, or in widely scattered log cabins, and the presence of an uneducated race forming nearly one half the population, have been great obstacles in the way of popular education.

Alabama is comparatively a new state. Admitted into the Union in 1819, her rise in importance has kept pace steadily with the progress of modern cotton cultivation. It sounds strange to hear planters still young refer to experiences in the early days of cotton in regions which are now celebrated for its production.

"I came to Montgomery County in 1834," said one. "I raised my first cotton crop in 1836. I had nine Negroes, and I made a bale to the hand. They didn't know how to pick it. So I hired thirty Indian girls to pick — as handsome young creatures as you ever saw. Cotton was then eighteen cents a pound. The Indian war disturbed us some; but I and a dozen more settlers went out and killed more Indians than all Scott's army. I now have two large plantations; this year I work a hundred and ten hands, and fifty-five mules and horses, on thirteen hundred acres of cotton and five hundred of corn; and I intend to make more money than ever before."

The principal railroads of the state were all in running condition, although the rolling stock was shabby and scarce. The Montgomery and West Point Road, which Wilson's raiders damaged to the amount of several millions, had been temporarily repaired. Depots were never plenty in the South, and where our forces had passed, not one was left — a great inconvenience especially to single gentlemen, going to take the train at two or three o'clock in the morning, finding the cars locked and guarded until the ladies should all be seated, and compelled to wait perhaps an hour, in the cold, for them to be opened.

XXIX
Atlanta

THE RAILROAD runs eastward from Montgomery, forks at Opelika, and enters Georgia by two divergent routes — the south branch crossing the Chattahoochee at Columbus, the north branch at West Point.

Wilson paid his respects to both these roads. The main body of his troops proceeded to Columbus (one of the principal towns of Georgia), which they carried by assault with a loss of but thirty men, capturing fifteen hundred prisoners, twenty-four pieces of artillery and immense military stores. At the same time a Union brigade took West Point. These were the closing battles of the great war of the Rebellion. Pushing on towards Macon, Wilson's advance was met not by bloody opposition but by a flag of truce announcing the surrender of Lee and the armistice between Sherman and Johnston.

Concerning our loss at West Point, I was not able to obtain exact information. A citizen who claimed to have been in the fight said, "We had seven men killed, and we just slaughtered over three hundred Yankees." A Negro said: "I saw five dead Yankees, and if there was any more, nobody knows what was done with 'em." A returned Confederate soldier, who regarded with great contempt the little affair the citizens bragged about, said it was no fight at all; the militia gave up the fort almost without a struggle, and there were not over a dozen men killed on both sides. The fort was situated on a high hill; and one old man, who was in it, told me they could not hold it because they couldn't use the guns effectively — they "couldn't elevate 'em down enough."

The Yankees had the credit of behaving very well at West Point. "They were going to burn the railroad depot, full of rolling stock, but a lady told 'em that would set her house, so they just run the cars off down the track, over a hundred of 'em, and fired 'em there" — the black ruins remaining to attest the fact.

Leaving West Point at noon I reached Atlanta at seven o'clock in the evening. It was a foggy night; the streets were not lighted, the hotels were full, and the mud was ankle deep on the crossings. I was at length fortunate enough to find lodgings with a clergyman and a cotton speculator in an ancient tavern room, where we were visited all night by troops of rats, scampering across the floor, rattling newspapers, and capering over our beds. In the morning, it was discovered that the irreverent rogues had stolen the clergyman's stockings.

A sun-bright morning did not transmute the town into a place of very great attractiveness. Everywhere were ruins and rubbish, mud and mortar and misery. The burned streets were rapidly rebuilding; but meanwhile, hundreds of inhabitants, white and black, rendered homeless by the destruction of the city, were living in wretched hovels, which made the suburbs look like a fantastic encampment of gypsies or Indians. Some of the Negro huts were covered entirely with ragged fragments of tin roofing from the burned government and railroad buildings. Others were constructed partly of these irregular blackened patches, and partly of old boards, with roofs of huge, warped, slouching shreds of tin, kept from blowing away by stones placed on the top.

Every business block in Atlanta was burned, except one. The railroad machine shops, the foundries, the immense rolling mill, the tent, pistol, gun-carriage, shot-and-shell factories and storehouses of the Confederacy had disappeared in flames and explosions. Half a mile of the principal street was destroyed. Private residences remained, with a few exceptions. The wooden houses of the suburbs had been already torn down, and their materials used to construct quarters for Sherman's men. The African Methodist Episcopal Church, built by the colored people with their hard earnings, was also demolished by our soldiers — at the instigation, it is said, of a white citizen living near, who thought the Negroes' religious shoutings a nuisance.

"When I came back in May," said a refugee, "the city was nothing but brick and ruins. It didn't seem it could ever be cleared. But in six weeks new blocks began to spring up, till now you see more stores actually in operation than we ever had before."

Here and there, between the new buildings, were rows of shanties used as stores, and gaps containing broken walls and heaps of rubbish. Rents were enormous. Fifteen and twenty dollars a month were charged for huts which a respectable farmer would hardly consider good enough for swine. One man had crowded into his back yard five of these little tenements, which rented for fifteen dollars a month each. Other speculators were permitting the construction on their premises of houses that were to be occupied rent free for one year by the poor families that built them, and afterwards to revert to the owners of the land.

The destitution among both white and black refugees was

very great. Many of the whites had lost everything by the war; and the Negroes that were run off by their masters in advance of Sherman's army had returned to a desolate place, with nothing but the rags on their backs. As at nearly every other town of any note in the South which I visited, the smallpox was raging at Atlanta, chiefly among the blacks and the suffering poor whites.

I stopped to talk with an old man building a fence before the lot containing the ruins of his burned house. He said: "The Yankees didn't generally burn private dwellings. It's my opinion these were set by our own citizens that remained after Sherman's orders that all women who had relatives in the Southern army should go South, and all males must leave the city except them that would work for government. I put for Chattanooga. My house was plundered, and I reckon burnt, by my own neighbors — for I've found some of my furniture in their houses. Some that stayed acted more honorably; they put out fires that had been set, and saved both houses and property. My family is now living in the shebang there. It was formerly my stable. The weatherboards had been ripped off, but I fixed it up the best I could to put my little 'uns in till we can do better."

Walking out to visit the fortifications, I stopped to look at a Negro's horse which had been crippled by a nail in his foot. While I was talking with the owner, a white man and two Negroes, who had been sitting by a fire in an open rail cabin close by, conversing on terms of perfect equality, came out to take part in the consultation around the sick beast. One proffered one remedy; another, another.

"If ye had some tare," said the white man (meaning tar), "open his huf, and bile tare and pour int' it."

His lank frame and slouching dress — his sallow visage, with its sickly, indolent expression — his lazy, spiritless movements and the social intimacy that appeared to exist between him and the Negroes, indicated that he belonged to the class known as "sand hillers" in South Carolina, "clay-eaters" in North Carolina, "crackers" in Georgia, and "white trash" and "poor whites" everywhere. Among all the individuals of this unfortunate and most uninteresting class whom I have seen, I do not remember a specimen better worth describing.

; He told me his name was Jesse Wade. "I lived down in Cobb," (that is, Cobb County) — seating himself on the neap of the Negro's wagon and mechanically scraping the mud from it with his thumbnail. "I was a Union man, I was, like my daddy befo'e me. Thar was no use me bein' a fule 'case my neighbors was. The Rebel Army treated us a heap wus'n Sherman did. I refugeed — left everything keer o' my wife. I had four bales o' cotton, and the Rebs burnt the last bale. I had hogs, and a mule, and a hoss, and they tuk all. They didn't leave my wife narry bed quilt. When they'd tuk what they wanted, they put her out the house and sot fire to 't.

"Narry one o' my boys fit agin the Union; they was conscripted with me, and one night we went out on guard together, we did, and jest put for the Yankees. All the men that had a little property went in for the wa', but the po' people was agin it. Sherman was up yer to Kennesaw Mountain then, and I left, I did, to jine him."

He was very poor. "I've got two hosses and a wagon, and I shouldn't have them if Sherman hadn't gin 'em tu me." He looked at his toes protruding through great gaps in his shoes. "I cain't git money enough to buy me a new pair, to save my life."

I asked Wade how old he was. "I'm fifty-one year old," he replied, "and thar's eight on us in the family, and tu hosses."

I inquired concerning education in his country. "Thar's a heap o' po' men in Cobb that cain't read nor write. I'm one. I never went to skule narry time."

Wade's theory of Reconstruction was simple. "We should of tuk the land, as we did the niggers, and split it, and gin part to the niggers and part to me and t' other Union fellers. They'd have had to submit to it, as they did to the niggers."

"Wade," I said, "tell me which you think will do the most work — a white man or a nigger?"

"The nigger," said Wade, surprised at so simple a question.

"Do you mean to say that one of these black men will do more work than you?"

"Yes, sho'."

"What's the reason of that?"

" 'Case they was allus put mo'e at it."

By this time a large number of Negroes had assembled on the spot, dressed in their Sunday clothes, and such an animated discussion of their political rights ensued that, concluding I had strayed by mistake into an outdoor convention of the freed people, I quietly withdrew — followed by my friend Wade, who wished to know if I could accommodate him to a "chaw of tobacker."

XXX

Macon

A S MY first view of Atlanta was had on a dismal night, so my last impression of it was received on a foggy morning, which showed me, as I sat in the cars of the Macon train, waiting at the depot, groups of rain-drenched Negroes around outdoor fires; the dimly seen trees of the park; tall ruins looming through the mist; Masonic Hall standing alone (having escaped destruction) ; squat wooden buildings of recent, hasty construction beside it; windrows of bent railroad iron by the track; piles of brick; a small mountain of old bones from the battlefields, foul and wet with the drizzle; a heavy coffin box, marked "glass," on the platform; with mud and litter all around.

A tide of Negro emigration was flowing westward from the comparatively barren hills of northern Georgia to the rich cotton plantations of the Mississippi. Every day anxious planters from the Great Valley were to be met with, inquiring for unemployed freedmen, or returning home with colonies of laborers who had been persuaded to quit their old haunts by the promise of double wages in a new country. As it cost no more to transport able-bodied young men and women than the old and the feeble, the former were generally selected and the latter left behind. Thus it happened that an unusually large proportion of poor families remained about Atlanta and other Georgia towns.

There were two such families huddled that morning under the open shed of the depot. They claimed that they had been hired by a planter who had brought them thus far, and for some reason, abandoned them. They had been at the depot a week or more, sleeping in piles of old rags and subsisting on rations issued by the bureau: stolid-looking mothers, hardened by field labor, smoking short black pipes; and older children tending younger ones, feeding them out of tin cups and rocking them to sleep in their arms. But to me the most noticeable feature of the scene was the spirit manifested towards these poor creatures by spectators of my own color.

"That baby's going to die," said one man. "Half your children will be dead before spring."

"How do you like freedom?" said another.

"Niggers are fated," said a third. "About one out of fifty will take care of himself; the rest are gone up."

The remarks of the ladies in the car were equally edifying.

"How much better off they were with somebody to take care of 'em!"

"Oh dear, yes! I declare it makes me hate an abolitionist!"

"Do see that little baby! It's a-kicking and screaming! I declare, it's white! One of the young Federals, I reckon."

From Atlanta until within about twenty-five miles of Macon, the railroad runs upon a ridge. The doorways of the log huts and shabby framed houses we passed were crowded with black, yellow and sallow-white faces — women, children and slatternly, barefoot girls, with long, uncombed hair on their shoulders — staring at the train. The country is better a little back from the railroad, as is frequently the case in the South.

Macon, at the head of steamboat navigation on the Ocmulgee River and the most important interior town in the state, is a place of broad, pleasant streets. In 1860, it had eight thousand inhabitants. As it was a sort of city of refuge, "where everybody was run to" during the latter years of the war, its population had greatly increased. Hundreds of white refugees from other parts of the country were still crowded into it, having no means of returning to their homes, or having no homes to return to. They were kept from starvation by the government. "To get rid of feeding them," said Colonel Lambert, Sub-Assistant Commissioner of the Freedmen's Bureau, "we are now giving them free transportation wherever they wish to go."

Colonel Lambert had on hand sixteen cases of murder and felonious shooting by white persons, Negroes being the victims. The seventeenth case was reported from Twiggs County while I was at Macon. A chivalrous sportsman, apparently for the fun of the thing, took a shot at a Negro walking peaceably along the street and killed him. The colonel sent out twenty-five mounted men to hunt the murderer; but it was almost impossible to make arrests in such cases. There were in every place unprincipled men who approved the crime and helped to shield the criminal.

Crimes of this description were more or less frequent in districts remote from the military posts. Said Colonel Lambert: "To prevent these outrages, we need a much greater military force. But the force we have is being reduced by the mustering out of more troops. We are thus prevented from carrying out the intentions of the government; and there is danger that before long, the continuance of its authority here will be regarded as a mere farce. What we need is cavalry; but our troops are all infantry. I mount them in a case of emergency, where some desperado is to be hunted, by seizing horses at the first livery stable, which we return after we have got through with them, politely thanking the proprietor in the name of the government."

The Negro of middle Georgia is a creature in whom the emotions entirely predominate over the intellectual faculties. He has little of that shrewdness which town life cultivates in the black race. The agents of the bureau complained that they had sometimes great difficulty in persuading him to act in accordance with his own interests. If a stranger offered him twelve dollars a month, and a former master in whom he had confidence, appealing to his gratitude and affection, offered him one dollar, he would exclaim impulsively, "I work for you, Mass'r Will!"

Sometimes, when he had been induced by his friends to enter a complaint against his master or mistress for wrongs done him, ludicrous and embarrassing scenes occurred in the freedmen's courts. "Now, Thomas," says a good lady, "can you have the heart to speak a word against your old, dear, kind mistress?"

"No, missus, I neber will!" blubbers Thomas; and that is all the court can get out of him.

The reverence shown by the colored people toward the officers of the bureau was often amusing. They looked to them for what they had formerly depended upon their masters for. If they had lost a pig, they seemed to think such great and all-powerful men could find it for them without any trouble. They cheered them in the streets, and paid them at all times the most abject respect.

There were four freedmen's schools in Macon, with eleven teachers and a thousand pupils. There was a night school of two hundred children and adults, where I saw men of my own age learning their letters, and gray-haired old men and women forming, with slowness and difficulty, with the aid of spectacles, the first characters in the writing book. The teachers were furnished by the American Missionary Association — the freedmen paying for their own books and for fuel and lights.

Mr. Eddy, the superintendent and an old experienced teacher, said to me: "The children of these schools have made in a given time more progress in the ordinary branches of education than any white schools I ever taught. The eagerness of the older ones to learn is a continual wonder to me. The men and women say, 'We work all day, but we'll come to you in the evening for learning, and we want you to make us learn. We're dull, but we want you to beat it into us!' "

XXXI

Andersonville

J UST across the railroad track below Macon, in a pleasant pine grove, is the Fair Ground, where was located that thing of misery known to us as the Macon Prison. It was the "Yankee Prison" down here.

I visited the spot one bright morning after a shower, when breezes and sunshine were in the pinetops overhead. The ground was covered with a thin growth of brown grass, wet with rain, stepping along which I came suddenly to a quadrangular space as arid as the hill of Golgotha. No marks were necessary to show where the stockade had stood, with its elevated scaffolding on which walked the Rebel guard. The stockade had been removed; but the blasted and barren earth remained to testify to the homesick feet that had trodden it into dreary sterility.

A little stream runs through a hollow below the Fair Ground, carrying off much of the filth of the town. From that stream our prisoners drank. The tub set in the side of the bank at the foot of the hill, and the ditch that conducted into it the water for their use, were still there. Guarded, they came down from the stockade to this tub, of the contents of which they were not always permitted to have enough.

"I used to hear 'em yell for water," said a Negro living near.

"I was bad off as a slave, but I never begun to be so bad off as they was. Some of 'em had no shoes for winter, and almost no clothes."

In the pine woods on the hill above the stockade is "Death's Acre" — the prison burying ground, enclosed by a plain board fence and containing little rows of humble graves marked with stakes, and numbered. I noticed numbers as high as two hundred and thirty. How many National soldiers lie buried in this lot I do not know.

I shall not dwell upon the sufferings endured by the inmates of this prison. They shrink into insignificance compared with the horrors of the great military prison of Georgia and the South. Enough, and more than enough has been spoken and written about them. The infamy of Andersonville is world-wide.

Passing through Washington in August, 1865, I looked into the hot and steaming courtroom where Captain Henry Wirz was on trial. In a worn broadcloth coat, with his counsel at his side occasionally whispering to him, his elbow on a table, and his thin uneasy hand fingering his dark beard or supporting his chin, attenuated, bent, and harassed with the most terrible anxieties — for however indifferent he may have been to the lives of other and better men, there was one life to which he was not indifferent, and which was now at stake; down-looking for the most part, but frequently glancing his quick sharp eye at the court or the witnesses, there sat the miserable man, listening to minutely detailed accounts of the atrocities of which he had been the instrument.

The cause he had served with such savage fidelity had perished; and the original authors of the enormities he had been employed to commit stalked at large or lay in temporary con-

finement, confidently expecting executive clemency; while this
wretched hireling, whose sin consisted in having done their
work too well, was to suffer not the just for the unjust but the
guilty dog for the still more guilty masters.

Fifty-eight miles below Macon, by the Southwestern Railroad, is the scene of the crimes against humanity for which
Wirz was punished with death. The place is set down as *Anderson* on maps and in guidebooks; and that is the name by which
it was known to the inhabitants of the country, until the immense hideous business the war dignified it with the title of
ville.

It is a disagreeable town, with absolutely no point of interest about it except the prison. Before the war it had but five
buildings: a church without a steeple, a small railroad depot,
a little framed box in which was the country post office, and
two dwellings. There were other dwellings within a mile.

Such was Anderson. Anderson*ville* contains some forty additional cheap-looking, unpainted buildings of various sizes, all
of which were constructed with reference to the prison, such
as officers' houses, government storehouses, hospital buildings
(for troops on duty), and so forth. The hospital is now used
as a hotel. The entire atmosphere of the place is ugly and re-
pulsive.

The village lies on the railroad and west of it. Between a
third and one half of a mile east of it is the prison. The space
enclosed by the rough stockade contains twenty-five acres, divided by a sluggish stream flowing through it. It looks like a
great horseyard. Much of the land is swampy, but the rest is elevated, rising on the south side gradually, and on the north side
quite steeply from the brook. It was from this shallow stream,
defiled with refuse from the camp of the Georgia Reserves, that

the thirty thousand prisoners who were sometimes crowded into this broken oblong space drew their chief supply of water. There were a few little springs in the banks, very precious to them.

The walls of the stockade are of upright logs about a foot in diameter, twenty feet high above ground, in which they are set close together, deep enough to be kept firmly in their position. There are an outer and an inner wall of this description, with a space fifty yards in breadth between them. There were sentry boxes for the soldiers on guard, hung like bird nests near the top of the inner wall. These were reached by ladders. For further security, the stockade was partly surrounded by a deep ditch; and on portions of two sides there is an unfinished third line of upright logs.

The outer wall of the stockade has but one entrance. Through this the newly arrived prisoners were marched, and along the space between the two walls to one of two gates which gave admission to the interior of the prison. How many thousands of brave soldiers entered these infernal doors, from which only ghostly skeleton-men, or the corpses of skeleton-men, ever issued forth again!

The prisoners were of course confined within the inner wall. And not only so, but they were prevented from approaching within twenty feet of it by the dead line. Or if not prevented — for much of the way this fatal boundary was marked only by posts set at intervals of six or seven yards — he who, in blindness and sickness and despair, perhaps jostled out of his way by the blind, sick, despairing multitude crowded within, set his foot one inch beyond the strict limits, as some Rebel on guard chose to *imagine* them, crack went a musket, a light puff of smoke curled up from one of the bird nests and the poor wretch lay in his blood, groaning out the last of many groans, which ended his long misery.

I learned that when the stockade was first built, the ground it encloses was covered with trees. Why were they not left — at least a few — to bless with their cooling shade the captives in the heat of those terrible summers? Not a tree remained. Nearby were forests of beautiful timber, to which they were not even permitted to go and cut wood for fuel and huts.

One can imagine nothing more dreary and disheartening than the interior view of the stockade as it is today, except the stockade as it was during the war. The holes in which the prisoners burrowed for protection from the weather have been mostly destroyed by rain. Nearly all the huts are in ruins. The barrack sheds, in which but a mere handful of the thirty thousand prisoners could find place, still remain, marked with sad relics — bunks with the names of the occupants cut upon them, or fragments of benches, knives, old pipes and old shoes.

Between the outer and inner walls were the bakehouse, the pen for sick call, and the log sheds in which the stocks were kept. The cookhouse was outside.

Besides the great stockade there was a small stockade for officers, and a hospital stockade containing some eight acres, and surrounded by upright logs ten or twelve feet high.

In pleasant pine woods, about a hundred rods north of the stockade, is the original burying ground of the Andersonville prison, enlarged and converted into a national cemetery since the war. A whitewashed fence encloses a square space of near fifty acres, divided into four main sections by two avenues crossing it and cutting each other at right angles. Two of these sections are subdivided by alleys into five smaller sections, where the dead lie in long, silent rows, by hundreds. Here are about seven thousand graves. The northeast quarter of the cemetery is undivided; and here, in a single vast encampment, sleep five thousand men.

There are in all near thirteen thousand graves, each with its little white headboard commemorating the name, rank, company, regiment, and date of death of its inmate. The records show that the first death occurred on February 27, 1864, and the last on April 28, 1865. From April 1, 1864, to April 1, 1865, the average rate of mortality was over a thousand a month. It sometimes reached a hundred a day.

Apart from the rest, in the northwestern corner of the cemetery are the graves of the Georgia Reserves who died while on duty here — one hundred and fifteen out of four regiments. The mortality among them appears also to have been great; and indeed one cannot conceive how it should be otherwise within the pestiferous influence of the prison atmosphere.

At the intersection of the avenues rises the flagstaff planted by Miss Clara Barton's party, who laid out the cemetery grounds in the summer of 1865. Here, on the soil of Georgia, above the graves of our dead, waves the broad symbol of the nation's power and victory; while all round this sanctified ground stand the ancient pines, waving their green arms and murmuring requiems for the weary ones at rest. The Rebel owner of the land occupied by the prison has been pardoned by the President; and I learned from the Freedman's Bureau that he has asked for the restoration of his property — demanding even that the cemetery grounds should be turned over to him.

In conclusion, I may state that citizens of Georgia, living at a distance from Andersonville, said to me they knew of the atrocities permitted there, and that they did not think it possible for the Rebel leaders to have been ignorant of them.

XXXII

Sherman in Georgia

ACCORDING to a tradition which I found current in middle Georgia, General Sherman remarked, while on his grand march through the state, that he had his gloves on as yet, but that he would take them off in South Carolina. Afterwards, in North Carolina, I heard the counterpart of this story. As soon as he had crossed the state line, "Boys," said he to his soldiers, "remember we are in the old North State now" — which was equivalent to putting on his gloves again.

At mention of these anecdotes, however, many good Georgians and North Carolinians blazed with indignation: "If he had his gloves on here, I should like to know what he did with his gloves off!" A Confederate brigadier general said to me:

"One could track the line of Sherman's march all through Georgia and South Carolina by the fires on the horizon. He burned the ginhouses, cotton presses, railroad depots, bridges, freighthouses and unoccupied dwellings, with some that were occupied. He stripped our people of everything. He deserves to be called the great robber of the nineteenth century. He did a sort of retail business in North Carolina, but it was a wholesale business, and no mistake, in Georgia, though perhaps not quite so smashing as his South Carolina operations."

Confederate soldiers delight in anecdotes of this famous campaign. Here are two samples:

"When we were retreating before old Sherman, he sent word to Johnston that he wished he would leave just a horseshoe or something to show where he had been. Hood always left enough; but Johnston licked the ground clean behind him."

"The approach to Savannah was defended by splendid, proud forts, bristling with cannon, and our cowardly militia just run without firing a shot!"

The citizens talked with equal freedom of the doings of the "Great Robber." A gentleman of Jones County said:

"I had a noble field of corn, not yet harvested. Old Sherman came along and turned his droves of cattle right into it, and in the morning there was no more corn there than there is on the back of my hand. His devils robbed me of all my flour and bacon and corn meal. They took all the pillow-slips, ladies' dresses, drawers, chemises, sheets and bed quilts they could find in the house to tie their plunder in. You couldn't hide anything but they'd find it.

"I sunk a cask of molasses in a hog wallow; that I think I should have saved, but a nigger boy the rascals had with 'em said he 'lowed there was something hid there; so he went to feeling with a stick, and found the molasses. Then they just robbed my house of every pail, cup, dish, what-not that they could carry molasses off to their camping ground in. After they'd broke open the cask and took what they wanted, they left the rest to run in a river along the ground. There was one sweet hog wallow, if there never was another!"

A lady living near Milledgeville was the president of a sol-diers'-aid society. At the time of Sherman's visit she had in her house a box full of stockings knit by patriotic ladies for the feet of the brave defenders of their country. This box she buried in a field which was afterwards ploughed, in order to obliterate all marks of concealment. A squadron of cavalry arriving at this field formed in line, charged over it, and discovered the box by a hollow sound it gave forth under the hoofs. The box was straightway brought to light, to the joy of many a stockingless invader, who had the fair ladies of Milledgeville to thank for his warm feet that winter.

Sherman's field orders show that it was not his intention to permit indiscriminate destruction and plundering. Yet these orders appear to have been interpreted very liberally. A regiment was usually sent ahead with instructions to guard private dwellings; but as soon as the guards were removed, a legion of stragglers and Negroes rushed in to pillage; and I am convinced that in some cases even the guards pilfered industriously.

Wilson's men, when they seized fresh horses for their use, turned the jaded ones loose in the country. Sherman's army corps acted on a different principle. The deliberate aim seemed to be to *leave no stock whatever in the line of march.* Whenever fresh horses were taken, the used-up animals were shot. Such also was the fate of horses and mules found in the country and not deemed worth taking. The best herds of cattle were driven off; inferior herds were slaughtered in the fields, and left. A company of soldiers would shoot down a drove of hogs, cut out the hindquarters and abandon what remained.

"The Federal Army generally behaved very well in this state," said a Confederate officer. "The destruction of railroads, mills and ginhouses, if designed to cripple us, was perfectly justifiable. But you did have as mean a set of stragglers following your army as ever broke jail. I'll do you the credit to say, though, that there were more foreigners than Yankees among them.

"Your fellows hung several men in my neighborhood to

make 'em tell where their money was. Some gave it up after a little hanging; but I know one man who went to the limb three times, and saved his money and his life too. Another man had three hundred dollars in gold hid in his garden. He is very fat; weighs, I suppose, two hundred and fifty pounds. He held out till they got the rope around his neck, then he caved in. 'I'm dogged,' says he, 'if I'm going to risk my weight on a rope just for a little money!' "

An old gentleman in Putnam County related the following: "Sherman's men gave my son-in-law sut! He had made thirty-two hundred gallons of syrup — more than he had casks for; so he sunk a tank in the ground and buried it. The Yankee soldiers came and helped themselves to it. He had the finest flower garden in the county; they made his own slaves scatter salt all over it, then turned their horses on and finished it. They made my own daughter wait at table. She said she kept servants for such work; but they replied: 'You are none too good.' "

Sherman's invasion cannot properly be called a raid: even Wilson's brilliant expedition with twelve thousand cavalry is belittled by that epithet. Sherman had under his command four infantry corps and a corps of cavalry, pursuing different routes, their caterpillar tracks sometimes crossing each other, braiding a belt of devastation from twenty-five to fifty miles in breadth, and upwards of six hundred miles in extent. The flanking parties driving the light-footed Rebel cavalry before them; bridges fired by the fugitives; pontoon trains hurrying to the front of the advancing columns when streams were to be crossed; the hasty corduroying of bad roads; the jubilant foraging parties sweeping the surrounding country of whatever was needful to support life and vigor in those immense crawling and bristling creatures called army corps; the amazing quantity and variety of plunder collected together on the routes of the wagon trains — the soldiers sitting proudly on their heaped-up stores as the trains approached, then, in lively fashion, thrusting portions into each wagon as it passed — for no halt was allowed; the ripping up of railroads; the burning and plundering of plantations; the encampment at evening; the kindling of fires; the sudden disappearance of fences and the equally sudden springing up of shelter-tents, like mushrooms, all over the ground; the sleep of the vast, silent, guarded hosts; and the hilarious awakening to the toil and adventures of a new day — such are the scenes of this most momentous expedition, which painters, historians, romancers will in future labor to conceive and portray.

Warned by the flying cavalry, and the smoke and flames of plantations on the horizon, the panic-stricken inhabitants thought only of saving their property and their lives from the invaders. Many fled from their homes carrying the most valuable of their possessions, or those which could be most conveniently removed. Mules, horses, cattle, sheep, hogs were driven wildly across the country, avoiding one foraging party perhaps only to fall into the hands of another. The mother caught up her infant; the father, mounting, took his terrified boy upon the back of his horse behind him; the old man clutched his moneybag and ran; not even the poultry, not even the dogs were forgotten; men and women shouldered their household stuffs, and abandoned their houses to the mercies of the soldiers, whose waving banners and bright steel were already appearing on the distant hilltops.

The flight from Milledgeville, including the stampede of the Rebel state legislators, who barely escaped being entrapped by our army — the crushing of passengers and private effects into overloaded cars, the demand for wheeled vehicles and the exorbitant prices paid for them, the freight, the confusion, the separation of families — formed a scene which neither the spectators nor the actors in it will soon forget.

The Negroes had all along been told that if they fell into the hands of the Yankees, they would be worked to death on fortifications, or put into the front of the battle and shot if they did not fight, or sent to Cuba and sold; and that the old women and young children would be drowned like cats and blind puppies. And now the masters showed their affection for these servants by running off the able-bodied ones, who were competent to take care of themselves, and leaving the aged, the infirm and the children to the "cruelties" of the invaders. The manner in which the great mass of the remaining Negro population received the Yankees showed how little they had been imposed upon by such stories, and how true their faith was in the armed deliverance which Providence had ordained for their race.

Traveling by private conveyance from Eatonton — northern terminus of the Milledgeville and Eatonton Railroad — over to Madison on the Georgia Road, on my way to Augusta, I passed a night at a planter's house of the middle class. It was a plain, one-and-a-half story, weather-browned framed dwelling with a porch in front and two front windows. The floors were carpetless, but clean swept. There was a glowing fire in the fireplace, beside which sat a neatly attired, fine-looking but remarkably silent grandmother, taking snuff.

The house had three other inmates — the planter and his wife, and their son, a well-educated young man who sat in the evening reading *Handy Andy* by the light of the oak-wood fire. No candle was lighted, except for me at bedtime.

This was not the house of a small farmer, but of the owner of two plantations, of a thousand acres each. He had had fifty-nine Negroes before the war. There was a branch running through his estate, on the bottomland of which he could make a bale of cotton to the acre. On the uplands it took three or four acres to make a bale. This year his son had undertaken to run the plantation we were on, while he was to oversee the other. The young man was far more hopeful of success than his father.

"The great trouble in this country is, the people are mad at the niggers because they're free. They always believed they wouldn't do well if they were emancipated, and now they maintain, and some of them even hope, they won't do well — that too in the face of actual facts. The old planters have no confidence in the niggers, and as a matter of course the niggers have no confidence in them. They have a heap more confidence in their young masters, and they work well for us."

"I wish we older ones had the faculty you say you have for making the free niggers work," said the young man's mother. "I always kept two women just to weave. The same women are with me now. Before they were declared free, they could weave six and eight yards of cloth a day, easy. Now the most they do is about one yard."

The home was on the main road traversed by the Fifteenth Corps, belonging to the left wing of Sherman's army, on its way from Madison to Milledgeville.

"I never would have thought I could stay home while the Yankees were passing," said the mother, "but I did. They commenced passing early in the morning, and there wasn't an hour in the day that they were not as thick as blue pigeons along the road.

"I was very excited at first. My husband was away, and I had nobody with me but our Negroes. A German soldier came into the house first of any. He was as ugly-looking fellow as ever I saw; but I suppose any man would have looked ugly under such circumstances. Said he, 'I've orders to get a saddle from this house.' I told him my husband had done gone off with the only saddle we had. Then he said, 'A pistol will do.' I said I had no pistol. Then he told me he must have a watch of me. I had a watch, but it was put out of the way where I hoped no Yankee could find it; so I told him I had none for him.

"He then looked all around the room and said, 'Madam, I have orders to burn this house,' I replied that I hoped the Federals were too magnanimous to burn houses over the heads of defenseless women. He said, 'I'll insure it for fifty dollars'; for that's the way they got a heap of money out of our people. I said, 'I've no fifty dollars to pay for insuring it; and if it depends upon that, it must burn.'

"Soon as he saw he couldn't frighten me into giving him anything, he went to plundering. He had found a purse with five dollars in Confederate money in it, when he saw an officer coming in the front door and escaped through the back door. He was a very great villain, and the officer said if he was caught he would be punished.

"I don't know what I should have done if it hadn't been for the Yankee officers. They treated me politely in every way. They couldn't prevent my meal and bacon from being taken by the foraging parties — all except what I had hid; but they gave me a guard to keep soldiers from plundering the house, and when one guard was taken away I had another in his place. Some families on this road, who had no guard, were so broken up they had nothing left to keep house with."

*   *   *

At Milledgeville — a mere village surrounded by beautiful hilly and wooded country — I saw something of the Georgia State Legislature. It was at work on a cumbersome and rather useless freedmen's code, which, however, contained no very objectionable features. In intelligence and political views this body represented the state very fairly. I was told that its members, like the inhabitants of the state at large, were, with scarce an exception, believers in the right of secession. The only questions that ever divided them on that subject were not as to the right but as to the policy; and whether the state should secede separately, or cooperate with the other seceding states.

Since the Rebel state debt had been repudiated, there existed a feeling among both legislators and people that all debts, public and private, ought to be wiped out with it. I remember well the argument of a gentleman of Morgan County. "Two thirds of the people in this county are left hopelessly involved by the loss of the war debt. The more loyal portion of our citizens would not invest in Confederate scrip, but put their money into state bonds, which they thought safe from repudiation. A large number of debts are for Negro property. Now, since slavery is abolished, all debts growing out of slavery ought to be abolished.

"Four or five men in this county," he added, "have the power to ruin over thirty families, whose obligations they bought up with Confederate money. As that money turns out to have never been legally good for anything, all such obligations should be canceled."

Throughout the state I heard the bitterest complaints against the Davis despotism. "There was first a tax of ten per cent levied on all our produce; then of twelve per cent on all property. Worse still, our property was seized at the will of the government and scrip given in exchange, which was not good for taxes or anything else. There was public robbery by the government, and private robbery by the officers of the government. The secretary of war, Seddon, had grain to sell; so he raised the price of it to forty dollars a bushel, when it should have sold for two dollars and a half.

"The Conscript Act was executed with criminal partiality. A man of an influential family had no difficulty in evading it. During the last year of the war, there were one hundred and twenty-two thousand young Confederates in bombproof situations. But an ordinary conscript was treated like a prisoner, thrown into jail, and often handcuffed."

I found the freedmen's schools in Georgia supported by the New England Freedmen's Aid Society and the American Missionary Association. These were confined to a few localities — principally the large towns. The opposition to freedmen's schools on the part of the whites was generally bitter; and in several counties schoolhouses had been burned and the teachers driven away on the withdrawal of the troops. Occasionally, however, I would hear an intelligent planter remark: "The South has been guilty of the greatest inconsistency in the world, in sending missionaries to enlighten the heathen and forbidding the education of our own servants."

At Augusta, I visited a number of colored schools, including a private one kept by Mr. Baird, a colored man, in a little room where he had secretly taught thirty pupils during the war. The building, containing a store below and tenements above, was owned and occupied by persons of his own race; the children entered by different doors, the girls with their books strapped under their skirts, the boys with theirs concealed under their coats, all finding their way in due season to the little schoolroom. I was shown the doors and passages by which they used to escape and disperse at the approach of white persons.

Baird told me that during ten years previous to the war, he taught a similar school in Charleston, South Carolina. The laws prohibited persons of color from teaching, so he employed a white woman to assist him. She sat and sewed and kept watch until the patrol looked in, when she appeared as the teacher, and the real teacher (a small man) fell back as a pupil. It was ostensibly a school for free colored children, the teaching of slaves to read being a criminal offense; yet many of those were taught.

On the road to Augusta, my attention was attracted by the conversation of a Georgian and a Mississippian sitting behind me in the car. We had just passed Union Point, where there was considerable excitement about an unknown Negro found lying in the woods, sick with smallpox. Nobody went to his relief, and the citizens, standing with hands in pockets, allowed that if he did not die of disease, he would soon perish from exposure and starvation.

"The trouble is just here," said the Georgian behind me. "The niggers have never been used to taking care of their own sick. Formerly, if anything was the matter with them, their masters had them taken care of; and now they don't mind anything about disease, except to be afraid of it. If they've a sick baby, they let it die. They're like so many children themselves in respect to sickness."

"How much better off they were when slaves!" said the Mississippian. "A man would see to his own niggers, like he would to his own stock. But the niggers now don't belong to anybody, and it's no man's business whether they live or die."

"I exercise the same care over *my* niggers I always did," replied the Georgian. "They are all with me yet. Only one ever left me. He was a good, faithful servant, but sickly. He said one day he thought he ought to have wages, and I told him if he could find anybody to do better by him than I was doing, he'd better go. He went, and took his family; and in six weeks he came back again.

" 'Edward,' I said, 'how's this?' 'I want to come and live with you again, master, like I always have,' he said. 'I find I ain't strong enough to work for wages.' 'Edward,' I said, 'I am very sorry; you wanted to go, and I got another man in your place; now I have nothing for you to do, and your cabin is occupied.' He just burst into tears. 'I've lived with you all my days, master,' he said, 'and now I have no home!'

"I couldn't stand that. 'Take an ax,' I said, 'go into the woods, cut some poles and build you a cabin. As long as I have a home, you shall have one.' He was the happiest man you ever saw!"

"A Yankee wouldn't have done that," said the Mississippian. "Yankees won't take care of a poor white man. I've traveled in the North, and seen people there go barefoot in winter with ice on the ground."

"Indeed!" said I, turning and facing the speaker. "What state was that in?"

"In New York," he replied. "I've seen hundreds of poor whites barefoot there in the depth of winter."

"That is singular," I remarked. "I am a native of that state; I lived in it until I was twenty years old, and have traveled through it repeatedly since; and I never happened to see what you describe."

"I have seen the same thing in Massachusetts, too."

"I have been for some years a resident of Massachusetts, and have never yet seen a man there barefoot in the snow." The Mississippian made no direct reply to this, but ran on in a strain of vehement and venomous abuse of the Yankees, in which he was cordially joined by his friend the Georgian.

The track of the Central Railroad, one hundred and ninety-one miles in length, was destroyed with conscientious thoroughness by Sherman's army. From Gordon, twenty miles below Macon, to Scarborough Station, nine miles below Millen, a distance of one hundred miles, there was still an impassable hiatus of bent rails and burned bridges at the time of my journey; and in order to reach Savannah from Macon, it was necessary to proceed by the Georgia Road to Augusta, either returning by railroad to Atlanta, or crossing over by railroad and stage to Madison, between which places the Georgia Road, destroyed for a distance of sixty-seven miles, had been restored.

From Augusta I went down on the Augusta and Savannah Road to a station a few miles below Waynesboro, where a break in that road rendered it necessary to proceed by stages to Scarborough. From Scarborough to Savannah, the road was once more in operation.

The relaid tracks were very rough, many of the old rails having been straightened and put down again. "General Grant and his staff passed over this road a short time ago," said a citizen, "and as they went jolting along in an old boxcar, on plain board seats, they seemed to think it was great fun: they said they were riding on Sherman's *hairpins*" — an apt name applied to the most frequent form in which the rails were bent.

"Sherman's men had all sorts of machinery for destroying the track. They could rip it up as fast as they could count. They burned the ties and fences to heat the iron; then two men would take a bar and twist it or wrap it around a tree or telegraph post. Our people found some of their iron benders, and they helped mightily in straightening the rails again. Only the best could be used. The rest the devil can't straighten."

Riding along by the destroyed tracks, it was amusing to see the curious shapes in which the iron had been left. Hairpins predominated. Corkscrews were also abundant. Sometimes we found four or five rails wound around the trunk of a tree, which would have to be cut before they could be got off again.

The inhabitants of eastern Georgia suffered even more than those of middle Georgia from our army operations — the men having got used to their wild business by the time they arrived there, and the general having, I suspect, slipped one glove off. Here is the story of an old gentleman of Burke County:

"It was the Fourteenth Corps that came through my place. They looked like a blue cloud coming. They had all kinds of music — horns, cowbells, tin pans, everything they could pick up that would make a hideous noise. It was like Bedlam broke loose.

"They burned everything but occupied dwellings. They cut the belluses at the blacksmith shops. They took every knife and fork and cooking utensil we had. My wife just saved a frying pan by hanging on to it; she was considerable courageous, and they left it in her hands. After that they came back to get her to cook them some biscuits.

" 'How can I cook for you when you've carried off everything?' she said.

"They told her if she would make them a batch of biscuit, they would bring back a sack of her own flour and she should have the balance of it. She agreed to it; but while the biscuit was baking, another party came along and carried the sack off again.

"General Sherman went into the house of an old woman after his men had been pillaging it. He sat down and drank a glass of water. Says she to him, 'I don't wonder people say you're a smart man; for you've been to the bad place and got scrapings the devil wouldn't have.' His soldiers heard of it, and they took her dresses and hung them all up in the highest trees, and drowned the cat in the well.

"My wife did the neatest thing. She took all our valuables, such as watches and silver spoons, and hid them in the cornfield. With a knife she would just make a slit in the ground, open it a little, put in one or two things, and then let the earth down, just like it was before. Then she'd go on and do the same thing in another place. The soldiers went all over that cornfield sticking in their bayonets, but they didn't find a thing. The joke of it was, she came very near never finding them again herself."

The following story was related to me by a Northern man who had been twenty-five years settled in eastern Georgia:

"My neighbors were too much frightened to do anything in good order. But I determined I'd save as much of my property as I could drive on its own feet or load onto wagons. I took two loads of goods, and all my cattle and hogs, and run 'em off twenty miles into Screven County. I found a spot of rising ground covered with gall bushes, in the middle of a low, wet place. I went through water six inches deep, got to the knoll, cut a road through the bushes, run my wagons in and stuck the bushes down into the wet ground where I had cut them. They were six or eight feet high, and hid everything. My cattle and hogs I turned off in a bushy field. After that, I went to the house of a poor planter and stayed. That was Friday night.

"Sunday, the soldiers came. I lay hid in the woods, and saw 'em pass close by the knoll where my goods were, running in their bayonets everywhere. The bushes were green yet, and they didn't discover anything, though they passed right by the edge of them.

"All at once I heard the women of the house scream murder. Thinks I, 'It won't do for me to be lying here looking out only for my own interests, while the soldiers are abusing the women.' I crawled out of the bushes and was hurrying back to the house when five cavalrymen overtook me. They put their carbines to my head and told me to give 'em my money.

" 'Gentlemen,' I said, 'I've got some Confederate money, but it will do you no good.'

" 'Give me your pistol,' one said. I told him I had no pistol. They thought I lied, for they saw something in my pocket; but come to snatch it out, it was only my pipe. Then they demanded my knife.

" 'I've nothing but an old knife I cut my tobacco with; you won't take an old man's knife!'

"They let me go, and I hurried on to the house. It was full of soldiers. I certainly thought something dreadful was happening to the women; but they were screeching because the soldiers were carrying off their butter and honey and corn meal. They were making all that fuss over the loss of their property; and I thought I might as well have stayed to watch mine.

"Monday I returned home and found my family living on corn-meal bran. They had been robbed of everything. The soldiers had even taken the hat from my little grandson's head, six years old. There were fifty or a hundred soldiers in the house all one day, breaking open chests and bureaus; and those that come after took what the first had left.

"My folks asked for protection, being Northern people; and there was one officer who knew them; but he could control only his own men. So we fared no better than our neighbors."

The staging to Scarborough was very rough; but our route lay through beautiful pine woods, carpeted with wild grass. It was January, but the spring frogs were singing. The best rolling stock of the Central Road had been run up to Macon on Sherman's approach, and could not be got down again. So I had the pleasure of riding from Scarborough to Savannah in an old car crowded full of wooden chairs, in place of the usual seats.

Our route lay along the low, level borders of the Ogeechee River, the soil of which is too cold for cotton. We passed immense swamps, in the perfectly still waters of which the great tree trunks were mirrored. And all the way the spring frogs kept up their shrill singing.

At some of the stations I saw bales of Northern hay that had come up from Savannah. "There is a commentary on our style of farming," said an intelligent planter from near Millen. "This land, though worthless for cotton, could be made to grow splendid crops of grass — and we import our hay!"

XXXIII

Savannah

O N NOVEMBER 16, 1864, Sherman began his grand march from Atlanta. In less than a month his army had made a journey of three hundred miles, consuming and devastating the country. On December 13, by the light of the setting sun, General Hazen's division of the Fifteenth Corps made its brilliant assault on Fort McAlister on the Ogeechee, opening the gate to Savannah and the sea. On the night of the twentieth, Savannah was hurriedly evacuated by the Rebels, and occupied by Sherman on the twenty-first. The city, with a thousand prisoners, thirty-five thousand bales of cotton, two hundred guns, three steamers and valuable stores thus fell into our hands without a battle. Within forty-eight hours a United States transport steamer came to the wharf, and the new base of supplies, about which we were all at that time so anxious, was established.

The city was on fire during the evacuation. Six squares and portions of other squares were burned. At the same time a mob commenced breaking into stores and dwellings. The destroyers of railroads were in time to save the city from the violence of its own citizens.

A vast multitude of Negroes had followed the army to the sea. This exodus of bondmen from the interior had been permitted not simply as a boon to them but as an injury to the resources of the Confederacy, like the destruction of plantations and railroads. What to do with them now became a serious problem. Of his conference with Secretary Stanton at Savannah, General Sherman says:

"We agreed that the young and able-bodied men should be enlisted as soldiers or employed by the quartermaster in unloading ships and for other army purposes; but this left the old and feeble, the women and children, who had to be fed by the United States. Mr. Stanton summoned a large number of the old Negroes, mostly preachers, with whom he held a long conference. After this conference he was satisfied the Negroes could, with some little aid from the United States by means of abandoned plantations on the Sea Islands and along the navigable rivers, take care of themselves."

Sherman's "General Orders No. 15" were the result, giving Negro settlers "possessory titles" to these lands. Thus originated the knotty Sea Islands controversy, of which more by-and-by.

The aspect of Savannah is peculiarly Southern and not without a certain charm. Its uniform squares, its moist and heavy atmosphere, the dead level of its sandy streets shaded by moss-draped trees, and its frequent parks of oaks and magnolias impress you singularly. The surrounding country is an almost unbroken level. Just across the Savannah lie the low, marshy shores of South Carolina. It is the largest city of Georgia, having something like twenty-five thousand inhabitants. Here, before the war, dwelt the aristocracy of the country, living in luxurious style upon the income of slave labor on rice and cotton plantations.

There were sixteen hundred colored children in Savannah, twelve hundred of whom attended school. Three hundred and fifty attended schools of the Savannah Educational Association, organized and supported by the colored population. I visited one of these schools, taught by colored persons, in a building which was a famous slave mart in the good old days of the institution. In the large auction room, and behind barred windows of the jail over it, the children of slaves were now enjoying one of the first, inestimable advantages of freedom.

If you go to Savannah, do not fail to visit Bonaventure Cemetery, six miles from the city. You drive southward on Thunderbolt Road, past the fortifications, through fields of stumps and piny undergrowths, whose timber was cut away to give range to the guns, to the fragrant, sighing solitude of pine woods beyond. Leaving the main road, you pass beneath the low roof of young evergreen oaks overarching the path. This leads you into avenues of indescribable beauty and gloom.

Whichever way you look, colonnades of huge live-oak trunks open before you, solemn, still and hoary. The great limbs meeting above are draped and festooned with long, fine moss. Over all is a thick canopy of living green, shutting out the glare of day. Beneath is a sparse undergrowth of evergreen bushes, half concealing a few neglected old family monuments. The area is small, but a more fitting scene for a cemetery is not conceivable.

XXXIV

Charleston

THE RAILROAD from Savannah to Charleston, one hundred and four miles in length, running through a country of rice plantations, was smashed by Sherman in his march *from* the sea. As it never was a paying road before the war, I could see no prospect of its being soon repaired. The highway of the ocean supplies its place. There was little travel between the two cities, two or three small steamers a week being sufficient to accommodate all. Going on board one of these inferior boats at three o'clock one afternoon at Savannah, I awoke next morning in Charleston Harbor.

A warm, soft, misty morning it was. What is that great bulk away on our left? We have just left Fort Moultrie on our right; the low shores on which it crouches lie off there still visible, like banks of heavier mist. That obscure phenomenon ahead turns out to be Fort Ripley. The mist clears and we see, far on our right, Castle Pinckney; and on our left a gloomy line of pine forests which is James Island.

This is historic ground we are traversing — or rather historic water. What is that at anchor yonder? A monitor! A man in its low flat deck walks almost level with the water. Two noticeable objects follow us: one is a high-breasted, proud-beaked New

York steamer; the other, the wonderful light of dawn dancing upon the waves.

Before us all the while, rising and expanding as we approach, its wharves and shipping, its warehouses and church steeples gradually taking shape on its low peninsula thrust out between the two rivers, is the haughty and defiant little city that inaugurated treason, that led the Rebellion, that kindled the fire it took the nation's blood to quench.

I gave my bag to a black boy on the wharf, who led the way to Mills House. The appearance of the city in the early morning was prepossessing. It is a well-built, light and airy city. It lacks the broad streets, the public squares and the trees which give Savannah its charm; but it strikes one as a more attractive place for a residence.

Charleston did not appear as a very cleanly town, and I doubt if it ever was. Its scavengers are turkey buzzards. About the slaughter pens on the outskirts of the city, at the markets, and wherever garbage abounds, these black, melancholy birds congregate in numbers. In contrast with these obscenities are the gardens of suburban residences, green in midwinter with semitropical shrubs and trees.

Here centered the fashion and aristocracy of South Carolina before the war. Charleston was the watering place where the rich planters, who lived upon their estates in winter, came to lounge away the summer season, thus inverting the Northern custom. It has still many fine residences, built in a variety of styles; but, since those recent days of its pride and prosperity, it has been woefully battered and desolated.

The great fire of 1861 swept diagonally across the city from river to river. A broad belt of ruin divides what remains. One eighth of the city was burned, comprising much of its fairest and wealthiest quarter. No effort had yet been made to rebuild it. The proud city lies humbled in its ashes, too poor to rise again without the helping hand of Northern capital.

The ruins of Charleston are the most picturesque of any I saw in the South. The gardens and broken walls of many of its fine residences remain to attest their former elegance. Broad, semicircular flights of marble steps, leading up once to proud doorways, now conduct you over cracked and calcined slabs to the level of high foundations swept of everything but the crushed fragments of former superstructures, with here and there a broken pillar, a windowless wall. Above the monotonous gloom of the ordinary ruins rise the churches — the stone tower and roofless walls of the Catholic cathedral, deserted and solitary, a roost for buzzards; the burned-out shell of the Circular Church with its dismantled columns still standing, like those of an antique temple.

There are additional ruins scattered throughout the lower city, a legacy of the Federal bombardment. Yet I found people who still maintained that the bombardment did not amount to much. A member of the city fire department said: "But few fires were set by shells. There were a good many fires, but they were mostly set by mischief makers. The object was to get us firemen down in shelling range. There was a spite against us, because we were exempt from military duty."

The fright of the inhabitants, however, was generally admitted. The greatest panic occurred immediately after the occupation of Morris Island by General Gillmore. "The first shells set the whole town in commotion. It looked like everybody was skedaddling. Some loaded their goods and left nothing but empty houses. Others just packed a few things in trunks and boxes and abandoned the rest. The poor people and Negroes took what they could carry on their backs or heads or in their arms, and put for dear life. Some women put on all their dresses to save them. For a while the streets were crowded with runaways — hurrying, hustling, driving — on horseback, in wagons and on foot — white folks, dogs and niggers. But when it was found the shells only fell down town, the people got over their scare; and many who went away came back again. Every once in a while, however, the Yankees would appear to mount a new gun or get a new gunner; and the shells would fall higher up. That would start the skedaddling once more. One shell would be enough to depopulate a whole neighborhood."

The shelling began in July, 1863, and was kept up pretty regularly until the surrender of the city on the eighteenth of February, 1865. Sherman's army having flanked the city, its evacuation was not unexpected; but when it came, confusion and dismay came with it. The Rebel troops, departing, adhered to their usual custom of leaving ruin behind them. They fired the upper part of the city, burning an immense quantity of cotton with railroad buildings and military stores. While the half-famished poor were rushing early in the morning to secure a little of the Confederate rice in one of the warehouses, two hundred kegs of powder blew up, killing and mutilating a large number of those unfortunate people. Here also it devolved upon the Union troops to save the city from the fires set by its own friends.

Many people rushed in from the suburbs, got caught inside the intrenchments and could not get out again. Others rushed out panic-stricken from the burning city, and when they wished to return, found they could not. Charleston, from the moment of occupation, was a sealed city. Families were divided. "It was two months before I could learn whether my husband was dead or alive," said a lady who took refuge in the interior. And some who remained in Charleston told me it was a month before they heard of the burning of Columbia; that they could not even learn which way Sherman's army had gone.

One morning I went on board the government supply steamer *Mayflower,* plying between the city and the forts below. As we steamed down to the rows of piles driven across the harbor to compel vessels to pass under the guns of the forts, I noticed that they were so nearly eaten off by worms that, had the war continued a year or two longer, it would have been necessary to replace them.

Fort Sumter loomed before us, an enormous mass of ruins. We approached on the northeast side, which appeared covered with blotches and patches of a most extraordinary description, commemorating the shots of our monitors. The notches in the half-demolished wall were mended with gabions. On the southeast side not a square foot of the original octagonal wall remained, but in its place was an irregular, steeply sloping bank of broken bricks, stones and sand — a half-pulverized mountain on which no amount of shelling could have any other effect than to pulverize it still more.

On the northwest side, facing the city, the perpendicular lofty wall stands in nearly its original condition, astonishing us by contrast with the other sides. Between this wall and the wreck of a Rebel steamer, sunk while bringing supplies to the fort, we landed. By wooden steps we reached the summit and looked down into the huge crater within. This is a sort of irregular amphitheater, with sloping banks of gabions and rubbish on all sides save one.

On the southeast side, where the exterior of the fort received the greatest damage from the guns on Morris Island, the interior received the least. There are no casemates left except on that side. In the center stands the flagstaff bearing the starry symbol of the national power, once humbled here, and afterwards trailed long through bloody dust, to float again higher and haughtier than ever on those rebellious shores.

The fort is built upon a mole which is flooded by high water. It was half tide that morning, and climbing down the slope of the southeast embankment, I walked upon the beach below — or rather upon the litter of old iron that strewed it. It was difficult to step without placing a foot upon a rusty cannon ball or fragment of shell. I suggested to an officer that this would be a valuable mine to work, and was told that the right to collect the old iron around the fort had already been sold to a speculator for thirty thousand dollars.

I found eighty-five United States soldiers in Sumter — a mere handful, yet they were five more than the garrison at the time of Beauregard's bombardment in April, 1861. My mind went back to those earlier days, and to that other little band. How anxiously we had watched the newspapers week after week, to see if the Rebels would *dare* to execute their threats! How our hearts throbbed in sympathy with Major Anderson and his seventy-nine heroes! Major, Colonel, General Anderson — well might he step swiftly up the degrees of rank, for he was already atop of our hearts.

Looking back coolly at the event from the walls of Sumter today, it is not easy to understand how a patriot and a soldier, who knew his duty, could have sat quiet in his fortress while Rebel batteries were rising all around him. He was acting on the defensive, you say — waiting for the Rebels to commence hostilities. But hostilities had already begun. The first spadeful

of earth thrown up to protect the first Rebel gun within range
of Sumter was an act of war upon Sumter. To wait until surrounded by a ring of fire, which could not be resisted, before
opening the guns of the fort, appears, by the light both of military duty and of common sense, absurd. But fortunately something else rules in a great revolution besides military duty and
common sense; and in the plan of that Providence which shapes
our ways, I suppose Major Anderson did the best that was to
be done. Besides, forbearance to the utmost, and sometimes a
little beyond, was the policy of the government he served.

"Is this your first visit to Charleston?" I asked General S——
as we dined together.

"My first visit," he replied, "occurred in the summer of 1864,
considerably against my inclination. I was lodged at the expense
of the Confederate Government in the Work House — not half
as comfortable a place as this hotel!"

Both visits were made in the service of the United States Government, but under what different circumstances! Then a
helpless, insulted prisoner, now he came in a capacity which
brought to him as humble petitioners some of the most rebellious citizens of those days. When sick and in prison, they did
not minister unto him; but since he sat in an office of public
power, nothing could exceed their polite, hat-in-hand attentions.

Dinner over, he proposed that we should look at his old
quarters in the Work House. It was a castlelike building,
flanked by two tall towers; built of brick but covered with a
cement in imitation of freestone. Before the war it was used as
a safe place of deposit for that property known as slaves. Negroes for sale and awaiting the auction day, Negroes who had or

had not merited chastisement not convenient for their city masters or mistresses to administer at home, Negroes who had run away or were in danger of running away, were sent here for safekeeping or scientific flogging, as the case might be. It was a mere jail with cells and bolts and bars, like any other.

During the war, the Negroes were transferred to another building near by and the "Work House" became a Yankee prison, in which officers were confined. In the same block was the City Jail, likewise turned into a prison for Federal officers. The Roper and Marine Hospitals, not far off, were put to the same use.

It was a dungeonlike entrance, dark and low and damp, to which we gained admittance through a heavy door that creaked harshly on its hinges. "When I first entered here," said General S——, "a cold shudder ran over me. I looked around for a chance to escape, and saw on each side two rows of bayonets, not encouraging to the most enterprising man!"

We walked through the foul and dismal passages, upstairs and downstairs; visited the various cells, the old Negro whipping room, the room in which General Stoneman, the captured raider, was confined; and at length came to a room in the second story of the west tower, which was occupied by General S—— and a dozen more Federal officers. There were several wooden bunks in it on which they slept, from among which the general singled out his own.

"This is the old thing I lay on! Here is my mark!" He looked up. "Do you see that patched place in the roof? A shell came in there one day when we were lying on our bunks. It made these holes in the floor. But it hurt no one."

We went down into the yard. "I never got outside of this enclosure but once. Then I went through that gate for a load of wood. I had a taste of the pure air, and I can't tell you how good it was! It exhilarated me like wine."

On the other side of the yard was the building to which the Negroes were transferred. "Every day we could hear the yells of those who were being whipped."

In the yard is a wooden tower of observation, which we climbed and had a view of the city. It was occupied as a lookout by the Rebel guard. "Near the foot of this tower," said General S——, "was a small mountain of offal — fragments of food, old bones and the like, thrown out from the prison; a horrible heap — all a moving mass of maggots — left to engender disease. Luckily for us, the men on guard were made sick by it, and it was finally removed.

"The officer who had control of the prison has been appointed United States Marshal for the State of South Carolina for his kindness to us," he continued. "It is strange I never heard of his kindness when I was here. We were not whipped like the Negroes; but in other respects our treatment was no better. Out of curiosity I once measured my rations for ten days and counted just fifty-five spoonfuls — five and a half spoonfuls a day!

"I hadn't been here a week before we had three schemes for getting out. One was to cut through a board in the yard fence; but we found we were watched too closely for that. Another was to make a tunnel to the sewer in the street in front of the prison, as I will show you."

Descending the tower, he took me to an iron grating that covered a dark cavity in the ground under one of the prison passages. "Here is a large cistern, which we had exhausted of its contents. One day I pulled up this grate, dropped down into the hole, lighted a candle and made an exploration. On coming out I gave a favorable report, and that night we went to digging. We tunneled first through the cistern wall, then through the foundation wall of the prison, and got into the sand under the street. We half filled the old cistern with the stones and dirt we dug out, with sticks, old bones and any bits of iron we could lay our hands on.

"We worked like rats. Two or three of us were constantly in the tunnel, while others kept watch above. A friend outside had given us information with regard to the position of the sewer; we had already struck it, and the next night we should have got into it, and into the street beyond the prison guard, when we were betrayed by another prisoner. He had to be removed from the prison to save his life.

"We had our third and great plan in reserve. There were six hundred prisoners in the Work House, three hundred in the City Jail adjoining, and one thousand in the Roper and Marine Hospitals, within an arrow's shot. These were officers. At the Race Course Prison, on the outskirts of town, there were four thousand enlisted men. Our guard at the Work House consisted of three reliefs of thirty-three men each. They were mere militia that had never seen service. Old soldiers like us were not afraid of such fellows; and we knew that if we made a demonstration, they would be afraid of us.

"Our plan was for two prisoners, at a given signal, to leap on the back of each guard in the prison, and disarm him. Possibly some of us might get hurt, but we were pretty sure of success. Then, with the arms thus secured, we could easily capture the second relief guard as it marched in. Then we were to rush out immediately and seize the third relief. This would give us ninety-nine guns.

"With these we were to march directly upon the arsenal, capture it, and provide ourselves with all the arms and ammunition we needed. Then to release the thirteen hundred officers at the jail and hospitals, and the four thousand privates at the Race Course would have been easy; and we should have had a force of near six thousand men. With these, the city would have been in our power.

"Our plan then was to set fires clear across it, from river to river, to make a barricade of burning buildings against the Rebel artillery that would have been coming down to look after us. Of course, the panic and confusion of the citizens would have been extreme, and the military would hardly have known what we were about; while our plans were laid with mathematical precision. Our friend outside had smuggled in to us, done up in balls of bread, a map of Charleston, with explanations of every point about which we needed information; and through him we had communicated with our friends on Morris Island. We were to seize the shipping, capture the water batteries, and hold the lower part of the town until our friends, under cover of a furious bombardment, could come to our assistance.

"My whole heart was in this scheme, and the time was set for its execution. The very day before the day appointed, I was exchanged, together with the principal leaders in it. To be let out just on the eve of what promised to be such a brilliant exploit was almost a disappointment."

XXXV

The Sea Islands

THE PLANTATION Negro of the great cotton- and rice-growing states is a far more ignorant and degraded creature than the Negro of Virginia and Tennessee. This difference is traceable to a variety of causes. First, the farmers of the slave-breeding states were formerly accustomed to select from among their servants the most stupid and vicious class to be sold in the Southern market. To the same destination went all the more modern importations of raw savages from Africa.

The Negro is susceptible to civilization; and in the border states, his intelligence was developed by much intercourse with the white race. His veins also received a generous infusion of the superior blood. The same may be said of house and town servants throughout the South. The slaves of large and isolated plantations, however, enjoyed but limited advantages of this sort, seeing little of civilized society beyond the overseer, whose lessons were not those of grace, and the poor whites around them, scarcely more elevated in the scale than themselves.

In South Carolina the results of these combined causes are more striking than in any other state. The excess of her black population, and the unmitigated character of slavery within her borders, afford perhaps a sufficient explanation of this fact. In 1860, she had 291,388 white, 402,406 slave, and 9,914 free col-

ored inhabitants. Even these figures do not indicate the overwhelming predominance of black numbers in certain localities.
In the poorer districts, as counties are here called, the whites
were in a majority; while in certain others there were three and
four times as many Negroes as white persons. Herded together
in great numbers, and worked like cattle, the habits of these
wretched people were little above those of the brute.

Owing to this excessive black population and its degraded
character, labor appeared to be more disorganized and the
freedmen in worse condition in South Carolina than elsewhere.
The Sea Islands question, however, had had a very marked and
injurious effect upon labor in the state, and should be taken
into consideration.

The most ignorant of the blacks have certain true and strong
instincts which stand them in place of actual knowledge. Their
faith in Providence has a depth and integrity which shames the
halting belief of the more enlightened Christian. Next to that,
and strangely blended with it, is the faith in the government
which has brought them out of bondage. Along with these goes
the simple conviction that, in order to be altogether free, they
must have homes of their own.

The government encouraged them in that belief and hope.
Conscious of their own loyalty, and having a clear understanding of the disloyalty of their masters, they expected confidently,
long after the war had closed, that the forfeited lands of these
masters would be divided among them. It was only after earnest
and persistent efforts on the part of officers of the bureau to convince them this hope was futile, that they finally abandoned it.

But by this time it had become known among the freed people of South Carolina and Georgia that extensive tracts of land
on the coast had been set aside by military authority for their

use. There the forty thousand bondmen who followed Sherman out of Georgia, together with other thousands who had preceded them, or come after, were established upon independent farms, in self-governing communities from which all white intruders were excluded. These settlements were chiefly upon the rich and delightful Sea Islands which the Rebel owners had abandoned, and which now became the paradise of the freedmen's hopes.

"Go there," they said, "and every man can pick out his lot of forty acres, and have it secured to him."

With such fancies in his brain, the Negro of the interior was not likely to remain contented on the old plantation, after learning that no acre of it was to be given him. And so the emigration to the coast set in.

In October, 1865, orders were issued that no more allotments of land should be made to freedmen. But this did not stop entirely the tide of emigration; nor did it inspire with contentment those who remained in the interior. "If a freedman has forty acres on the coast," they reasoned, "why shouldn't we have as much here?" Hence one of the most serious troubles the bureau had to contend with.

In October, General Howard visited the Sea Islands with the intention of restoring to the pardoned owners the lands on which freedmen had been settled, under General Sherman's order. According to the President's theory, a pardon entitled the person pardoned to immediate restoration of his property. Hence arose a conflict of authority and endless confusion.

Secretary Stanton had approved of Sherman's order, and advised the freedmen to secure homesteads under the government's protection. General Saxton, assistant commissioner of the bureau, had in every way encouraged them to do the same.

So had General Hunter. Chief Justice Chase had given them similar counsel. General Howard found the landowners urgent in pressing their claims, and the freedmen equally determined in resisting them.

Impressed by the immense difficulty of the problem, he postponed its immediate solution by a compromise, leaving the main question to be settled by Congress. Congress settled it after a fashion in the provisions of the Freedmen's Bureau Bill; but that, in consequence of the President's veto, did not become a law.

By Howard's plan, abandoned lands on which there were no freedmen settled under Sherman's order, or only "a few," were to be restored to pardoned owners. Other estates, on which there were more than "a few," were also to be restored, provided arrangements could be made satisfactory to both the owners and the freedmen. So nothing was settled. The owners claimed the lands, and wished the freedmen to make contracts to work for them. The freedmen claimed the lands, and positively refused to make contracts.

A company of South Carolina planters who were going over to look at their estates on James Island, and learn if any arrangements could be made with the freedmen, invited me to accompany them; and on the morning of the day appointed, I left my hotel for the wharf from which we were to embark.

Opposite lay James Island, with its marshy borders and dark-green line of pines. Boats — mostly huge cypress dugouts manned by Negroes — were passing to and fro, some coming from the island with loads of wood, others returning laden with families of freedmen going to their new homes, and with household goods and supplies.

"This is interesting," said one planter. "That wood comes from our plantations. The Negroes cut it off, bring it over to the city, and perhaps sell it to the actual owners of the land they have taken it from. We are buying our own wood of the darky squatters. The Negroes are still going to the island, picking their lands and staking out forty-acre lots, though the bureau is giving no more titles."

A large cypress dugout came to the wharf, rowed by a black man and his son. "These boats all belonged to the planters, till the Negroes took possession. Now a man has to hire passage in his own canoe."

The grim, silent boatman seemed to understand well that he was master of the situation. There were seven in our party, and his charge for taking us over to the island and back was ten dollars. He made no words about it: we could accept his terms, or find another boat. The gravity and taciturnity of this man indicated no mean capacity for self-ownership. As he and his son rowed us across the river, he attended strictly to business, hearing the talk of the planters about the race he represented — talk by no means complimentary — with an impenetrability of countenance quite astonishing.

This was the third visit of the planters to the island since the war. On the first occasion, they were met by a party of Negroes, forty in number, who rushed to the landing armed with guns, and drove them away with threats to kill them if they came to disturb them in their homes again; whereupon they withdrew. On their second visit they were accompanied by Captain Ketchum, special agent of the bureau for the Sea Islands, to whose influence they probably owed their lives. They were met as before, surrounded by fierce black faces and leveled guns, captured, and not permitted to regain their boat until their leaders, who could read a little, became satisfied, from an examination of the captain's papers, that he was an officer of the government.

"We are ready to do anything for gov'ment," they said. "But we have nothing to do with these men."

They asked the captain who were the real owners of the land — they who had been placed there by the government, or the planters who had been fighting against the government?

"That is uncertain," replied the conscientious captain.

The planters, who had hoped for a different reply, were disgusted. "We may as well go back now," they said. And scarcely any effort was made to induce the Negroes to abandon their claims and make contracts.

This was now their third visit, and it remained to be seen how they would be received. We disembarked at a plantation belonging to three orphan children whose guardian was a member of our party. The freedmen, having learned that the mere presence of the planters on the soil could effect nothing, had changed their tactics and not one was to be seen. Although there were twenty-two hundred on the island, it appeared as solitary and silent as if it had not an inhabitant.

We found the plantation house occupied as headquarters by an officer of the bureau recently sent to the island. The guardian of the three orphans took me aside, showed me the desolated grounds without, shaded by magnificent live oaks, and the deserted chambers within.

"You can understand my feelings coming here," he said. "My sister expired in this room. She left her children to me. This estate, containing seventeen hundred acres and worth fifty thousand dollars, is all that remains to them; and you see the condition it is in. Why does the government of the United States persist in robbing orphan children? They have done nothing; they haven't earned the titles of Rebels and traitors. Why not give them back their land?"

I sympathized sincerely with this honest gentleman and his orphan wards. "But you forget," I said, "that such a war as we have passed through cannot be, without involving in calamities the innocent as well as the rest. It would have been well if that fact had not been overlooked in the beginning."

He made no reply. I afterwards learned that he was one of the original and most fiery secessionists of Charleston. He made a public speech early in 1861 in which he expressly pledged his life and fortune to the Confederate cause. His life he had managed to preserve; and of his fortune, sufficient remained for the elegant maintenance of his own and his sister's children, so that it appeared to me quite unreasonable for him to complain of the misfortune which he himself had been instrumental in bringing upon the orphans.

The party separated, each man going to look at his own estate. I accompanied one who had three fine plantations in the vicinity. A Northern man by birth, his sympathy had been with the government, while he found his private interest in working for the Confederate usurpation under profitable contracts. By holding his tongue and attending to business, he had accumulated a handsome fortune — wisely investing his Confederate scrip in real estate, which he thought somewhat more substantial. These plantations were a part of his earnings.

Being a Northern man, and at heart a Union man, he deemed it hard that they should not at once be restored to him. The fact that they were his reward for aiding the enemies of his country did not seem to have occurred to him as any bar to his claims.

At first we found all the freedmen's houses shut up. By pressing into some of them, we discovered a few women and children, but the men had disappeared. Since they were not to resist our coming, it seemed their policy to have nothing whatever to do with us. At last we found an old Negro too decrepit to run away, who sullenly awaited our approach.

"How did you come here?" I asked.

"Yankees fotch me."

"Don't you want to go back to St. John?"

"Yankees fotch me here," repeated the old man, "and I won't go back widout de Yankees send me back."

We inquired about his family and his prospects.

"My chil'n's out in soldiering. I made corn, peas, and potatoes; I got enough to carry me out de year. I had to bought my own clo'es, besides. Gov'ment don't help me none."

He had his forty acre lot, and would not peril his claim to it by talking about a contract.

We lingered at these cabins, waiting for a guard the officer at headquarters thought it prudent to send with us. At last he arrived — a shining black youngster in soldier clothes, overflowing with vanity and politeness. "I'm waiting on your occupation," he said, and we started on.

A mile from headquarters we found Negro men and women working in the fields. "Is this your farm?" my friend inquired of one of them.

"I calls it mine. General Saxton told me to come and stake out my forty acres, and he'd give me a ticket for it."

"Wouldn't it be better for you to contract for good wages than to work in this way?"

"No, I don't want to contract. I'll eat up my corn and peas fus'."

Observing a strange-looking thing of skin and bones standing in the weeds, I asked, "Is that a horse?"

"Dat's a piece o' one. When he gits tired, I can take my arms; I've good strong arms."

Seeing the immense disadvantage under which these poor people labored, without teams, without capital, and even without security in the possession of their little homesteads, I urged them to consider well what the planters had to offer.

"If I contract, what good does my forty acres do me?"

"But you are not sure of your forty acres. This year or next they may be given back to the former owner. Then you will have nothing, for you will have spent all your time and strength in trying to get a start. But if you work for wages, you will have, if you are prudent, a hundred and fifty dollars in clear cash at the end of the year. At that rate it will not be long before you will be able to buy a little place and stock it handsomely; then you will probably be much better off than you would be working here in this way."

I could see that this argument was not without its weight with the men. They appeared troubled by it, but not convinced. The women clamored against it, and almost made me feel that I was an enemy, giving them insidious ill advice. And when I saw the almost religious attachment of these people to their homes, it would have caused me remorse to know that I had persuaded any of them to give up their humble but honest aims.

We extended our walk as far as Fort Pemberton on Stono River, which bounded my friend's plantations in that direction. On our return, he thought he would try one more freedman with the offer of a contract.

The man was working with his wife on a little farm of indefinite extent. "I don't know how much land I have. I guessed off as near as I could forty acres." He could get along very well if he only had a horse. "But if I can git de land, I'll take my chances."

"But if you can't get the land?"

"If a man got to go crost de riber and he can't git a boat, he take a log. If I can't own de land, I'll hire or lease land, but I won't contract."

"Come, then," said my friend, "we may as well go home."

XXXVI

Sherman in the Carolinas

T HE MARCH of the Federals into our State," says a writer in the Columbia *Phoenix*, "was characterized by such scenes of license, plunder and conflagration as showed that the threats of the Northern press, and of their soldiery, were not to be regarded as a mere *brutum fulmen*. Daily, long trains of fugitives lined the roads, with wives and children, and horses and stock and cattle, seeking refuge from the pursuers. Long lines of wagons covered the highways. Half-naked people cowered from the winter under bush-tents in the thickets, under the eaves of houses, under the railroad sheds and in old cars left along the route. All these repeated the same story of suffering, violence, poverty and nakedness. Habitation after habitation, village after village — one sending up its signal flames to the other, presaging for it the same fate — lighted the winter and midnight sky with crimson horrors.

"No language can describe, nor can any catalogue furnish, an adequate detail of the widespread destruction of homes and property. Granaries were emptied, and where the grain was not carried off, it was strewn to waste under the feet of the cavalry, or consigned to the fire which consumed the dwelling. The negroes were robbed equally with the whites of food and clothing. The roads were covered with butchered cattle, hogs, mules and the costliest furniture. Valuable cabinets, rich pianos, were not only hewn to pieces, but bottles of ink, turpentine, oil, whatever could efface or destroy, were employed to defile and ruin. Horses were ridden into the houses. People were forced from their beds, to permit the search after hidden treasures.

"The beautiful homesteads of the parish country, with their wonderful tropical gardens, were ruined; ancient dwellings of black cypress, one hundred years old, which had been reared by the fathers of the Republic — men whose names were famous in Revolutionary history — were given to the torch as recklessly as were the rude hovels; choice pictures and works of art from Europe, select and numerous libraries, were all destroyed. The inhabitants, black no less than white, were left to starve, compelled to feed only upon the garbage to be found in the abandoned camps of the soldiers. The corn scraped up from the spots where the horses fed has been the only means of life left to thousands but lately in affluence.

"The villages of Buford's Bridge, of Barnwell, Blackville, Graham's, Bamberg, Midway, were more or less destroyed; the inhabitants everywhere left homeless and without food. The horses and mules, all cattle and hogs, whenever fit for service or for food, were carried off, and the rest shot. Every implement of the workman or the farmer, tools, ploughs, hoes, gins, looms, wagons, vehicles, was made to feed the flames."

Passing northward through the state, by the way of Orangeburg, Columbia and Winnsboro, I heard stories corroborative of the general truthfulness of this somewhat highly colored picture. The following, related to me by a lady residing in the Orangeburg district, will serve as a sample of the narratives.

"The burning of the bridges by the Confederates, as the Yankees were chasing them, did no good but a deal of harm.

They couldn't stop such an army as Sherman's, but all they could do was to hinder it, and keep it a few days longer in the country, eating us up.

"It was the best disciplined army in the world. At sundown, not a soldier was to be seen, and you could rest in peace till morning. That convinces me that everything that was done was permitted, if not ordered.

"I had an old cook with me — one of the best old creatures you ever saw. She had a hard master before we bought her, and she carried the marks on her face and hands where he had thrown knives at her. Such treatment as she got from us was something new to her, and there was nothing she wouldn't do for us.

" 'For heaven's sake, missus,' says she, 'bury some flour for the chil'n!' I gave her the keys to the smokehouse and told her to do what she pleased. 'Send all the niggers off the place but me and my son,' she says, 'for I don't trust 'em.' Then she and her son buried two barrels of flour, the silver pitcher and goblets, and a box of clothes. But that night she dreamed that the Yankees came and found the place; so next morning she dug up all the things but the flour, which she hadn't time to remove, and buried them under the hogpen.

"Sure enough, when the Yankees came, they found the flour but her dream saved the rest. She was afraid they would get hold of her son and make him tell, so she kept him in the chimney corner right under her eyes all day, pretending he was sick.

"Some of the Negroes were much excited by the Yankees' coming. One of our black girls jumped up and shouted, 'Glory to God! De Yankees is comin' to marry all we niggers!' But they generally behaved very well. A black man named Charles, belonging to one of our neighbors, started with a load of goods and flanked the Yankees for three days, and eluded them.

"The foragers loaded up our old family carriage with bacon and sweet potatoes, and drove it away. They took our last potatoes. Three or four had just been roasted for the children. 'Damn the children!' they said, and they ate the potatoes.

"The soldiers were full of fun and mischief. Says one, 'I'm going to the smokehouse to sweeten my mouth with molasses, and then I'm coming in to kiss these dumb perty girls.' They emptied out the molasses, then walked through it and tracked it all over the house. They dressed their horses in women's clothes. They tore up our dresses and tied them to their horses' tails. They dressed up the Negroes that followed them. They strung cowbells all around their horses and cattle. They killed chickens and brought them into the house on their bayonets, all dripping.

"For three nights we never lay down at all. I just sat one side of the fireplace and another young lady the other, thinking what had happened during the day and wondering what dreadful things would come next.

"Some of the officers had colored girls with them. One stopped overnight with his miss at the house of one of our neighbors. When they came downstairs in the morning, she was dressed magnificently in Mrs. J——'s best clothes.

"I never gave the Negroes a single order, but they went to work after the Yankees had passed and cleared up the whole place. They took corn and ground it; and they went to the Yankee camp for meat and cooked it for us. Our horses were taken, but they planted rice and corn with their hoes. There were scarcely any white men in the country. Most were in the army; and the Yankees took prisoner all who came under the conscript act. They carried some away who have never been heard from since.

"My husband was in Charleston, and for weeks neither of us knew if the other was alive. I walked seventeen miles to mail a letter to him. The old cook went with me and carried my child. From seven in the morning until dark, the first day, I walked twelve miles; and five the next. The old cook didn't feel tired a bit, though she carried the baby; but she kept saying to me, 'Don't set down dar, missus. We'll neber git dar!' We were two days coming home again."

Almost until the last moment, the people of South Carolina, relying upon the immense prestige of their little state's sovereignty, even after the state was invaded, believed that the capital was safe. Already, during the war, thousands of citizens from Charleston and other places had sought the retirement of its beautiful shady streets and supposedly impregnable walls. The population of Columbia had thus increased in two or three years from fourteen to thirty-seven thousand. Then Sherman appeared, driving clouds of fugitives before him into the city. Still the inhabitants cherished their delusion, until it was dispelled by the sound of the Federal cannon at their gates. The Confederate troops fell back into the city, followed by bursting shells.

Then commenced the usual scenes of panic. Numbers of the poorer classes took advantage of this confusion to plunder the city. They broke into the South Carolina Railroad Depot, which was crowded with the stores of merchants and planters, trunks of treasure, innumerable wares and goods of fugitives, all of great value. Among its contents were some kegs of powder. The plunderers paid, and suddenly, the penalties of

their crime. Using their lights freely and hurriedly, they fired
a train of powder leading to the kegs. A fearful explosion followed, destructive to property and life.

Early on Friday the Confederate quartermaster and commissary stores were thrown open to the people. Old men, women,
children and Negroes loaded themselves with plunder. Wheel-
er's cavalry rushed in for their share, and several troopers were
seen riding off "with huge bales of cotton on their saddles."

The same day — Friday, February 17th — Sherman entered
Columbia. To the anxious mayor he said: "Not a finger's
breadth of your city shall be harmed. You may lie down and
sleep, satisfied that your town will be as safe in my hands as in
your own." That night Columbia was destroyed.

It is still a question, who is responsible for this calamity.
Sherman denies that he authorized it, and we are bound to believe him. But did he not permit it? Or was it not in his power
at least to have prevented it? General Howard is reported to
have said to a clergyman of the place that no orders were given
to burn Columbia, but the soldiers had got the impression that
its destruction would be acceptable at headquarters. Were the
soldiers correct?

A member of Sherman's staff speaks thus of the origin of the
fire: "I am quite sure it originated in sparks flying from the
hundreds of bales of cotton which the Rebels had placed along
the main street, and fired as they left the city. Fire from a
tightly compressed bale of cotton is unlike that of a more open
material, which burns itself out. The fire lies smoldering in a
bale long after it appears to be extinguished; and in this instance, when our soldiers supposed they had extinguished the
fire, it suddenly broke out again with disastrous effect.

"There were fires, however, which must have been started

independent of the above-named cause. The source of these is ascribed to revenge from some two hundred of our prisoners, who had escaped from the cars as they were being conveyed from this city to Charlotte, and with the memories of long sufferings in the miserable pens I visited yesterday on the other side of the river, sought this means of retaliation."

But is this the whole truth with regard to the burning of Columbia? I visited the place nearly a year after its great disaster, when the passions of men had had time to cool a little. Through the courtesy of Governor Orr I made acquaintance with prominent and responsible citizens. To these gentlemen I am indebted for the following statements.

Early in the evening, as the inhabitants, quieted by Sherman's assurance, were retiring to their beds, a rocket went up in the lower part of the city. Then another in the center, and a third in the upper part of the town. Dr. R. W. Gibbes, father of the present mayor, was in the street near one of the Federal guards, who exclaimed, on seeing the signals, "My God! I pity your city!" Mr. Goodwyn, who was mayor at the time, reports a similar remark from an Iowa soldier. "Your city is doomed! These rockets are the signal!" Immediately afterwards fires broke out in twenty different places.

The dwellings of Secretary Trenholm and General Wade Hampton were among the first to burst into flames. Soldiers went from house to house, spreading the conflagration. Fireballs, composed of cotton saturated with turpentine, were thrown in at doors and windows. Many houses were entered and fired by means of combustible liquids poured upon beds and clothing, and ignited by wads of burning cotton, or matches from a soldier's pocket. The fire department came out in force, but the hose pipes were cut to pieces and the men driven from the streets. At the same time universal plundering and robbery began.

The burning of the house of Dr. Gibbes was described to me by his son: "He had a guard at the front door; but some soldiers climbed in at the rear of the house, got into the parlor, heaped together sheets, poured turpentine over them, piled chairs on them, and set them on fire. As he remonstrated with them, they laughed at him. The guard at the front door could do nothing, for if he left his post, other soldiers would come in that way.

"The guard had a disabled foot, which my father had dressed for him. He appeared grateful for the favor, and earnestly advised my father to save his valuables. The house was full of costly paintings, and curiosities of art and natural history, and my father did not know what to save and what to leave behind. He finally tied up in a bed quilt a quantity of silver and gems. As he was going out of the door — the house was already on fire behind him — the guard said, 'Is that all you can save?' 'It is all I can carry,' said my father. 'Leave that with me,' said the guard. 'I will take charge of it, while you go back and get another bundle.'

"My father thought he was very kind. He went back for another bundle and while he was gone, the guard ran off with his lame leg and all the gems and silver."

One of Gibbes's neighbors, a widow lady, had an equally conscientious guard. He said to her, "I can guard the front of the house, but not the rear; and if you have anything valuable buried you had better look after it." She threw up her hands and exclaimed, "Oh, my silver and my fine old wine, buried under the peach tree!" The guard immediately called a squad of men, and told them to respect the widow lady's wine and silver, buried under that peach tree. He went with them, and they dug a little to see if the treasures were safe. Finding the wine, they tasted it to see if it merited the epithet "fine old." Discovering that it did, they showed their approbation of her good sense and truthfulness by drinking it up. They then carried off the silver.

Fortunately the streets of Columbia were broad, else many of the fleeing fugitives must have perished in the flames which met them on all sides. The exodus of homeless families, flying between walls of fire, was a terrible and piteous spectacle. I have already described a similar scene in Chambersburg, and shall not dwell upon this. The fact that these were the wives and children and flaming homes of our enemies does not lessen the feeling of sympathy for sufferers.

Three fifths of the city was destroyed. No more respect seems to have been shown for buildings commonly deemed sacred than for others. The churches were pillaged, and afterwards burned. St. Mary's College, a Catholic institution, shared their fate. The Catholic convent, to which had been confided for safety many young ladies not nuns, and stores of treasure, was ruthlessly sacked. The soldiers drank the sacramental wine and profaned with fiery draughts of vulgar whiskey the goblets of the communion service. Some went off reeling under the weight of priestly robes, holy vessels and candlesticks.

Not much drunkenness was observed among the soldiers until after the sacking of the city had been some time in progress. Then the stores of liquors consumed exhibited their natural effect; and it is stated that many perished in fires of their own kindling.

Yet the army of Sherman did not, in its wildest orgies, forget its splendid discipline. "When will these horrors cease?" asked a lady of an officer at her house. "You will hear the bugles at

sunrise," he replied. "Then they will cease, and not till then."
He prophesied truly. "At daybreak on Saturday morning," said
Mayor Gibbes, "I saw two men galloping through the streets,
blowing horns. Not a dwelling was fired after that, immediately
the town became quiet."

During the looting, some curious incidents occurred. One
man's treasure, concealed by his garden fence, escaped the soldiers' divining rods but was afterwards discovered by a hitched
horse pawing the earth from the buried box. Some hidden guns
had defied the most diligent search until a chicken, chased by a
soldier, ran into a hole beneath a house. The soldier, crawling
after and putting in his hand for the chicken, found the guns.

A soldier, passing in the streets and seeing some children
playing with a beautiful little greyhound, amused himself by
beating its brains out. Another soldier with a kinder heart told
them not to cry, and proposed to have a funeral over the remains of their little favorite. He put it in a box and went to
bury it in the garden, directly *on the spot where the family
treasures were concealed.* The proprietor, in great distress,
watched the proceedings, fearful of exciting suspicion if he opposed it, and trembling lest each thrust of the spade should re-
veal the secret. A corner of the box was actually laid bare, when,
kicking some dirt over it, he said, "There, that will do, children!" and hastened the burial.

It is curious to consider what has become of all the jewels and
finery of which our armies robbed the people of the South. On
two or three occasions gentlemen of respectability have shown
me, with considerably more pride than I could have felt under
the circumstances, vases and trinkets which they "picked up
when they were in the army." Some of these curiosities have
been heard from by their rightful owners.

A ring worn by a lady of Philadelphia was last summer recognized by a Southern gentleman, who remarked that he thought he had seen it before. "Very possibly," was the reply. "It was given me by Captain —— of General Sherman's staff; and it was presented to him by a lady of Columbia for his efforts in saving her property." But the lady of Columbia, who knew nothing of any such efforts in her behalf, avers that the gallant captain stole the ring.

Mrs. Minegault, daughter of the late Judge Huger of Charleston, while on a visit to New York last summer, was kneeling in Grace Church one Sunday morning when she saw, upon the shoulders of a lady kneeling before her, a shawl which had been lost when her plantation, between Charleston and Savannah, was plundered by the Federals. Her attention being thus attracted, she next observed on the lady's arm a bracelet which was taken from her at the same time. This was to her a very precious souvenir, for it had been presented to her by her father, and it contained his picture.

The services ended, she followed the lady home and rang at the door. She was shown into the parlor, and presently the lady appeared with the shawl upon her shoulders and the bracelet on her arm. Frankly the visitor related the story of the bracelet, and at once the wearer restored it to her with apologies and regrets. The visitor, quite overcome by this generosity and delighted at recovery of the bracelet, had not the heart to say a word about the shawl, but left it in the possession of the innocent wearer.

Columbia must have been a beautiful city, judging by its ruins. The streets were broad and well shaded. Many fine residences still remain on the outskirts, but the entire heart of the city is a wilderness of crumbling walls, naked chimneys and trees killed by flames. The fountains of the desolated gardens are dry, the basins cracked; the pillars of the houses are dismantled or overthrown; the marble steps are broken. Fortunately the unfinished new State House, one of the handsomest public edifices in the whole country, received but trifling injury.

At a distance from the Sea Islands, the free-labor system in South Carolina was fast settling down upon a satisfactory basis. General Richardson, commanding the eastern district of the state, assured me that there was going to be more cotton raised in those districts this year than ever before.

The finances of South Carolina were at a low ebb. Governor Orr told me that there had not been a dollar in the state treasury since his inauguration. The current expenses of the war were mostly met by taxation; and the annual interest on the foreign debt of two and a half millions had been promptly paid up to July, 1865, by the exportation of cotton. The state bank was obliged to suspend its operations, but the faith of the state was pledged for the redemption of the bills. The other banks had been ruined by loans made to the Confederate Government.

South Carolina suffered more than any other state by the sale of lands for United States taxes during the war. I heard of one estate, worth fifteen thousand dollars, which had been sold for three hundred dollars. Governor Orr instanced another, the market value of which was twenty-four thousand dollars, which was bought in by the government for eighty dollars. Such was the fate of abandoned coastlands held by the United States forces. Their owners, absent in the interior, were in most instances ignorant even of the proceedings by which their estates were sacrificed.

The prevalence of crime in remote districts was alarming. I was assured by General Sickles that the perpetrators were in most cases outlaws from the other states, to which they dared not return. Union soldiers and Negroes were their favorite victims. They rode in armed bands through the country, defying military authorities. The people would not inform against them for fear of vengeance. Many robberies and murders of soldiers and freedmen, however, were unmistakably committed by citizens.

Much ill feeling had been kept alive by United States treasury agents searching the country for Confederate cotton and branded mules and horses. Many of these agents, as far as I could learn, were mere rogues and fortune hunters. They would propose to seize a man's property in the name of the United States, but abandon the claim on the payment of heavy bribes, which went into their own pockets. Sometimes, having seized "C.S.A." cotton, they would have the marks on the bales changed, get some man to claim it and divide with him the profits.

I found in South Carolina a more virulent animosity existing in common people against the government and people of the North than in any other state I visited. Only in South Carolina was I treated with gross personal insults on account of my Northern origin. Yet there is in this state a class of men whom I remember with admiration for their courteous hospitality and liberal views. Instead of insulting and repelling Northern men, they seem eager to learn of them the secret of Northern enterprise and prosperity. Their ideas, although not those of New England radicals, are hopeful and progressive. Considering that they have advanced from the Southern side of the national question, their position is notable and praiseworthy.

This class is small, but it possesses a vital energy of which great results may be predicted. From it the freedmen have much to hope and little to fear. It is not so far in advance of the people that it cannot lead them; nor so far behind the most advanced sentiment of the times that we may not expect them soon to come up to it.

On my way to Winnsboro, some miles north of Columbia, I had an interesting experience of staging over that portion of the Charlotte and South Carolina Railroad destroyed by Sherman. Much of the way the stage route ran beside or near the track. Gangs of laborers were engaged in putting down new ties and rails, but most of the old iron lay where our boys left it.

It was the Seventeenth Corps that did this little job, and it did it well. It was curious to note the different styles of the destroying parties. The point where one detail appeared to have left off and another to have begun was generally unmistakable. For a mile or two you would see nothing but hairpins, and bars wound around telegraph posts and trees. Then you would have corkscrews and twists for about the same distance. Then came a party that gave each heated rail one sharp wrench in the middle and left it perhaps nearly straight, but facing both ways. Here was a plain business method, and there a fantastic style which showed that its authors took a wild delight in their work.

Within the coach, an animated political discussion was at its height. Two South Carolinians and a planter from Arkansas were dissecting the Yankees in liveliest fashion, while a bitter South Carolina lady and a good-natured Virginian occasionally put in a word.

It was some time before I was recognized as a representative of all that was mean and criminal in the world. At length something I said seemed to excite suspicion; and the Arkansan wrote something on a card, which was passed to everyone except me. An alarming hush of several minutes ensued. It was as if a skeleton had appeared at a banquet. The abuse of the Yankees was the banquet; and I was perfectly well aware that I was the skeleton. At last the awful silence was broken by the Arkansan.

"What is thought of Negro suffrage in the North?"

I replied that opinion was divided; but that many people believed some such security was necessary for the freedmen's rights. "They do not think it quite safe," I said, "to leave him without any voice in making the laws by which he is to be governed — subject entirely to the legislation of a class that cannot forget that he was born a slave."

"I believe," said one of the South Carolinians, "all that is owing to the lies of the newspaper correspondents traveling through the South, and writing home whatever they think will injure us. I wish every one of 'em was killed off. If it wasn't for them, we should be left to attend to our own business instead of being ridden to death by Yankee masters. It isn't fair to take solitary instances reported by them as representing the condition of the niggers and the disposition of the whites. Some impudent darky, who deserved it, gets a knock on the head, or a white man speaks his mind rather too freely to some Yankee who has purposely provoked him, and a long newspaper story is made out of it, showing that every nigger in the South is in danger of being killed, and every white man is disloyal."

"Certainly," I said, "isolated cases do not represent a whole people. But the acts of a legislative body may be supposed to represent the spirit and wishes of its constituents. We consider the Negro code enacted by your special legislature simply abominable. It is enough in itself to show that you are not quite ready to do the freedmen justice. Your present governor appears to be of the same opinion, judged by his veto of the act to amend the patrol laws, and his excellent advice to your representatives who passed it. You are wholly mistaken, my friend, in supposing that the people of the North wish anything of you that is unnecessary, unreasonable or unjust."

"All we want," said the South Carolinian, "is that our Yankee rulers should give us the same privileges with regard to the control of labor which they themselves have."

"What privileges have they which you have not?"

"In Massachusetts, a laborer is obliged by law to make a contract for a year. If he leaves his employer without his consent, or before the contract expires, he can be put in jail. And if another man hires him, he can be fined. It is not lawful there to hire a laborer who does not bring a certificate from his last employer. All we want is the same or a similar code of laws here."

"My dear sir," said I, "all any man could wish is that you might have just such laws here as they have in Massachusetts. But with regard to the code you speak of, it does not exist there, and it does not exist in any Northern state with which I am acquainted. There is nothing like it anywhere."

"How do you manage without such laws? How can you get work out of a man unless you *compel* him in some way?"

"Natural laws compel him; we need no others. A man must work if he would eat. A faithful laborer is soon discovered, and he commands the best wages. An idle fellow is detected quite as soon, and is discharged. Thus the system regulates itself."

"You can't do that with niggers."

"Have you ever tried? Have you ever called your freedmen together and explained to them their new condition?"

"Well, there may be something to that. I can't say, for I never thought of trying but one way with a nigger. But nigger suffrage the South a'n't going to stand anyhow. We've already got a class of voters that's enough to corrupt the politics of any country. I used to think the nigger was the meanest of God's creatures. But I've found a meaner brute than he, and that's the low-down white man. If a respectable man hires a nigger for wages, one of those low-down cusses will offer him twice as much to get him away. They want him to prowl for them.

"A heap of these no-account whites are getting rich, stealing cotton; they're too lazy or cowardly to do it themselves, so they get the niggers to do it for 'em. These very men hold the balance of political power in this district. Just before the war, at an election in Columbia, over a hundred sand-hillers sold their votes beforehand, and were put into jail till the polls opened and then marched out to vote."

"By what right were they put in jail?"

"It was in the bargain. They knew they couldn't be trusted not to sell their votes to the next man that offered more whiskey, and they like going to jail well enough if they can go drunk. Make the niggers voters, and you'll have just such another class to be bought up with whiskey."

"It seems to me more reasonable," I replied, "to suppose that the franchise will elevate the Negro; and by elevating him you will elevate the white man who has been degraded by the Negro's degradation. Some of both races will no doubt be found willing to sell their votes for whiskey; but that is no more reason why all blacks should be deprived of the right of suffrage than that all whites should be."

This is a specimen of the talk that was kept up during the day. Finally, we reached a point to which the railroad had been repaired and took the cars for Winnsboro. While we were waiting by moonlight in the shelterless camping ground which served as a station, one of my South Carolina friends said: "We may as well tell the whole truth as half. The Yankees treated us mighty badly; but a heap of our own people followed in their track and robbed on their credit."

On the train I found a hotelkeeper from Winnsboro drumming for customers. He was abusing the Yankees with great violence until he found that I was one. After that he kept quiet, and even apologized for his remarks, until I told him I had concluded to go to the house of a rival runner. Thereupon he broke forth again.

"They've left me one inestimable privilege — to hate 'em. I git up at half-past four in the morning and sit up till twelve at night to hate 'em. Talk about Union! They had no object in coming down here but just to steal. I'm like a whipped cur; I have to cave in; but that don't say I shall love 'em. I owned my own house, my own servants, my own garden, and in one night they reduced me to poverty.

"My house was near the State House in Columbia. It was occupied by Howard's headquarters. When they left, they just poured camphene over the beds, set 'em afire, locked up the house and threw away the key. That was after the burning of the town, and that's what made it so hard. Some one had told 'em I was one of the worst Rebels in the world, and that's the only truth I reckon that was told. I brought up seven boys, and what they hadn't killed was fighting against 'em then. Now I have to keep a boardinghouse in Winnsboro to support my wife and children."

At Winnsboro I passed the night. A portion of that town also had been destroyed, and there too Sherman's "bummers" were said to have behaved very naughtily. For instance: "When the

Episcopal Church was burning, they took out the melodeon and
played the devil's tunes on it till the church was well burned
down. Then they threw on the melodeon."

Next day I entered North Carolina. Almost immediately on
crossing the state line, a change of scene was perceptible. The
natural features of the country improved; the appearance of its
farms improved still more. That night I passed at the house of
a Connecticut man in a country village — a warm and comfortable New England home transported to a Southern community — and went on next day to Raleigh.

At Raleigh I found the legislature, composed mostly of a respectable and worthy-looking yeomanry, battling over the question of Negro testimony in the civil courts, spending day after
day in the discussion of a subject which could be settled in only
one way, and which ought to have been settled at once. One
member remarked outside: "I'll never vote for that bill unless
driven to it by the bayonet." Another said: "I'm opposed to giving niggers *any* privileges."

These men represent a large class of North Carolina farmers;
but fortunately there is another class of more progressive and
liberal ideas which are sure at last to prevail.

The business of Raleigh was dull, the money in the country
being exhausted. A few Northern men who had gone into trade
there were discouraged, and anxious to get away. "So great is
the impoverishment of our state," Governor Worth said to me,
"that a tax of any considerable amount would bring real estate
at once into the market."

The freedmen throughout the central and northern part of
the state had generally made contracts and were at work. In the
southern part, fewer contracts had been made in consequence

of the inability of the large planters to pay promptly. "When paid promptly, the freedmen are everywhere working well," I was assured by the officers of the bureau.

From Governor Worth I received a rather sorry account of the doings of Sherman's "bummers" in this state. Even after the pacification, they continued their lawless marauding.

"They visited my place, near Raleigh, and drove off a fine flock of ewes and lambs. I was state treasurer at the time, and having to go away on public business, I gave my Negroes their bacon, which they hid behind the ceiling of the house. The Yankees came and held an ax over the head of one of the Negroes, and by threats compelled him to tell where it was. They tore off the ceiling and stole all the bacon. They took all my cows. Three cows afterwards came back; but they recently disappeared again, and I found them in the possession of a man who says he bought them of the bummers. I had a grindstone, and as they couldn't carry it off, they smashed it. There was on my place a poor, old, blind Negro woman — the last creature in the world against whom I should suppose any person would have wished to commit a wrong. She had a new dress; and they stole even that.

"I was known as a peace man," said the governor, "and for that reason I did not suffer as heavily as my neighbors." He gave this testimony with regard to that class which served, but did not honor, our cause. "Of all the malignant wretches that ever cursed the earth, the hangers-on of Sherman's army were the worst," adding: "It can't be expected that the people should love a government that has subjugated them in this way."

XXXVII

The Desolate South

I MADE but a brief stay in North Carolina, then passed on homeward and reached the beautiful snowy hills and frosted forests of New England early in February. It now only remains for me to sum up briefly my answers to certain questions which are constantly put to me regarding Southern emigration, the loyalty of the people, and the future of the country.

The South is in the condition of a man recovering from a dangerous malady: the crisis is past, appetite is boundless, and only sustenance and purifying air are needed to bring health and life in fresh waves. The exhausted country calls for supplies. It has been drained of its wealth and of its young men. Capital is eagerly welcomed and absorbed. Labor is also needed. There is much shallow talk about getting rid of the Negroes and of filling their places with foreigners. But war and disease have already removed more of the colored race than can be well spared; and I am confident that, for the next five or ten years, leaving the blacks where they are, the strongest tide of emigration that can be poured into the country will be insufficient to meet the increasing demand for labor.

Northern enterprise, emancipation, improved modes of culture and the high prices of cotton, rice, sugar and tobacco cannot fail to bring about this result. Nor will planting alone flourish. Burned cities and plantation buildings must be restored, new towns and villages will spring up, old losses must be repaired and a thousand new wants supplied. Trade, manufactures, the mechanic arts, all are invited to share in this teeming activity.

Particular location the emigrant must select according to his own judgment, tastes and means. Just now I should not advise Northern men to settle far back from the main routes of travel unless they go in communities, purchasing and dividing large plantations, and forming societies independent of any hostile sentiment that may be shown by the native inhabitants. But I trust that in a year or two, all danger of discomfort of disturbance arising from this source will have mostly passed by.

The loyalty of the people is generally of a negative sort: it is simply disloyalty subdued. They submit to the power which has mastered them but they do not love it; nor is it reasonable to expect that they should. Many of them lately in rebellion are, I think, honestly convinced that secession was a great mistake, and that the preservation of the Union, even with the loss of slavery, is better for them than any such separate government as that of which they had a bitter taste. Yet they do not feel much affection for the hand which corrected their error. There is another class which would still be glad to dismember the country, and whose hatred of the government is radical and intense. But this class is small.

The poor whites may be divided into three classes: those who, to their hatred of the Negro, join a hatred of the government that has set him free; those who associate with the Negro and care nothing for any government; and those who, cherishing more or less Union sentiment, rejoice to see the old aristocracy overthrown.

Of another armed rebellion, not the least apprehension need

be entertained. The South has had enough of war for a long time to come. The habiliments of mourning, which one sees everywhere in its towns and cities, will cast their dark shadow upon any future attempt at secession long after they have been put away in the silent wardrobes of the past. Only in the case of a foreign war might we expect to see a party of malignant malcontents go over to the side of the enemy. They would doubtless endeavor to drag their states with them, but they would not succeed. Fortunately, those who are still so anxious to see the old issue fought out are not themselves fighting men, and are dangerous only with their tongues.

Of *unarmed* rebellion, of continued sectional strife, stirred up by Southern politicians, there exists very great danger. Their aims are distinct, and they command the sympathy of the Southern people. To obtain the exclusive control of the freedmen and to make such laws for them as shall embody the prejudices of the late slave-holding society; to govern not only their own states but to regain their forfeited leadership in the affairs of the nation; to effect the repudiation of the national debt or to get the Confederate debt and the Rebel state debts assumed by the whole country; to secure payment for their slaves, and for all injuries and losses occasioned by the war; these are among the chief designs of a class who will pursue them with recklessness and persistency.

How to prevent them from agitating the nation in the future as in the past and from destroying its prosperity is the most serious of questions. If you succeed in capturing an antagonist who has made a murderous assault upon you, common sense and a regard for your own safety and the peace of society require at least that his weapons, or the power of using them, should be taken from him. These perilous schemes are the present weapons of the nation's conquered enemy; and does not prudent statesmanship demand that they should be laid forever at rest before he walks again at large in the pride of his power?

All that just and good men can ask is this security. Vindictiveness, or a wish to hold the rebellious states under an iron rule, should have no place in our hearts. But if the blood of our brothers was shed in a righteous cause, let us honor our brothers and the cause by seeing that reality established. If treason is a crime, surely it can receive no more fitting or merciful punishment than to be deprived of its power to do more mischief. Let peace, founded upon true principles, be the only retribution we demand.

It was my original intention to speak of the various schemes of reconstruction claiming the consideration of the country. But they have become too numerous and are generally too well known to be detailed here. The Southern plan is simple: that the states lately so eager to destroy the Union are now entitled to all their former rights and privileges in that Union. Their haste to withdraw their representatives from Congress is more than equaled by their anxiety to get them back in their seats.

They consider it hard that at the end of the bloodiest civil war that ever shook the planet, they cannot quietly slip back in their places and take up once more the scepter of political power.

Often, in conversation with candid Southern men, I was able to convince them it was hardly to be expected that the government, emerging victorious from such a struggle and finding its foot on that scepter, should take it off with alacrity. And they were forced to acknowledge that, had the South proved victorious, its enemies would not have escaped so easily.

This plan does not tolerate the impediment of any Congressional test oath. When I said to my Southern friends that I should be glad to see those representatives who could take the test oath admitted to Congress, this was the usual reply: "We would not vote for such men. We had rather have no representatives at all. We want representatives to *represent* us, and no man *represents* us who can take your test oath. We are Rebels, if you choose to call us so, and only a good Rebel can properly represent us."

This is the strongest argument I have heard against the admission of loyal Southern members to Congress. And if the white masses of the lately rebellious states are alone, and indiscriminately, to be recognized as the people of those states, it is certainly a valid argument.

"It is enough," they maintained, "that a representative in Congress takes the ordinary oath to support the government; *that* is a sufficient test of his loyalty" — forgetting that, at the outbreak of the Rebellion, this proved no test at all.

Such is the Southern plan of reconstruction. Opposed to it is the plan on which I believe a majority of the people of the loyal states are agreed, namely, that certain guarantees of future national tranquillity should be required of those who have caused so great a national convulsion. But as to what those guarantees should be, opinions are divided, and a hundred conflicting measures are proposed.

For my own part, I see but one plain rule by which our troubles can be finally and satisfactorily adjusted; that is, the enactment of simple justice for all men. Anything that falls short of this falls short of the solution of the problem.

The "Civil Rights Bill" — enacted since the greater portion of these pages were written — is a step in the direction in which this country is inevitably moving. The principles of the Declaration of Independence, supposed to be our starting point in history, are in reality the goal towards which we are tending. Far in advance of our actual civilization, the pioneers of the Republic set up those shining pillars. Not until all men are equal before the law, and none is hindered from rising or from sinking by any impediment which does not exist in his own constitution and private circumstances, will that goal be reached.

Soon or late the next step is surely coming. That step is universal suffrage. It may be wise to make some moral or intellectual qualification a test of a man's fitness for the franchise; but anything which does not apply alike to all classes is inconsistent with the spirit of American nationality.

But will the Southern people ever submit to Negro suffrage? They will submit to it quite as willingly as they submitted to Negro emancipation. They fought against that as long as any power of resistance was in them; then they accepted it; they are now becoming reconciled to it; and soon they will rejoice over it. Such is always the history of progressive ideas. The first advance is opposed with all the might of the world until its triumph is achieved; then the world says "Very well," and employs all its arts and energies to defeat the next movement, which triumphs and is finally welcomed in its turn.

But are the emancipated blacks prepared for the franchise? They are, by all moral and intellectual qualifications, as well prepared for it as the mass of poor whites in the South. Although ignorant, they possess, as has been said, a strong instinct which stands them in the place of actual knowledge. That instinct inspires them with loyalty to the government, and it will never permit them to vote so unwisely and mischievously as the white people of the South voted in the days of secession.

Moreover, there are among them men of fine intelligence and leading influence by whom, and not by their old masters, they will be instructed in their duty at the polls. And this fact is most certain — that they are far better prepared to have a hand in making the laws by which they are to be governed than the whites are to make those laws for them.

How this step is now to be brought about is not easy to determine; and it may not be brought about for some time to come. Meanwhile, it is neither wise nor just to allow the representation of the Southern states in Congress to be increased by the emancipation of a race that has no voice in that representation; and some constitutional remedy against this evil is required.

The present high price of cotton, and the extraordinary demand for labor, seem providential circumstances designed to teach both races a great lesson. The freedmen are fast learning the responsibilities of their new situation, and gaining a position from which they cannot easily be displaced. Their eagerness to acquire knowledge is a bright sign of hope for their future. By degrees the dominant class must learn to respect those who, as chattels, could only be despised.

Respect for labor rises with the condition of the laborer. The whites of the South are not by choice ignorant or unjust, but circumstances have made them so. Teach them that the laborer is a man, and that labor is manly — a truth that is now dawning upon them — and the necessity of mediation between the two races will no longer exist.

Then the institutions of the South will spontaneously assimilate to our own. Then we shall have a Union of states not in form only but in spirit also. Then shall we see established the reality of the cause that has cost so many priceless lives and such lavish outpouring of treasure. Then will disloyalty die of inanition, and its deeds live only in legend and in story. Then breaks upon America the morning glory of that future which shall behold it the Home of Man, and the Lawgiver among the nations.